Voices of World War II

Recent Titles in
Voices of an Era

Voices of Ancient Egypt: Contemporary Accounts of Daily Life
Rosalie David, editor

Voices of Ancient Greece and Rome: Contemporary Accounts of Daily Life
David Matz, editor

Voices of Civil War America: Contemporary Accounts of Daily Life
Lawrence A. Kreiser, Jr. and Ray B. Browne, editors

Voices of Early Christianity: Documents from the Origins of Christianity
Kevin W. Kaatz, editor

Voices of Early Modern Japan: Contemporary Accounts of Daily Life during the Age of the Shoguns
Constantine Vaporis, editor

Voices of Revolutionary America: Contemporary Accounts of Daily Life
Carol Sue Humphrey, editor

Voices of Shakespeare's England: Contemporary Accounts of Elizabethan Daily Life
John A. Wagner, editor

Voices of Victorian England: Contemporary Accounts of Daily Life
John A. Wagner, editor

Voices of World War II

Contemporary Accounts of Daily Life

Priscilla Roberts, Editor

Voices of an Era

AN IMPRINT OF ABC-CLIO, LLC
Santa Barbara, California • Denver, Colorado • Oxford, England

Library of Congress Cataloging-in-Publication Data

Voices of World War II : contemporary accounts of daily life / Priscilla Roberts, Editor.
pages cm. — (Voices of an era)
Includes bibliographical references and index.
ISBN 978-0-313-38662-6 (hardcopy : alk. paper) — ISBN 978-0-313-38663-3 (ebooks)
1. World War, 1939–1945—Personal narratives. 2. World War, 1939–1945—Sources.
I. Roberts, Priscilla, editor.
D811.A2V587 2012
940.53092'2—dc23 2012010300

ISBN: 978-0-313-38662-6
EISBN: 978-0-313-38663-3

16 15 14 13 12 1 2 3 4 5

This book is also available on the World Wide Web as an eBook.
Visit www.abc-clio.com for details.

Greenwood
An Imprint of ABC-CLIO, LLC

ABC-CLIO, LLC
130 Cremona Drive, P.O. Box 1911
Santa Barbara, California 93116-1911

This book is printed on acid-free paper ∞

Manufactured in the United States of America

For my father, Donald Roberts, who lived through it

Contents

Preface

World War II was a pivotal event in 20th-century history, with its impact felt in some way by almost every human being across the entire planet. Inevitably, the 32 documents gathered in this collection can only constitute an introduction to the historic conflict, its ramifications, and the variety of experiences participants in the war encountered or endured. All were generated during, immediately before, or after and as a result of the war, and encapsulate different aspects of the multifaceted and global undertakings and endeavors involved in World War II and its widely varying impact on individual lives. Included in this book are writings and speeches by some of the war's most prominent, even notorious figures, among them Franklin D. Roosevelt, Heinrich Himmler, Henry R. Luce, and Charles A. Lindbergh; official documents that in some cases affected millions of lives, notably the minutes of the meeting of German bureaucrats that planned the "Final Solution," the attempt to murder all of Europe's Jewish population; accounts by journalists and professional historians who observed and reported on key moments and events in the war and its aftermath; speeches, statements, manifestoes, and articles by private individuals—some prominent, some less so—who sought to influence public thinking on the war; diaries and letters written during the war; oral histories and memoirs produced after the war, some by military personnel of both sexes, some by women, children, prisoners, or civilian officials; and even some contemporary poetry featuring the war and its consequences.

At times, the same event or issue is viewed from different perspectives. An account by the lead Japanese pilot at Pearl Harbor is juxtaposed with President Franklin D. Roosevelt's "Date which Will Live in Infamy" speech to the American nation. German and American accounts of D-Day stand next to each other, as do German and Russian recollections of fighting and sieges on the Eastern Front. An American bomber pilot writes with some pride of the skills needed to pilot a Lancaster airplane on a destructive raid over Germany, while the atomic attack on Hiroshima is viewed from the perspective of a German priest living on the outskirts of the city. Several documents focus upon the sufferings and brutal persecution of European Jews, while others illustrate still more facets of the savagery and cruelty of war, describing the ordeals of prisoners of war, comfort women, and civilians in occupied areas. Some accounts, including the publisher Henry Luce's famous article "The American Century," attempt to imagine, influence, and shape the postwar world.

This volume attempts to place documents in context, to enable the reader to evaluate them as historical sources, and to suggest analogies with current issues of interest to people today. Each document includes an "Introduction" that provides some background on its creation; information for the reader to bear in mind when reading the document; and a brief account of the "Aftermath" and consequences of that document. An "Ask Yourself" section presents readers with a selection of related questions, followed by a number of "Topics to Consider," intended to generate wide-ranging discussion of the implications of the issues raised by that particular document. In some cases, additional sidebars provide information on specific individuals, events, or issues related to the document. Each document is accompanied by a short bibliography, listing books, Internet resources, and films and television programs that shed further light on the document and issues arising from it for those who wish to pursue more research on the topic.

In the past, before digital technology made it possible to dispatch information from one place to another without necessarily using paper of any kind, documents were usually physical artifacts, generally written on paper of some sort. In World War II, when electronic media were essentially limited to the telegraph, whose wires could transmit text around the world, admittedly at considerable expense, this was very much the case. Although all the documents included in this volume are printed in a uniform typeface, the originals, of course, appeared in many different formats—some handwritten, others typewritten—before they were eventually published. To supplement the printed versions, the volume includes facsimiles of several original documents from World War II, accompanied by descriptions of exactly how these were produced. It is worth remembering that in these years documents were normally either written by hand or rather laboriously typed on a manual typewriter—in some cases deciphering a handwritten original or following verbal dictation—after which they were sometimes corrected or revised by hand and then retyped.

This volume also includes several general sections, offering additional background and reference information. An introduction provides a broad-brush overview of the most significant aspects of World War II. A detailed chronology gives a timeline of the war from the rise of Adolf Hitler in 1933 to the establishment of international war crimes tribunals shortly after the war ended. A biographical appendix identifies and describes the most significant historical figures—their names are highlighted in **Bold Small Capitals** in the text—mentioned in the book, while a glossary explains the meaning of specific terms and concepts. A general bibliography lists a selection of major historical books, Web sites, movies, and television programs dealing with World War II. One section is devoted to discussing in detail "How to Evaluate Primary Documents" as historical sources. All these tools are intended to help readers to hone the skills needed to analyze and appreciate primary source documents and materials from World War II from the perspective of a well-trained, sophisticated, and knowledgeable historian.

INTRODUCTION

World War II was a truly global conflict, a conflagration that engulfed almost all the Eurasian land mass, drew in most of the countries and territories of North Africa, North and South America, Australasia, Southeast Asia, and the North and South Pacific, and reshaped the entire international system. In Asia, fighting began in 1937, expanded in 1941, and lasted until 1945; in Europe, hostilities started in September 1939 and continued for almost six years. In a broader perspective, the causes of World War II can be traced back at least to World War I (1914–1918), which fragmented and weakened the existing international order, creating a set of problems that helped to precipitate World War II; nor did the consequences of World War II end when fighting ceased in 1945. The power vacuum it created in large parts of the world was effectively filled by the Cold War, which evolved out of the balance of forces that existed when the war ended and from long-standing ideological and geopolitical conflicts with a far more venerable ancestry. World War II brought both U.S. and Soviet power into the center of Europe, where they confronted each other; it also made the United States a major player in the Asia-Pacific region. The rise of nationalist and communist political movements in Asia was clearly apparent even before World War II began, but the war enormously enhanced the position of both forces and ultimately did much to end formal Western colonialism around the globe.

Politicians, diplomats, and generals made—or tried to make—the war's biggest decisions, but their ultimate success in implementing these policies depended on their ability to win support or at least acquiescence from their populations. Around the world, the experience of war helped to unleash forces for social reform, generating demands that in future ordinary people should receive far more in terms of social benefits, their reward for fighting the war, enduring hardships on the home front, and laboring in the economic war effort. It was no coincidence that after World War II, generously funded social welfare states became the norm across most of Europe, nor that there and elsewhere aristocratic military elites were largely discredited and lost much of their political status and power. Across the globe, from World War II onward politicians—even in authoritarian one-party states—found it necessary to pay at least rhetorical lip service to democracy and popular rule. Nor was it coincidental that in Europe, which had endured two brutal wars in 30 years, liberals sought to integrate at least the Western portion of the continent politically and economically as a means of preventing further destructive conflagrations.

Almost throughout the globe, average men and women found it impossible to avoid or ignore the impact of World War II. Tens of millions of ordinary people fought in the war, as soldiers or irregular partisans. At least as many worked in the war industries and hundreds of millions lived in territories that were fought over, bombed, or occupied. Tens of millions of soldiers and civilians died, in combat, as prisoners of war, or as the victims of bombing, atrocities, concentration camps, exposure, starvation, and disease. Estimates of total wartime deaths range from 62 million to 79 million, between 3 and 4 percent of the world's population at the time. Of those who died, between 22 and 25 million were military personnel, while figures for civilian casualties—including those from war-related disease and famine—range from 32 to almost 50 million, plus an additional 5.75 million deaths in the genocidal German campaign against Europe's Jewish population known as the Holocaust. Germany lost between 6.7 and 9 million people in World War II, 8–10 percent of its population; the Soviet Union an estimated 26 million, 14 percent of its population, of whom military personnel represented well under half; China between 10 and 20 million, three-quarters of them civilians; Poland perhaps 5.5 million, 16 percent of its population; and Japan between 2.5 and 3 million, including up to 1 million civilians, around 4 percent of the entire population. Statistics alone do not convey the human cost. These figures do not include those who survived the war but were seriously wounded or psychologically traumatized. In addition, around the world, tens of millions of refugees who saw their homes and often their countries devastated were forcibly uprooted from their former lives—some for years, others permanently. This global Diaspora reshaped the demographics of the nations from which they fled and those—generally less domestically turbulent, the United States, Canada, and Australia, for example—to which they migrated.

From small children to the elderly, even among those fortunate enough to escape the war's worst ravages, its effects were still felt long after the actual fighting ceased. For many, the war was a time of brutal hardship; of battles and experiences they would rather forget. For others more fortunate, the war meant years of camaraderie and excitement, of using their skills and living their lives with an intensity they would never again attain, and of shared effort in a common and uplifting cause. And for many, maybe even the majority, the war and its effects were simply there to be endured and if possible survived. Although one can perhaps discern common themes, the impact of war varied widely, making every person's story in some way different and distinctive. No single collection of documents could ever hope to encapsulate the vast range of individual experiences in and responses to World War II. Even though some documents here were chosen at least in part because they seemed broadly representative of a particular group of wartime participants, the small selection of private letters, memoirs, and diaries gathered in this volume perhaps suggests how very differently the same war could be felt by each man, woman, or child involved.

At every level, World War II generated an enormous mass of documents, supplemented after the end of the conflict by a vast assortment of published and unpublished recollections, memoirs, and oral histories. Selecting representative documents for this volume has been an almost impossible task. Some date to the war itself, while others were created by participants looking back on their experiences, on occasion from a distance of several decades. Speeches or writings by prominent wartime figures—Franklin D. Roosevelt, Charles A. Lindbergh, Henry R. Luce—that won audiences of many millions are included. So too are significant accounts of particular aspects of the war written or broadcast by well-known popular journalists, and some widely circulated essays and poems. This volume includes just one highly secret official document distributed only to an extremely restricted readership: the minutes of the January 1942 Wannsee conference of top German leaders that decided on a systematic program to exterminate Europe's Jewish population. So many millions of deaths resulted from the implementation of this meeting's conclusions that its impact on everyday life seemed to justify its presence in this collection. Everything else contemporaneous with the war was fairly readily available at the time to the man or woman on the street and often the subject of extensive public commentary and discussion. We hope that this collection will within its brief compass convey something of the flavor of everyday life for at least a few diverse representatives of the millions of participants in World War II.

How to Evaluate Primary Documents

This collection can only at best offer an introduction to the complex documentary record of World War II. The supporting material on these documents seeks to highlight some of the issues—often still highly politicized and controversial—that continue to bedevil efforts to write the history of the war. What individuals and societies choose to remember and—even more—what they prefer to forget about a given set of events represent highly revealing decisions, in which current preoccupations and priorities often play a substantial part. Several documents in this volume, for example, discuss sensitive topics—the experiences of "comfort women" forced into prostitution, the mass rape of German women in 1945, medical experimentation on human subjects, racial discrimination against African Americans in the U.S. armed services, anti-Semitism within Allied nations—that governments involved often sedulously sought to ignore, deliberately suppressing information on these subjects when possible.

Documents are the raw materials of history. For the 20th century, they exist in great abundance, take many different forms, and are produced for a wide range of purposes. And, as with most raw materials, the historian has to recognize their varying properties and exercise great caution when handling them. The story they tell may or may not be true, and each type of document has its own advantages and drawbacks. One distinguished World War II historian, Sir John Wheeler-Bennett, who edited collections of German documents on interwar foreign policy and termed documents "the bare bones of history," recalled how, as "a young and budding historian I had a thing about documents. I believed that in documents lay the real truth of history." He nonetheless confessed that, while never losing his fundamental interest in documents, he later:

> discovered . . . that historical truth—in that it exists at all—lies not in documents alone, nor in memoirs, diaries, biographies or oral history. All these are essential and invaluable factors in the historian's armoury but, when the chips are down, the final result depends on the historian himself alone, on his ability to weigh, assay and analyse the accumulated material at his disposal and to come up with his own honest opinions and conclusions. There are no answers at the back of the book.[1]

No document can ever be treated as simply a neutral, objective, unbiased account of events. Every document is written for a purpose, even if it is simply to record one's own private experiences and feelings. In no circumstances can one approach a document in a vacuum; the more one knows about its context, the better one can appreciate it. One also needs to be aware that the documentary record is never complete. During World War II, governments and officials, especially when facing defeat and possible retribution, destroyed many compromising documents, particularly those detailing atrocities and abuses of power and materials relating to intelligence operations. Many documents have also been casualties of war itself, immolated in bombing raids and other military operations. Personal and even official records are sometimes simply jettisoned when people and organizations move house or need more storage space. And even today, many surviving documents from World War II remain closed to researchers, as governments still consider them too sensitive to release.

Every document comes out of certain circumstances, produced by one or more individuals or organizations at a given time for specific reasons, usually framed with a particular audience or audiences in mind. Confronting this evidence, a historian must ask: *Who* wrote this, *When, Where, For Whom,* and *Why?* Precisely *what kind* of document is it, and in *what context* was it written or produced? *How* accurate or truthful is this document? *How* and where was it circulated? The historian must also consider the *Results* and *Consequences,* short- and long-term, of the document in question. The more one knows, the better equipped one is to appreciate all the ramifications and complications surrounding a given document.

Who can be complicated. Some documents—a soldier's letter to his girlfriend, or a personal diary—are relatively straightforward, with a single, readily obvious author. Other documents may have multiple authors. More often than not, government documents are products of many hands. U.S. president Franklin D. Roosevelt employed several speech writers and consulted other officials and confidants as he drafted his public addresses, even though the final call on what to include was his. Oral histories are often the outcome of interviews, their text first recorded or taken down in note form and then transcribed, with corrections sometimes made by the interviewee, sometimes by the interviewer, before a smooth final text emerges. Much of their content may reflect the interviewer's own questions, interests, and preoccupations. Professional secretaries frequently write memoranda of conversations or minutes of meetings that summarize the proceedings, sometimes accurately, sometimes with major omissions or inaccuracies; full verbal transcripts of such interchanges are far rarer. Public statements by individuals or organizations often represent a collective effort, even when only one person's name is given as author.

Who requires the historian not simply to identify the author(s) of these varied accounts, but also to appreciate just who or what that author was. Each human being is the product of a unique set of experiences and circumstances, living in a specific time, place, and situation, carrying highly individual baggage in terms of assumptions, background, education, class, gender, race, nationality, and outlook. Each of us filters our understanding of both past and present through this apparatus, much of which we take for granted. Forty years after World War II ended, a radical American Jewish woman welder from Brooklyn, New York, continued to view Stalin's Russia with warm affection, while a top German diplomat who fought against Russia from 1941 to 1945 still regretted his country's failure to capitalize on popular Russian and Ukrainian resentment of Stalinist rule by organizing Russian prisoners of war into effective anti-Soviet military units that he believed might have overthrown the Soviet communist regime. Yet a Russian general who likewise spent four years fighting on the Eastern front, and was present when Soviet and American forces met up at Torgau on the Elbe in late April 1945, highlighted his memories of numerous savage German atrocities against

Russian civilians and prisoners of war. Each retrospectively viewed World War II through very different spectacles.

When refers not just to the actual date on which a given document is written, but also to the broader context. A pacifist manifesto produced a year before the United States entered World War II, when the issue of American intervention in the conflict was highly controversial, must be seen as a deliberate attempt to influence the ongoing political debate on the subject. In June 1944, professional historians accompanied the Allied forces launching the D-Day invasion of Western Europe and interviewed the soldiers involved within days or at most weeks of the Normandy landings. Such interviews are likely to have a freshness that may be missing from veterans' war stories many years later, when certain tales have been retold on numerous occasions and have settled into a formulaic account. But maturity, distance, the passage of time, and hindsight may give those whose memories of war date back to when they were children or in their teens or early 20s different and more reflective perspectives on their experiences and how and where these fitted into broader historical trends. A letter writer, diarist, or journalist describing events of the previous few hours—the German invasion of Poland, the nightly bombing of London in 1940, or a raid over Germany—will write with more immediacy than one recounting these events months or years later.

Where can be equally important. Individual diaries written in the Warsaw ghetto as German restrictions caused ever growing numbers of death from starvation and disease, or in besieged Leningrad in somewhat similar conditions, will almost inevitably be less exuberant than an account by a prominent American official of the Allied liberation of Paris after four years of German occupation. Knowing that the great majority of inhabitants of the Warsaw ghetto died during the war while many of those in Leningrad survived is significant to understanding the different diaries. Predictably, a farewell letter to his parents from a Japanese Kamikaze pilot who killed himself shortly afterwards in a suicide attack during the Battle of Okinawa is far more somber in tone than a highly trained American bomber pilot's letter from Britain to his future wife. Even though the American was flying dangerous missions, his chances of survival were appreciably higher, and it was clear to him that the war would end in an Allied victory. The fact that W. H. Auden wrote his poem "September 1, 1939," in New York, in a country that was officially neutral and detached from the European war just beginning, gave him a measure of distance from the conflict. The degree of censorship, official or self-imposed, in any location affected what individuals or organizations felt free to write and circulate to others, whether as unpublished personal letters or published accounts.

The questions of *For Whom* and *Why* a given document is written or produced are not always straightforward. Personal letters are usually intended for the stated recipient, though the writer often knows that they will be circulated to others, possibly interested friends and family, perhaps even beyond. Diaries can represent a permanent record of interesting events where the writer is a participant or witness; a focus of self-examination; or a repository for indiscreet observations and even frustrations impossible to express elsewhere. Wartime speeches by top officials often had multiple audiences. Speaking one day after Pearl Harbor, Roosevelt needed to obtain a declaration of war from Congress; to reassure the American people and prepare them for a long, hard, but winnable war; and to set out his country's official position, that Japan had launched an unprovoked sneak attack on a peaceable, innocent United States. American journalists reporting from Germany and Britain early in the war often sought to expose the brutality of Nazi Germany, while encouraging support for Britain, especially after Winston Churchill became Britain's prime minister. Public statements, such as those of the Reverend Arle Brooks on pacifism or French resistance figures on the future of their country and Europe, are usually intended to advocate a particular policy or stance, win political and popular support for it, and perhaps bolster the standing and influence of the authors.

Autobiographical writing and oral histories can be particularly slippery sources. The past is too often tailored to meet present requirements and expectations. Memoirs or oral recollections produced many years after certain episodes can be exercises in self-justification. They may seek to distort the historical record by exaggerating, diminishing, altering, concealing, or ignoring the author's role and responsibility, or that of the author's country, organization, army unit, or colleagues, for specific actions or policies, especially if these are later considered discreditable. After the war ended, novel technology, especially light and easily operable recording machines, contributed to the development of the new field of oral history, whose practitioners made dedicated efforts to collect, transcribe, and make available the recollections of all levels of wartime participants, from those who were children at the time to high-ranking officials. The growing interest in family history likewise impelled individuals to set down their recollections for future generations. Some such efforts had additional motivations. In the early 1990s, assorted Russians and Americans who had been involved in some aspect of Soviet-American collaboration during World War II took part in teleconferences and other meetings where they recalled their experiences. In their reminiscences, most tended to emphasize positive aspects of the Soviet-American wartime relationship.

Other activists of various political stripes gathered collections of oral histories that focused upon unsavory topics once officially ignored or minimized, including the sufferings of "comfort women" working for the Japanese military, the wartime internment of Japanese Americans in the United States, and Japan's secret program using captured prisoners for biological warfare experiments, something U.S. occupation authorities allegedly deliberately concealed after 1945 in return for access to the data collected. On occasion, the reminiscences so compiled became ammunition in campaigns to win compensation for the victims. However poignant such accounts may be, historians need to remember that they were often written and perhaps edited with this purpose in mind. In some cases, recalling hardships that the losers of World War II endured became a controversial exercise. Efforts by German and Japanese representatives to bring up the rape of German women by Russian soldiers, the deaths and sufferings of millions of German refugees fleeing westward as Soviet forces advanced, ferociously destructive Allied bombing raids on both German and Japanese cities, and the use of atomic weapons against Nagasaki and Hiroshima, attracted heavy criticism as being attempts to cast Germany and Japan in the role of victims of World War II and implicitly exonerate those countries and their people from responsibility for the savagery and suffering they inflicted on others during the war. Debate still rages today over whether Stalin's Russia or Hitler's Germany showed more brutality toward opponents, internal and external, and whether Soviet communism and Nazi fascism should be considered as morally equivalent.

When analyzing any document, text, context, and the form in which it was circulated are all important. Literary skills are useful here. Language often reveals much about the writer and his or her objectives and mindset. The chillingly matter-of-fact bureaucratic prose of the Wannsee memorandum detailing the "Final Solution" indicates how Nazi officials deliberately dehumanized the Jews they intended to exterminate, treating mass murder almost as a technical problem. President Franklin D. Roosevelt's rather understated, utilitarian style when telling the American people of the Japanese attack on Pearl Harbor, enlivened by the use of the words "infamy," "treachery," and "dastardly" to characterize Japanese behavior, proved extremely effective in terms of winning popular support. The oral histories included here have probably undergone some editing, and are in many cases translations, but even so most convey a strong sense of their subjects' personalities. The diary of the elderly Russian artist Anna Ostroumova-Lebedeva, trapped in Leningrad throughout its lengthy siege, uses dramatic metaphors and philosophical speculation to express her sense of a world grown mad, trapped in a romantic infatuation with war, reflections evocative of the St. Petersburg intelligentsia to which she belonged. The athletic and beautiful flying ace Olga Lisikova, another Leningrad native, was by contrast far less poetic in her forceful but straightforward account of her wartime aviation career, whose blunt tone seems an expression of her own fiery and resourceful determination.

Every document has its own theme, key concepts, and assumptions, which the reader needs to identify. Charles Lindbergh and Arle Brooks, opposing American intervention in World War II, appealed to democratic values that they assumed all Americans shared; but their opponents who supported U.S. involvement in the war likewise highlighted the cause of freedom and democracy. Roosevelt—like his British counterpart, Prime Minister Winston Churchill—invoked God in his wartime speeches, aligning his own nation's cause with Christian values and principles that Brooks too claimed to represent through his pacifism. Japanese Americans seeking redress for past internment emphasized not just their own patriotism but their staunch belief in American values and their firm Christian faith, implicitly arguing that these made them more deserving of compensation. The Filipino politician Claro Recto, trying to mitigate harsh Japanese occupation policies against his own countrymen, appealed to stated Japanese support for Philippine independence and the ideals of pan-Asian solidarity and brotherhood expressed in Japan's declaration of a Greater East Asia Co-Prosperity Sphere. Several documents in this collection demonstrate how in both Europe and Asia, issues of resistance, collaboration, treachery, patriotism, and how best to serve one's country could become extremely complicated, especially in times of occupation or when an individual or group disagreed with the policies of their own government. Even a seemingly simple letter from an American bomber pilot trying to relax after a difficult raid on Germany to a cousin back in Kansas gains added interest when one realizes that for some time the writer had been trying to persuade this woman to marry him.

The way in which documents are circulated has important implications. Journalists normally wrote or broadcast for the general public and hoped extensive audiences would read or listen to them. The publisher Henry Luce, seeking maximum exposure for his essay "The American Century," which urged the United States to move aggressively to make itself the world's greatest power, not only gave it top billing in *Life* magazine but reprinted millions of copies, distributing these in bulk throughout the United States, a deliberate effort to generate public support for his views. Arle Brooks, who engineered his own arrest and trial to ensure maximum publicity for his presentencing declaration of pacifist beliefs, undoubtedly hoped to draw comparable attention to his own statement of faith. He did not succeed: the Christian press covered it extensively, but the *New York Times,* the leading newspaper of record in the United States, forbore to mention the entire episode, quite possibly an indication of the pro-Allied outlook of the newspaper's proprietors. For Jews confined to the Warsaw ghetto, well aware that their chances of living through the war were slim, keeping diaries, letters, and other written records of their life there and preserving every scrap of documentary evidence was a means of affirming their existence and defying efforts to destroy their entire community. Hiding caches of such materials, in the hope that some at least would survive, was an act of faith. Some official documents—the minutes of the Wannsee conference mandating the "final solution," for example—were highly secret, intended only for a limited audience. Many of the more compromising among these were destroyed in the course of the war. Nazi Interior Minister Heinrich Himmler encouraged unmarried SS men to produce as many children as possible before going to war, but the outrage he provoked among Nazi women's leaders impelled him to soft-pedal and tone down such exhortations. Official proclamations and speeches by top political leaders, by contrast, were carefully crafted public statements intended to rally popular support for specific policies.

Even documents which were originally private often subsequently appeared in print. The published versions sometimes had major omissions, the result of personal or official censorship. Anna Ostroumova-Lebedeva's autobiographical memoirs of the siege of Leningrad, published in 1945 and 1951, included excerpts from her diary, but none of these mentioned inequities in food rationing, misbehavior by communist functionaries, or official callousness toward the city's population. Although her original diary was preserved and donated to a Leningrad museum, not until the 1990s, after the fall of the Soviet Union, was the full version published. Most of the oral histories here are drawn from larger published collections, compiled in the 1980s and 1990s for particular purposes, when elderly survivors of World War II were already reaching the end of their lifespans. Some compilers sought simply to gather personal memories of that period while the subjects were still available and make these parts of the historical record. In doing so, they often published reminiscences on sensitive matters, sexual abuse or personal knowledge of atrocities, for example, or recollections of savage combat experiences, that the speakers or writers would not have included at an earlier date. Historians also sought to unearth information on various compromising subjects—biological warfare, atrocities, rape and sexual exploitation, intelligence activities—that different governments had for their own convenience sought to deny or ignore. These endeavors often involved collecting verbal testimonies not merely from victims but also from individuals who had in some way participated in such activities. Some found this a long-sought opportunity to express their own sense of guilt; others, rather chillingly, justified their activities and found nothing in them to regret.

Always, however, there is a certain amount of self-selection, since those who do not wish to record their memories often simply decline to do so. When using such published collections, compiled many years after the event, the reader needs to be aware of various pitfalls. In some cases, for example, oft-told war stories, the account may have lost its original freshness and settled into a comfortable formulaic pattern. Published collections of oral histories and recollections may also omit substantial portions of each and only include those highlights that most appeal to the editors, sometimes scattered through a volume in several different locations. When compiling these collections, the editors may also have their agenda, and only include materials that accord with this. Memory is often unreliable at best, and over time many people have exaggerated or altered their recollections, sometimes deliberately, sometimes unconsciously, or omitted whatever they consider discreditable to themselves. Very often, it is impossible for those using oral histories or memoirs to verify the accuracy of recollections, though when a group of colleagues of some kind is involved, some degree of cross-checking is often possible.

One should exercise due skepticism and at least acknowledge the existence of a lengthy tradition of creative fictional memoirs and other documents—including faked diaries by Adolf Hitler—that later proved to be hoaxes. Diaries, letters, memoranda, and reports written separately but describing the same events can serve as controls. In no case, however, is there any guarantee of truth. The past is another country, one we view at a distance through our own contemporary perspective. Our reconstruction, however partial, of that past from documents and other evidence demands knowledge, skill, understanding, and the imagination to put ourselves in the place of those who first created these materials.

Note

1. John Wheeler-Bennett, *Friends, Enemies and Sovereigns* (London: Macmillan, 1976), 58.

Chronology

1933	January 30	Adolf Hitler is appointed chancellor of Germany.
1934	June 30	The political purge known as the Night of the Long Knives begins and will continue until July 2.
	August 2	Hitler merges the offices of chancellor and president, making himself absolute ruler of Germany.
1938	March 12	German troops enter Austria unopposed.
	March 13	Germany annexes Austria, creating the Anschluss.
	September 30	Germany, France, Britain, and Italy sign the Munich Agreement, which permits German annexation of the Czechoslovakian Sudetenland.
	November 9–10	Following violent attacks on Jewish homes, businesses, and synagogues in Germany, approximately 25,000–30,000 Jews are deported to concentration camps in an event that becomes known as Kristallnacht ("Night of Broken Glass").
	December 6	France signs a nonaggression pact with Germany.
1939	March 16	Czechoslovakia falls under German control.
	September 1	Germany invades Poland.
	September 3	Great Britain and France declare war on Germany.
	September 7	French forces cross the German border near Saarbrucken.
	September 17	The Soviet Union invades eastern Poland.
	October 5	Polish organized resistance ends at Kock.
	October 14	The German submarine U-57 sinks the British battleship *Royal Oak* at Scapa Flow in the Orkney Islands.
	November 30	The Soviet Union invades Finland.
	December 13	Battle of the River Plate.

	December 17	The German pocket battleship *Graf Spee* is scuttled off Montevideo, Uruguay.
1940	February 13	The Soviets breach the Mannerheim Line in Finland.
	March 12	The Soviets and Finns sign a peace treaty, ending the Finnish-Soviet War (Winter War).
	April	The Katyń Forest Massacre takes place throughout April and into early May.
	April 9	Germany invades Norway and Denmark.
	May 3	Vidkun Quisling becomes leader of Norway as King Haakon departs.
	May 10	Germany invades the Netherlands, Belgium, Luxembourg, and France. Winston L. S. Churchill becomes British prime minister.
	May 13	Queen Wilhelmina leaves the Netherlands for exile in London.
	May 14	Elements of the German Air Force bomb Rotterdam.
	May 15	The Netherlands army surrenders to Germany.
	May 19	The German ports of Hamburg and Bremen are bombed by the British.
	May 26	Operation Dynamo, the evacuation of British and French forces at Dunkirk, commences.
	May 28	Belgium capitulates to Germany.
	June 4	Operation Dynamo ends.
	June 8	Allied forces complete their evacuation from Norway.
	June 9	Norway signs an armistice with Germany.
	June 10	Italy declares war on France and Great Britain. Norway officially surrenders to the Germans.
	June 11	Italian forces invade southeastern France.
	June 14	Paris falls to the Germans.
	June 15	Soviet forces invade Estonia.
	June 16	Marshal Henri Philippe Pétain becomes French premier.
	June 17	Soviet forces invade Latvia.
	June 18	Neutral Sweden accedes to an agreement whereby German forces may pass through Swedish territory.
	June 22	France signs an armistice with Germany.
	June 27	Soviet forces invade Romania.
	June 28	The British government recognizes Charles de Gaulle as leader of the Free French. German forces bomb the British Channel Islands of Guernsey and Jersey.

July 1	German submarines attack merchant ships in the Atlantic Ocean.
July 3	In Operation Catapult, British Navy units secure portions of the French fleet but engage and sink a number of French warships at Mers-el-Kébir, Algeria.
July 9	Vichy becomes the temporary capital of France. The British government rejects Hitler's peace offer.
July 10	The Battle of Britain commences.
July 16	Hitler plans Operation Sea Lion, the invasion of Great Britain.
July 25	The United States announces an embargo of strategic materials to Japan.
August 5	Italian forces invade British Somaliland. Latvia and Lithuania are formally admitted into the Soviet Union.
August 6	Estonia is formally admitted into the Soviet Union.
August 17	Hitler declares a blockade of Great Britain.
September 3	The Destroyers for Bases deal between the United States and Britain is announced by U.S. president Franklin D. Roosevelt as an executive order. Britain receives 50 World War I–vintage U.S. destroyers in return for leases on base territory in North America.
September 13	Italian forces invade Egypt.
September 15	A major German air attack is made on London.
September 16	Conscription is introduced in the United States.
September 22	Vichy France allows Japanese air bases and troops in French Indochina.
September 23	British and Free French forces attack Dakar. Hitler and Spanish dictator Francisco Franco meet at Hendaye, France, on the border with Spain.
September 27	The Axis Tripartite Pact is signed between Germany, Italy, and Japan.
October 7	German forces enter Romania.
October 10	Operation Sea Lion is shelved.
October 28	Italian forces invade Greece from Italian-occupied Albania.
October 31	The Battle of Britain ends. The Germans switch to night bombings (the Blitz).
November 5	Roosevelt wins election to his third four-year term as U.S. president.

	November 11	British forces stage air attack on the Italian Fleet at Taranto, Italy.
	November 14–15	The Germans stage an air attack on Coventry, England, destroying much of the city.
	November 19–20	The Germans stage air attack on Birmingham, England.
	November 20	Hungary joins the Axis alliance.
	November 22	The Greeks defeat the Italians, capturing Koritsa, Albania.
	November 23	Romania joins the Axis alliance.
	December 9	British forces begin to drive the Italians from Egypt.
1941	January 19	British forces invade Italian Eritrea.
	January 22	Tobruk falls to Australian and British forces.
	February	*Life* magazine publishes "The American Century" by Henry Luce.
	February 5–7	The Battle of Beda Fomm takes place. The British defeat Italian forces in Libya.
	February 8	British forces take Benghazi, Libya. Bulgaria and Germany sign a military pact.
	February 12	German general Erwin Rommel arrives in North Africa.
	March 1	Bulgaria joins the Tripartite Pact.
	March 11	Roosevelt signs the Lend-Lease Bill.
	March 16	The British mount a counteroffensive in Somaliland and Ethiopia.
	March 24	Rommel commences the German offensive in Libya.
	March 25	The Yugoslavian government agrees to join the Axis alliance.
	March 26	The pro-Axis Yugoslav government is overthrown.
	March 28	Britain inflicts losses on the Italian fleet in the Battle of Cape Matapan.
	April 3	A pro-Axis regime is established in Iraq.
	April 6	Germany invades Greece and Yugoslavia. The British occupy Addis Abba, the capital of Ethiopia.
	April 11	The Axis siege of Tobruk commences.
	April 13	A five-year nonaggression pact is signed between Japan and the Soviet Union.
	April 17	The Yugoslavian army surrenders to the Germans.
	April 23	Greece signs an armistice with Germany.
	May 1	The British repulse the German attack on Tobruk.

May 2	The British invade Iraq.
May 5	Ethiopian emperor Haile Selassie returns to Addis Ababa.
May 10	German Deputy Führer Rudolf Hess flies to Scotland on an unauthorized peace-keeping mission.
May 20	The Germans mount an airborne assault against Crete.
May 24	The German battleship *Bismarck* sinks Britain's battle cruiser *Hood.*
May 27	The British sink the *Bismarck.*
May 31	Crete falls to the Germans.
June 4	A pro-Allied government is installed in Iraq.
June 8	British and Free French troops attack Syria and Lebanon.
June 14	Vichy French forces in Syria are defeated by the British.
June 15	The British counteroffensive in Libya is defeated.
June 22	Germany, Italy, and Romania declare war on the Soviet Union. Germany commences Operation Barbarossa, the invasion of the Soviet Union.
June 26	Finland declares war on the Soviet Union, launching the Continuation War.
June 27	Hungary declares war on the Soviet Union.
July 9	The Germans capture 300,000 Soviet troops near Minsk in the Soviet Union.
July 12	The Anglo-Soviet Treaty of Mutual Assistance is signed.
July 14	British forces occupy Syria and Lebanon.
July 24	Southern French Indochina is occupied by Japanese forces.
July 26	The United States suspends trade with Japan.
July 31	German preparations commence for the so-called Final Solution, a standardized method of annihilating the European Jews, which ultimately results in the Holocaust.
August 12	The Atlantic Charter is drawn up by Churchill and Roosevelt.
August 25	Soviet and British troops occupy Iran.
September 3	Gas chambers are used experimentally at the Auschwitz concentration camp.
September 8	German forces lay siege to Leningrad.
September 19	German forces capture Kiev.
September 29	The German army murders nearly 34,000 Jews in Kiev.
October 2	The Germans commence Operation Typhoon, the planned capture of Moscow.

	October 16	German and Romanian forces capture Odessa.
	October 17	General Tōjō Hideki becomes the premier of Japan.
	October 24	German forces take Kharkov in the Soviet Union.
	November 8	The Germans move onto the Crimean Peninsula.
	November 13	The British carrier *Ark Royal* is sunk by a German submarine.
	November 18	British forces launch a counteroffensive in Libya.
	November 20	The Germans take Rostov in the Soviet Union.
	November 27	Soviet forces retake Rostov.
	December 5	German forces suspend their attack on Moscow.
	December 7	Japanese forces bomb Pearl Harbor in the Hawaiian Islands.
	December 8	The United States, Great Britain, and other Allied powers declare war on Japan. Japanese forces attack Guam, Wake Island, and the Philippines. Japan invades Hong Kong, Malaya, and Thailand.
	December 9	Japan invades the Gilbert Islands. China declares war on Germany and Japan. Hitler issues his "Night and Fog" decree.
	December 10	British forces relieve the Tobruk garrison. Japanese aircraft sink the British battleship *Prince of Wales* and battle cruiser *Repulse* off Malaya. Japanese forces take Guam.
	December 11	Italy and Germany declare war on the United States. Japanese forces invade Burma (Myanmar).
	December 16	Japanese forces invade Borneo. Axis forces in North Africa retreat to El Agheila in Libya.
	December 19	Hitler assumes command of the German army.
	December 23	The Japanese offensive in the Philippines commences.
	December 24	British forces recapture Benghazi.
	December 25	Japanese forces take Hong Kong.
	December 31	Japanese forces occupy Manila in the Philippines.
1942	January 1	The United Nations (UN) declaration is signed by 26 nations. The Soviets begin an offensive in Finland.
	January 2	The Japanese capture Manila.
	January 11	The Japanese invade the Netherlands East Indies. Japanese forces capture Kuala Lumpur.
	January 13	Germany begins a U-boat offensive along the eastern coast of the United States. Soviet forces recapture Kiev.
	January 20	Japan commences its Burma offensive. The Wannsee Conference, a meeting of German officials, is held in Berlin to discuss procedures for the "final solution."

January 21	The Axis offensive against British forces in Libya commences.
January 25	Japanese forces land at Lae, New Guinea.
January 26	The first U.S. troops committed to the war effort arrive in northern Ireland.
January 28	German forces recapture Benghazi.
February 1	U.S. planes bomb the Marshall and Gilbert islands.
February 8	Japanese forces take Rangoon, Burma.
February 15	Singapore surrenders to Japanese forces.
February 19	Japanese forces capture Bali.
February 23	Japanese forces capture Timor.
February 27–28	The Battle of the Java Sea is waged.
March 2	Japanese forces land in Mindanao in the Philippines. Batavia in the Netherlands East Indies is evacuated, and the Dutch government is moved to Bandung on Java.
March 7	Japanese troops enter Rangoon.
March 9	Java surrenders to the Japanese.
March 13	Japanese forces land in the Solomon Islands.
March 17	U.S. general Douglas MacArthur reaches Australia from the Philippines.
March 19	The gas chamber is first used on human victims at Auschwitz-Birkenau.
April 5	Japanese naval forces raid Ceylon (Sri Lanka).
April 9	U.S. forces surrender to the Japanese on the Bataan Peninsula on Luzon in the Philippines.
April 18	U.S. B-25 bombers raid Tokyo.
May 1	Mandalay, Burma, surrenders to Japanese forces.
May 6	Corregidor falls to the Japanese. U.S. forces surrender in the Philippines.
May 7–8	The Battle of the Coral Sea, between Japanese and U.S.-Australian naval and air forces, is waged.
May 20	Japanese forces complete the conquest of Burma.
May 22	Mexico declares war on the Axis powers.
May 26	Axis forces begin their offensive in Libya.
May 27	Reichsprotektor of Bohemia and Moravia Reinhard Heydrich is attacked and wounded in Prague.
May 30	The Royal Air Force (RAF) bombs Köln (Cologne), Germany.

June 4	Japanese forces attack the Aleutian Islands.
June 4–6	The Battle of Midway is waged.
June 5	German forces besiege Sevastopol in the Crimea.
June 6	Heydrich dies in Prague after being attacked by assassins the week prior.
June 7	The village of Lidice in Bohemia is liquidated in retaliation for Heydrich's death.
June 21	Axis forces in North Africa capture Tobruk.
June 24	General Dwight D. Eisenhower is named to command U.S. forces in Europe.
June 25	The Germans are victorious at Kharkov.
July 1–3	The Germans secure Sevastopol.
July 1–4	The First Battle of El Alamein is waged in Egypt.
July 3	Japanese forces land on Guadalcanal in the Solomon Islands.
July 22	The first Warsaw ghetto deportations to death camps occur.
July 23	German forces capture Rostov-on-Don in the Soviet Union.
August 7	U.S. Marines land on Guadalcanal.
August 9	German forces capture oil fields in the Caucasus. A civil disobedience campaign begins in India.
August 12	Churchill and Averell Harriman accept Joseph Stalin's invitation and meet with him in Moscow.
August 13	General Bernard L. Montgomery becomes commander of the British Eighth Army in Egypt.
August 19	British and Canadian forces raid Dieppe, France. Brazil declares war on Germany and Italy.
August 23	The Battle for Stalingrad begins.
August 31	The Battle of Alam Halfa halts Axis advance in North Africa.
September 2	Axis forces retreat following the Battle of Alam Halfa.
September 22	German forces reach Stalingrad.
September 26	Australian ground forces stop Japanese land forces working overland toward Port Moresby, New Guinea.
October 18	Hitler issues the secret Commando Order.
October 23	The British Eighth Army attacks Axis forces at El Alamein.
November 1	British forces break through at El Alamein.
November 4	Axis forces retreat from El Alamein.
November 8	In Operation Torch, Allied forces land in Algeria and Morocco.

	November 11	Axis forces occupy Vichy-administered France.
	November 13	British forces retake Tobruk.
	November 16	Australian and U.S. forces attack Buna-Gona, New Guinea.
	November 19	The Soviet counteroffensive begins at Stalingrad.
	November 27	The French scuttle 77 warships at Toulon, France.
	November 28	The Allies are repulsed by Germans 20 miles outside Tunis, Tunisia.
	December 13	Axis forces withdraw from El Agheila.
	December 16	German forces try but fail to relieve Stalingrad.
	December 24	Admiral Jean Darlan is assassinated in Algiers.
	December 31	The Battle of the Barents Sea is waged.
1943	January 2	Australian and U.S. forces take Buna, New Guinea.
	January 14–24	The Casablanca Conference, involving Churchill and Roosevelt, takes place.
	January 23	Tripoli, Libya, is taken by the British Eighth Army.
	January 27	Wilhemshaven, Germany, is bombed by the U.S. Army Air Forces (USAAF).
	January 30	Admiral Karl Dönitz succeeds Admiral Erich Raeder as commander of the German navy.
	January 31	German field marshal Friedrich Paulus surrenders at Stalingrad.
	February 8	The Soviet Red Army recaptures Kursk.
	February 9	U.S. forces secure Guadalcanal.
	February 16	Soviet forces retake Kharkov.
	February 22	Rommel exits by the Kasserine Pass in Tunisia.
	February 25	Rommel is replaced by General Hans-Jürgen von Arnim as commander of German forces in North Africa.
	March 2–4	The Battle of the Bismarck Sea is fought between Japanese and U.S.-Australian forces.
	March 5	Allied aircraft bomb industrial targets in Germany's Ruhr Valley.
	March 14–15	German forces recapture Kharkov.
	March 20–28	The British Eighth Army breaks the Axis Mareth Line in Tunisia.
	April 1–22	Axis forces withdraw from Tunisia.
	April 18	Japanese admiral Yamamoto Isoroku's plane is shot down in a U.S. aerial ambush.

April 19	Elements of the German army begin an effort to liquidate the Warsaw ghetto.
April 22	The United States and Great Britain start the Allied offensive in North Africa.
May 11	The Japanese-held Attu Island in the Aleutians is attacked by U.S. troops.
May 13	The Allies capture Tunis and secure the surrender of 275,000 German and Italian troops in North Africa.
May 16	The Warsaw ghetto uprising ends.
May 16–17	The RAF makes Ruhr Valley dams a priority target.
May 21	French Resistance leader Jean Moulin is arrested by the Germans.
May 22	Dönitz suspends U-boat operations in the North Atlantic.
June 11	The Italian island of Pantellaria surrenders.
June 13	The Tunisia Campaign ends in defeat for the Axis powers.
June 30	U.S. forces retake Attu Island.
July 5–17	The Battle of Kursk is waged.
July 9	U.S. and British forces invade Sicily in Operation Husky.
July 19	U.S. aircraft bomb Rome.
July 22	U.S. forces capture Palermo, Sicily.
July 24	Allied aircraft bomb Norway. RAF bombings reduce Hamburg, Germany, to rubble.
July 25	King Victor Emmanuel III of Italy dismisses Benito Mussolini; Pietro Badoglio succeeds Mussolini as the leader of Italy.
August 1	The Japanese establish a puppet regime in Burma.
August 5	Soviet forces recapture Belgorod and Orel.
August 6	The Battle of Vella Gulf in the Solomon Islands is fought.
August 14–24	The Allied Quebec Conference is held.
August 17	British and U.S. forces conclude the conquest of Sicily. The USAAF conducts daylight raids on Regensburg and Schweinfurt, Germany.
August 23	Soviet forces retake Kharkov.
September 3	British forces land at Calabria, Italy.
September 8	The Italian government signs an armistice with the Allies.
September 9	Allied forces land at Taranto and Salerno, Italy, during Operation Avalanche.

	September 10–11	German forces occupy Rome.
	September 12	Mussolini is rescued by German commandos led by Otto Skorzeny.
	September 18	Allied forces capture Sardinia.
	September 22	Soviet forces secure a bridgehead on the Dnieper River.
	September 23	Mussolini establishes a new Fascist government in northern Italy.
	September 24	German forces retreat from Smolensk in the Soviet Union.
	September 25	Soviet forces retake Smolensk and Novorossisk in the Soviet Union.
	October 1	The Allies capture Naples.
	October 4	German forces capture the Greek island of Kos.
	October 5	Allied forces capture Corsica.
	October 13	Italy declares war on Germany. The USAAF conducts a second raid on Schweinfurt.
	October 14	Canadian forces take Campobasso, Italy. Soviet forces capture Zaporozhye, Ukraine.
	October 18	British, Soviet, and U.S. foreign ministers meet in Moscow.
	October 25	The Soviets take Dnepropetrovsk, Ukraine.
	November 1	U.S. forces invade Bougainville in the Solomon Islands.
	November 5	The Greater East Asia Conference is held in Tokyo.
	November 7	Soviet forces liberate Kiev.
	November 20	The Allies attack the Sangro River in Italy. Eduard Benes and Stalin sign a Soviet-Czech peace treaty.
	November 22–26	The Allies hold the Cairo Conference.
	November 28–December 1	The Tehran Conference between Churchill, Roosevelt, and Stalin.
	December 3–7	After a brief hiatus, the Cairo Conference resumes.
	December 24	Eisenhower receives command of the Allied European invasion.
	December 26	U.S. forces reach Cape Gloucester in the Solomon Islands.
1944	January 16	Eisenhower is appointed supreme commander of Allied forces in Western Europe.
	January 22	The Allied beachhead is established at Anzio, Italy.
	January 25	The Allies begin a counteroffensive in Burma.
	January 27	Soviet forces break the 900-day Siege of Leningrad.

February 3	The Allied offensive stalls at Cassino, Italy.
February 7	U.S. forces take Kwajalein in the Marshall Islands.
February 15	Allied aircraft bomb Monte Cassino, Italy. Soviet forces secure Estonia.
February 18	U.S. naval forces attack the Japanese on Truk in the Caroline Islands.
February 20–26	Allied forces coordinate the "Big Week" air strikes against German factories.
February 26	The Soviets bomb Helsinki, Finland.
March 8	Japanese forces begin an offensive in Burma.
March 15	Japanese forces invade India.
March 18	The RAF conducts a large-scale raid on Hamburg.
March 30	The RAF raids Nürnberg (Nuremberg), Germany.
April 2	Soviet troops enter Romania.
April 10	Soviet forces retake Odessa.
April 15	Soviet troops take Tarnopol, Ukraine.
April 19	Japanese forces capture Zhengzou, China.
May 1	Japanese forces take Xuchang, China.
May 9	The Soviets recapture Sevastopol.
May 11	Allied forces attack the Gustav Line near Rome.
May 12	German forces surrender in the Crimea.
May 17–18	German troops withdraw from Monte Cassino.
May 23	The Allies break out from the Anzio beachhead.
May 25	German forces withdraw from Anzio. Japanese forces take Luoyang, China.
June 4–5	Allied troops enter Rome.
June 6	Allied troops land in Normandy, France (D-Day).
June 9	Soviet forces attack Finland.
June 10	The Germans liquidate the town of Oradou-sur-Glane, France.
June 12–13	German V-1 buzz bombs hit London.
June 15	The USAAF bombs Tokyo. U.S. forces invade Saipan in the Mariana Islands.
June 19–21	The Battle of the Philippine Sea is fought.
June 22	Soviet forces commence an offensive in Belorussia. Japanese forces withdraw from Kohima, India.

June 27	Cherbourg, France, is liberated by the Allies.
July 3	The Soviets recover Belorussia.
July 4	The Allies defeat Japanese forces at Imphal, India.
July 9	British and Canadian forces capture Caen, France. U.S. forces declare Saipan secured.
July 18	U.S. forces liberate Saint-Lô, France. Tōjō resigns as Japanese premier and is succeeded by Koiso Kuniaki.
July 20	An assassination attempt on Hitler is unsuccessful, and the effort by the German Resistance to seize power fails.
July 21	U.S. forces invade Guam in the Mariana Islands.
July 23	Soviet forces take Lublin, Poland.
July 25	Soviet forces liberate the Majdanek concentration camp. In Operation Cobra, Allied forces break out from Normandy.
July 28	The Soviets retake Brest-Litovsk, Belorussia. U.S. forces take Coutances, France.
August 1	The Warsaw Rising against Germans begins. U.S. troops reach Avranches, France.
August 4	The last Jews leave the Netherlands, Anne Frank included. Allied forces capture Florence, Italy.
August 8	Japanese forces capture Hengyang, China.
August 10	U.S. forces declare Guam secured.
August 11	German forces withdraw from Florence.
August 15	In Operation Dragoon, Allied forces land in southern France.
August 16	Falaise, France, is liberated by the Allies. The French Resistance stages an uprising in Paris.
August 21	Allied forces trap 60,000 Germans in the Argentan-Falaise pocket.
August 22	The final Japanese withdrawal from Indian territory occurs.
August 23	Romania surrenders to the Allies.
August 24	Romania declares war on Germany. The Allies liberate Bordeaux, France.
August 25	Free French forces liberate Paris. The Allies begin an attack on the Gothic Line in Italy.
August 28	The Allies secure Toulon and Marseille, France.
August 30	German forces withdraw from Bulgaria.
August 31	Soviet forces take Bucharest.
September 1	Dieppe is liberated by British forces.

September 2	Allied forces take Pisa, Italy.
September 3	German forces withdraw from Finland. Brussels is liberated.
September 4	The Soviets and the Finns agree to a cease-fire. Antwerp is liberated.
September 5	The Soviets declare war on Bulgaria.
September 6	The Allies liberate the southern portion of the Netherlands.
September 8	Soviet and Bulgarian forces conclude an armistice. Bulgaria declares war on Germany. German V-2 rockets hit London.
September 17–26	Operation Market-Garden, the effort of the Western Allies to secure a crossing over the Rhine River at Arnhem, fails.
September 19	An armistice is concluded between the Allies and Finland.
September 22	Allied forces capture Boulogne, France.
September 25	Allied forces break through the Gothic Line in Italy. Hitler calls up all remaining 16- to 60-year-old males for military service.
September 26	Soviet forces occupy Estonia. The remaining Allied forces surrender at Arnhem.
September 28	Canadian forces liberate Calais, France.
October 2	The Germans end the Warsaw Rising. The Polish Home army surrenders to the Germans. The Allies enter western Germany.
October 10–29	The Soviets capture Riga in Latvia.
October 14	British forces liberate Athens, Greece. Rommel is forced to commit suicide.
October 18	Soviet forces enter Czechoslovakia.
October 20	Yugoslav partisans and Soviet forces enter Belgrade. U.S. troops land at Leyte in the Philippines.
October 21	German forces surrender at Aachen, Germany.
October 23	Charles de Gaulle is recognized by the United States as head of the French provisional government.
October 23–26	The Battle of Leyte Gulf is fought between Japanese and Allied naval and air forces.
October 23	Soviet forces enter East Prussia.
October 24	The Japanese employ kamikaze suicide aircraft for the first time, in the Battle of Leyte Gulf.
October 25	Soviet forces capture Kirkenes, Norway.
October 30	Gas is used for the last time in executions at Auschwitz.
November 4	Axis troops surrender in Greece.

	November 10	Japanese forces take Guilin and Liuzhou in China.
	November 20	French forces reach the Rhine through the Belfort Gap.
	November 24	French forces liberate Strasbourg, France. The USAAF begins the systematic bombing of Japan.
	November 28	Antwerp is opened to Allied supply ships.
	November 29	The Allies occupy Albania.
	December 3–4	Civil war in Greece commences, and martial law is proclaimed in Athens. Japanese forces retreat in Burma.
	December 16	The Battle of the Bulge (Ardennes Offensive) commences.
	December 17	Waffen-SS troops murder U.S. prisoners of war (POWs) at Malmedy, Belgium.
	December 26	U.S. forces relieve Bastogne, France.
	December 27	Soviet forces besiege Budapest.
1945	January 1–17	The Germans begin to leave the Ardennes.
	January 9	U.S. forces invade Luzon.
	January 16	The Battle of the Bulge ends in an impasse.
	January 17	Soviet troops occupy Warsaw.
	January 19	German forces retreat in large numbers across the Baltic Sea.
	January 20	The Hungarian government concludes an armistice with Soviet forces.
	January 26	Soviet troops liberate Auschwitz.
	January 27	Soviet forces occupy Lithuania.
	January 30	A Soviet submarine sinks the passenger ship *Wilhelm Gustloff,* killing 5,100 people.
	February 4–11	The Yalta Conference, involving Churchill, Roosevelt, and Stalin, takes place in the Crimea.
	February 8	The Allied offensive to the Rhine River begins.
	February 13	The remaining German forces in Budapest surrender to Soviet forces.
	February 13–14	The RAF and USAAF conduct the firebombing of Dresden, Germany.
	February 19	U.S. forces land on Iwo Jima in the Bonin Islands.
	February 20	Soviet forces take Danzig in East Prussia (present-day Gdansk, Poland).
	March 3	Finland declares war on Germany.
	March 4	U.S. forces secure Manila.

	March 7	Allied forces take Köln. U.S. forces seize the Remagen Bridge over the Rhine River.
	March 9	The USAAF firebombs Tokyo.
	March 16	U.S. forces secure Iwo Jima.
1945	March 20–21	Allied forces capture Mandalay, Burma.
	April 1	U.S. forces land on Okinawa.
	April 5	Admiral Suzuki Kantarō becomes Japanese premier.
	April 7	Soviet forces enter Vienna.
	April 10	Allied forces take Hanover, Germany.
	April 12	Roosevelt dies in Warm Springs, Georgia. Vice President Harry S. Truman becomes U.S. president.
	April 13	Soviet forces secure Vienna. The Allies take Arnhem.
	April 15	British forces liberate the Bergen-Belsen concentration camp.
	April 16	U.S. forces enter Nürnberg.
	April 18	The Germans in the Ruhr Valley surrender.
	April 23	Soviet forces reach Berlin. Allied forces reach the Po River in Italy.
	April 23–24	Heinrich Himmler offers surrender to the United States and Britain.
	April 25	U.S. and Soviet forces meet at the Elbe River in Germany. The San Francisco Conference begins.
	April 26	British forces capture Bremen.
	April 28	Italian partisans execute Mussolini at Lake Como, Italy. Allied forces take Venice.
	April 29	German forces in Italy surrender. American forces liberate the Dachau concentration camp. Soviet forces liberate the Ravensbrück concentration camp.
	April 30	Hitler commits suicide in Berlin.
	May 1	The Allies take Moulmein, Burma. Queen Wilhelmina returns to the Netherlands.
	May 2	German forces in Italy surrender. The Soviets capture Berlin.
	May 3	Rangoon, Burma, is liberated.
	May 5	An uprising against German occupation occurs in Prague. The Allies liberate Denmark. A truce is established on the Western Front.
	May 7	The Battle of the Atlantic ends. The Germans surrender unconditionally at Rheims, France.

	May 8	Victory in Europe Day (V-E Day) is celebrated. The Netherlands are liberated. Soviet forces enter Prague.
	May 9	Allied forces return to the Channel Islands.
	May 14	Australian troops capture Wewak, New Guinea. Members of the German High Command are imprisoned.
	June 5	The Allied powers divide Germany into four occupation zones.
	June 10	Australian forces invade Borneo.
	June 28	The U.S. Senate approves the United Nations Charter in a vote of 89–2.
	June 30	U.S. forces liberate Luzon in the Philippines.
	July 1	Allied troops move into Berlin.
	July 16	The first atomic weapon is successfully tested at Alamogordo, New Mexico.
	July 17–August 2	The Potsdam Conference between Churchill, Truman, and Stalin opens, running until August 2.
	July 21–22	U.S. forces secure Okinawa.
	July 26	Labour Party politician Clement Attlee becomes British prime minister.
	July 27	Chinese forces retake Guilin.
	August 6	A USAAF B-29 drops an atomic bomb on Hiroshima, Japan.
	August 8	The Soviet Union declares war on Japan.
	August 9	Soviet forces invade Manchuria. The United States drops an atomic bomb on Nagasaki, Japan.
	August 14	Japan capitulates unconditionally.
	September 2	The formal Japanese surrender takes place aboard the U.S. battleship *Missouri* in Tokyo Harbor. Victory over Japan Day (V-J Day) is celebrated.
	September 5	British forces reach Singapore.
	September 7	Japanese forces in Shanghai surrender.
	September 9	Japanese forces in China surrender.
	September 13	Japanese forces in Burma surrender. Japanese forces in New Guinea surrender.
	September 16	Japanese forces in Hong Kong surrender.
	October 24	The UN Charter comes into force with an initial 29 members.
	November 20	The International Military Tribunal in Nürnberg commences.
1946	May 3	The International Military Tribunal for the Far East begins.

THE COMING OF WAR IN EUROPE

1. Fascist Pageantry: William Shirer on the Nürnberg Rallies, 1934

INTRODUCTION

While dedicated Nazis sympathized with the ideological program **Adolf Hitler** set out in his political manifesto, the book *Mein Kampf,* many ordinary Germans found other aspects of the regime more attractive. Like the Italian **Fascist** leader **Benito Mussolini,** Hitler made the elimination of mass unemployment a high priority. In addition, authoritarian European states of both left and right often provided highly orchestrated public spectacles, glorifying the party and its leaders. Of none was this truer than Germany, where the **Nazi Party** staged grandiose annual week-long rallies at Nürnberg [Nuremberg] in Bavaria, the party's original home, carefully choreographed events in which many thousands of Nazi supporters participated. In 1934, the young American journalist William Shirer moved to Berlin, where he represented the *New York Herald* newspaper for several years. His first major assignment was to attend that year's Nürnberg rally. Shirer had never before seen Hitler in person, and the experience had a major impact on him.

A major preoccupation for the politically liberal Shirer was to first understand for himself and then explain to others why and how the Nazi Party, with its rather crude and brutal ideology and often less than appealing personnel, had been able to win the loyalties of the German working and middle class, so that, even if they had not originally supported the party, they were prepared to tolerate and acquiesce in the regime. Much as he detested Hitler, Shirer recognized the power of his almost mesmerizing rhetorical talents. His week at Nürnberg also forced him to acknowledge the skilful manner in which the Nazi Party deployed pageantry and organization to maximize the impact of its message upon the military, the general public, and "the little men of Germany who have made Nazism possible." European Fascist regimes of the interwar years followed the time-honored formula of keeping the masses happy with "bread and circuses." Although Shirer was personally deeply unsympathetic to Hitler's regime, he himself nonetheless clearly felt the emotional impact and exhilarating appeal of this week-long mass rally.

KEEP IN MIND AS YOU READ

1. Shirer did not publish this excerpt from his diaries until seven years after the events he described. At that time Americans were engaged in a fierce political debate over whether or not their country should assist Great Britain and

possibly join the war against Hitler's Germany. By recounting his experiences in Germany, Shirer sought to heighten the sensitivities of the American public to the evil, oppressive, and aggressive nature of the Nazi regime, and to convince his countrymen that it constituted a genuine threat, not just to other European nations, but also to the United States.

2. Relatively few of Shirer's potential American readers were likely to have attended the Nürnberg rallies or similar Nazi gatherings.
3. Shirer could be franker in his published diaries than in some of his reports as a journalist from Berlin, but for their own safety he still found it necessary in 1941 to conceal the identities of some of his sources and informants.

William Shirer, Diary Entry, 5 September 1934

I'm beginning to comprehend, I think, some of the reasons for Hitler's astounding success. Borrowing a chapter from the Roman [Catholic] Church, he is restoring pageantry and colour and mysticism to the drab lives of twentieth-century Germans. This morning's opening meeting in the Luitpold Hall on the outskirts of Nuremberg was more than a gorgeous show; it also had something of the mysticism and religious fervour of an Easter or Christmas Mass in a great Gothic cathedral. The hall was a sea of brightly coloured flags. Even Hitler's arrival was made dramatic. The band stopped playing. There was a hush over the thirty thousand people packed in the hall. Then the band struck up the *Badenweiler March,* a very catchy tune, and used only, I'm told, when Hitler makes his big entries. Hitler appeared in the back of the auditorium, and followed by his aides, **GOERING, GOEBBELS, HESS, HIMMLER,** and the others, he strode slowly down the long centre aisle while thirty thousand hands were raised in salute. It is a ritual, the old-timers say, which is always followed. Then an immense symphony orchestra played Beethoven's *Egmont* Overture. Great **Klieg lights** played on the stage, where Hitler sat surrounded by a hundred party officials and officers of the army and navy. Behind them the "blood flag," the one carried down the streets of Munich in the ill-fated **putsch**. Behind this, four or five hundred **S.A.** standards. When the music was over, Rudolf Hess, Hitler's closest confidant, rose and slowly read the names of the Nazi "martyrs"—**brown-shirts** who had been killed in the struggle for power—a roll-call of the dead, and the thirty thousand seemed very moved.

Klieg lights: flood lights, often used when filming
putsch: The abortive coup the Nazi Party mounted in Bavaria in 1924
S.A.: *Sturm Abteilung* or Storm Section of the Nazi Party, a paramilitary unit that terrorized those the party considered to be political opponents or in some way undesirable
brown-shirts: Nazi Party members and supporters identified themselves by wearing brown shirts

In such an atmosphere no wonder, then, that every word dropped by Hitler seemed like an inspired Word from on high. . . .

6 September 1934

Hitler sprang his *Arbeitdienst,* his Labour Service Corps, on the public for the first time today and it turned out to be a highly trained, semi-military group of fanatical Nazi youths. Standing there in the early morning sunlight which sparkled on their shiny spades, fifty thousand of them, with the first thousand bared above the waist, suddenly made the German spectators go mad with joy when, without warning, they broke into a perfect goose-step. Now, the goose-step has always seemed to me to be an outlandish exhibition of the human being in his most undignified and stupid state, but I felt for the first time this morning what an inner chord it strikes in the strange soul of the German people. Spontaneously they jumped up and shouted their applause. There was a ritual even for the Labour Service boys. They formed an immense *Sprechchor*—a chanting chorus—and with one voice intoned such words as these: "We want one Leader! Nothing for us! Everything for Germany! ***Heil Hitler!***"

* * *

7 September 1934

Another great pageant tonight. Two hundred thousand party officials packed in the Zeppelin Wiese with their twenty-one thousand flags unfurled in the searchlights like a forest of weird trees. "We are strong and will get stronger," Hitler shouted at them through the microphone, his words echoing across the hushed field from the loud-speakers. And there, in the flood-lit night, jammed together like sardines, in one mass formation, the little men of Germany who have made Nazism possible achieved the highest state of being the Germanic man knows: the shedding of their individual souls and minds—with the personal responsibilities and doubts and problems—until under the mystic lights and at the sound of the magic words of the **Austrian** they were merged completely in the Germanic herd. Later they recovered enough—fifteen thousand of them—to stage a torchlight parade through Nuremberg's ancient streets, Hitler taking the salute in front of the station across from our hotel. . . .

Heil Hitler! (literally, Hail to Hitler!) Standard words of greeting or farewell in Nazi Germany, usually accompanied by an uplifted right arm. Their use also indicated the pervasive cult of the leader that Nazi Germany encouraged

Austrian: Hitler was not originally German, but was born in the Austro-Hungarian Empire

10 September 1934

After seven days of almost ceaseless goose-stepping, speech-making, and pageantry, the party rally came to an end tonight. And though dead tired and rapidly developing a bad case of crowd-phobia, I'm glad I came. You have to go through one of these to understand Hitler's hold on the people, to feel the dynamic in the movement he's unleashed and the sheer, disciplined strength the Germans possess. And now—as Hitler told the correspondents yesterday in explaining his technique—the half-million men who've been here during the week will go back to their towns and villages and preach the new gospel with new fanaticism.

Source: William L. Shirer, *Berlin Diary: The Journal of a Foreign Correspondent 1934–1941* (New York: Alfred A. Knopf, 1941), 18–23. Reprinted by permission of Don Congdon Associates, Inc.

AFTERMATH

Shirer worked as a journalist in Berlin from 1934 to 1937, and again from September 1939 until December 1940, sending sometimes censored reports back to the United States, and even making some radio broadcasts to Americans from occupied France and wartime Germany. Throughout these years he also kept a diary, which had as one of its major themes how to explain the level of German support for the Nazi government and acquiescence in its destruction of civil liberties, elimination of all political rivals, and persecution of dissidents and Jews. Shirer recorded how many of his middle-class friends, formerly liberals, socialists, or even communists, often artists and students, praised National Socialism for restoring national pride and dignity to the German Fatherland, reversing the humiliations the **Treaty of**

Versailles inflicted on Germany in 1919, and providing order, authority, stability, and firm rule. In return for such reinvigoration, they were prepared to compromise individual and collective rights and liberties. The working class made a similar bargain, acquiescing in Hitler's eradication of the trade union movement in return for well-paid steady jobs, good benefits, and the psychological boost the participation in national regeneration bestowed. Even some of Shirer's most apparently helpful German informants were eventually revealed to be government spies.

Although the United States was still officially neutral, by December 1940, the anti-Nazi Shirer's position in wartime Berlin had become increasingly untenable, and he returned to his own country. Shirer later dramatically described how he managed, at considerable personal risk, to smuggle his diary out of Germany, packing it in two suitcases, well hidden under stamped copies of his government-censored radio broadcasts, which he then persuaded the gestapo (the Nazi secret police) to approve and seal up the day before he took them to the airport. Within months, he published a 600-page volume based upon these journals.

ASK YOURSELF

1. After World War II, Shirer published a massive history of the Third Reich and several volumes of memoirs, in which he felt free to be considerably more frank on certain subjects, for example, precisely how he smuggled his journal out of Germany, than in this published diary. What kind of circumstances are likely to cause writers close to events to conceal relevant facts about them?
2. Exposure to the atrocities and excesses of Hitler's Germany during the 1930s caused several well-known liberal American journalists, such as Ed Murrow and Dorothy Thompson, to become fiercely anti-Nazi, and to support American intervention in the war against Germany. In the 1960s, by contrast, their personal experiences caused several prominent American journalists reporting on American involvement in the fighting in Vietnam, notably David Halberstam and Neil Sheehan, to become public opponents of U.S. military intervention in Indochina. In the 2000s, American war correspondents have displayed similar skepticism towards the U.S.-led wars in Iraq and Afghanistan. Why did American newspapermen react so differently on these later occasions?
3. When working in a totalitarian state which seeks to control all information, including information about itself disseminated outside its own boundaries, is it ever possible—or even desirable—for a media representative to be merely an objective and impartial spectator?

TOPICS TO CONSIDER

1. Journalists and reporters are by no means always simply neutral observers. On returning to the United States, Shirer began a sustained campaign to awaken Americans to the evils of Nazism in Germany, lecturing around the country on the subject. The publication of his *Berlin Diary*, which became an immediate best seller, was part of this effort. In one of its final entries Shirer asked himself: "[D]oes Hitler contemplate war with the United States?" He answered: "I am firmly convinced that he does contemplate it and that if he wins in Europe and

Africa he will in the end launch it unless we are prepared to give up our way of life and adapt ourselves to a subservient place in his totalitarian scheme of things." Taking issue with such American opponents of war as the celebrated aviator Colonel **Charles Lindbergh**, he suggested potential scenarios whereby Germany might attack the United States, either by moving across the North Atlantic by way of Greenland, Iceland, Labrador, and Newfoundland, or by basing German forces in South America. Did the fact that Shirer was pursuing a particular political agenda in any way invalidate the insights contained in his diaries?

2. Shirer left his readers with no illusions as to the level of broad German support for the Nazi regime. He sometimes attributed this to the pervasive egotism of the national character, a belief that whatever was beneficial to Germany was right, and a corresponding popular inability to comprehend general concepts of international rights, as opposed to what was in the German national interest. Do you believe that "national character" is a useful concept to apply when seeking to understand the behavior of people from a particular country?

Further Information

Burden, Hamilton T. *The Nuremberg Party Rallies: 1923–39.* New York: Praeger, 1967.

Olson, Lynne, and Stanley W. Cloud. *The Murrow Boys: Pioneers on the Front Lines of Broadcast Journalism.* Boston, MA: Houghton Mifflin, 1996.

Shirer, William L. *End of a Berlin Diary.* New York: Alfred A. Knopf, 1947.

Shirer, William L. *The Rise and Fall of the Third Reich: A History of Nazi Germany.* New York: Simon & Schuster, 1960.

Shirer, William L. *"This is Berlin": Broadcasts from Nazi Germany.* Woodstock, NY: Overlook Press, 1999.

Shirer, William L. *20th Century Journey: A Memoir of a Life and the Times,* 3 vols. New York: Simon & Schuster, 1976–1990.

Wick, Steve. *The Long Night: William Shirer and the Rise and Fall of the Third Reich.* New York: Palgrave Macmillan, 2011.

Wykes, Alan. *The Nuremberg Rallies.* New York: Ballantine Books, 1970.

Films

Der Sieg des Glaubens (Victory of Faith) (1933), directed by Leni Riefenstahl.

Triumph of the Will (Triumph des Willens) (1935), directed by Leni Riefenstahl. This film of the 1934 Nürnberg rallies was made at Hitler's express request, after he had been impressed by Riefenstahl's previous documentary of the 1933 rallies.

2. Clare Hollingworth Describes the German Invasion of Poland, September 1939

INTRODUCTION

Throughout the 1930s, **Adolf Hitler** moved steadily to expand German territory at the expense of neighboring states. Early in 1938, German forces took over Austria, incorporating that state in the German **Reich**; later that year, Germany annexed half of Czechoslovakia, the **Sudetenland**, which possessed a substantial ethnic German population, a prelude to Germany's seizure of the remainder of Czechoslovakia in the spring of 1939. Almost immediately, Hitler directed his attention toward Poland, making emotional speeches demanding the return of the free city of Danzig (Gdansk) to Germany and condemning the treatment of ethnic Germans in Poland. As reconstituted in 1919, after more than a century in which its lands had been divided among Prussia, Austria, and Russia, Poland included substantial territory that had previously been part of Germany. At this stage, British prime minister **Neville Chamberlain** finally resolved to change the policy of effective British acquiescence in German expansion. Addressing the House of Commons at the end of March 1939, Chamberlain pledged that, should Germany attack Poland, Britain would go to war on Poland's behalf. Hitler's rhetorical demands on Poland continued, and in April he directed the German Army general staff to prepare plans for Operation White, a potential war against Poland and, if necessary, against Britain and France too. In the final days of August the same year, the governments of Great Britain and France issued formal guarantees of Poland's territorial integrity, but these had no deterrent effect. German military forces massed on the frontier with Poland. On August 31, 1939 German officials staged incidents in which, they claimed, ethnic Poles living in the German border town of Gleiwitz unsuccessfully attacked a German radio station and customs house, scattering the corpses of Poles from their own concentration camps around the scenes of these alleged atrocities to add verisimilitude. These episodes were cited as the immediate pretext for the German invasion of Poland, which began when German airplanes attacked Danzig at 4:45 A.M. on September 1, 1939, while German troops moved into Poland.

On August 30, 1939, the journalist Clare Hollingworth (1911–), newly employed by the British newspaper the *Daily Telegraph* and beginning what would become a long and renowned career as a war correspondent, was staying with the British Vice-Consul in Katowice, Poland, on the border with Germany. War was generally considered imminent, and she had left the German capital Berlin after officials made it clear that British citizens were no longer welcome there. She decided to cross the frontier into Germany, borrowing the British Vice-Consul's official car for the purpose. A few months later, Hollingworth published the following account of her journey and its aftermath in a book describing her experiences of the early days of the war.

KEEP IN MIND AS YOU READ

1. Clare Hollingworth later became a renowned military correspondent. At the time she wrote this story, however, she was not quite 28, and the *Daily Telegraph* had only hired her a few weeks earlier.
2. This was the first important story that Hollingworth ever submitted. The outbreak of World War II in Europe was a scoop of mammoth proportions, a story that she told and retold on hundreds if not thousands of occasions during her very long life.
3. Clare Hollingworth was a well-connected young Englishwoman from a good family, who had originally been expected to be a debutante and marry well, but chose instead first to study at the University of London, then to work with refugees, and finally to join the press corps, a career her family considered rather distasteful. Her connections with the British political elite stood her in good stead throughout her journalistic career, not least at this juncture, when she was able to stay with the British Vice-Consul and borrow his car.

Clare Hollingworth, The Coming of World War II in Katowice, Poland, 1939

Since all British correspondents had been expelled from Berlin some days before, I decided to have a look round in German Silesia. Katowice was too quiet for news. I crossed the frontier at Beuthen without trouble. (Though news of my crossing so upset the Polish Foreign Office that the British Embassy were required to vouch for me.) The German frontier town was nearly deserted. It was open to **enfilading** fire from Polish batteries, and the Germans evidently thought it prudent to evacuate civilians. Those who remained looked depressed and unhappy. I spoke to old acquaintances and found increased trust in Hitler, even among those who had been critical—but, linked with this, a refusal to believe in war.

'It won't come to that, **liebes Fräulein**, don't you worry. The **Führer** will get Germany her rights without war this time, just as he did before.'

They told me stories of the 'atrocities' committed by Poland against her **German minority**, and asked me if I had seen such things. I had not.

'Ah, you don't see them, but they happen every day. Why do you suppose our people come across the frontier to escape the Poles?' Then I learned an interesting thing. German 'refugees' from Poland were not being allowed into the Reich. They were being kept for use on the frontier. We were to hear much of them before the end of the war . . .

enfilading: cross fire
liebes Fräulein: dear girl
Führer: the Leader, the official title for German Hitler
German minority: The population of Poland included a substantial number of ethnic Germans, whose purported maltreatment was one of the excuses Hitler invoked for invading Poland

I drove along the fortified frontier road via **Hindenburg**, (which in the nineteen-twenties the townsfolk voted to call '**Leninburg**') to Gleiwitz, which had become a military town. On the road were parties of **motor-cycle despatch-riders**, bunched together and riding hard. As we came over the little ridge into the town, sixty-five of them burst past us, each about ten yards behind the other. From the road I could see bodies of troops, and at the roadside hundreds of tanks, armoured cars and field guns stood or moved off toward the frontier. Here and there were screens of canvas or planking, concealing the big guns; they seemed not to be camouflaged against air-attack. I guessed that the German Command was preparing to strike to the north of Katowice and its fortified lines: the advance which was to reach Czestochowa in two days of war.

In the middle of all this I bought odd things—wine, electric torches—and drove back peacefully. Now and then a trooper would spot the **Union Jack** on my car and give a sudden, astonished gape. As we reached a length of road which lies parallel with the frontier, I looked across a hollow, some wire and tank-barricades, and watched the peasant-women moving about the Polish fields, a few hundred yards away. In the evening I returned to Poland, without trouble, the feverish preparations of the German military uppermost in my mind.

[The next day, Hollingworth learned that in her absence the Polish authorities had uncovered and, so they believed, squelched various plots by German-Polish nationals, activities in which the German Consul was openly implicated, a fact which "showed me again that we stood on the edge of war." She nonetheless retired to bed, but was awoken in the early hours of September 1, 1939.]

Slam! Slam! . . . a noise like doors banging. I woke up. It could not be later than five in the morning. Next, the roar of airplanes and more doors banging. Running to the window I could pick out the 'planes, riding high, with the guns blowing smoke-rings below them. There was a long flash into the town park, another, another. Incendiary bombs? I wondered. As I opened my door I ran against the friends with whom I was staying, in their dressing-gowns.

'What is all this about?'

'We aren't sure. A big air-raid practice was announced for to-day. Or it may be something more. We are trying to reach Zoltaszek' (my old friend the Chief of Police). Just then the Polish maid appeared.

'Only Mrs. Zoltaszek is at home.'

'Then ask her what's going on. Is this an air-raid practice? What does she know?' they pressed the girl. She spoke into the telephone for a moment and then turned, her eyes wide open.

'She . . . she says it's the beginning of war! . . . '

I grabbed the telephone, reached the ***Telegraph* correspondent in Warsaw** and told him my news. I heard later that he rang straight through to the Polish Foreign Office, who had had no word of the attack. The *Telegraph* was not only the first paper to hear that Poland

Hindenburg/Leninburg: the military hero Field Marshal Paul von Hindenburg was chief of the German General Staff during World War I. Renaming the town after the Russian Communist leader Lenin during the 1920s was an indication that radical socialists had temporarily won power there

motor-cycle despatch-riders: German soldiers on motorcycles, used to carry urgent military messages

Union Jack: The British flag of the United Kingdom, which unites the English St. George's Cross, the Scottish St. Andrew's Cross, and the Irish St. Patrick's Cross. Small national flags are generally flown on diplomatic vehicles

***Telegraph* correspondent in Warsaw:** Hugh Carleton Greene, a prominent British journalist, later director general of the British Broadcasting Corporation (BBC), was also a brother of the famous novelist Graham Greene

The [British Vice-]Consul: John Anthony Thwaites, vice-consul in Katowice, also a notable art critic and collector. He had to abandon his art collection when he fled Katowice, and it was never recovered

was at war—it had, too, the odd privilege of informing the Polish Government itself.

I had arranged for a car to come on the first hint of alarm, but it did not arrive. We stood, drank coffee, walked about the rooms and waited; I was alternately cursing my driver and wondering whether the *Telegraph* would produce a Special Edition for my news. The war, as a tragic disaster, was not yet a reality. When my driver came at last, he met my fury with a pitying smile.

'It's only an air-raid practice,' he said.

We ran down to the British Consulate, which I knew well. On our way I noticed smiles on the faces turned up to the sky. 'Well,' they seemed to be saying, 'so this is the air-raid practice.'

'But of course it's an air-raid practice, Herr Konsul,' the Secretary of the Consulate was saying as I arrived. My own reaction, for the moment, was actual fear: fear that I had made the *gaffe* of my life by reporting a non-existent war.

However, official confirmation of the war came soon enough. At once the Secretary—one of the German minority, who had worked at the Consulate since its opening in 1920—burst into tears.

'This is the end of poor Germany,' she wept.

Just then my sympathy with 'poor Germany' was not all that it might have been.

Everyone at the Consulate was working furiously. Papers were being stuffed into the big, old-fashioned stoves until ashes fluffed under one's feet. **The Consul** was whipping round by telephone to ensure the departure of those British subjects who remained.

Source: Clare Hollingworth, *The Three Weeks' War in Poland* (London: Duckworth, 1940), 11–17. Used by permission of Gerald Duckworth & Co. Ltd.

AFTERMATH

Later on September 1, Great Britain and France demanded that Germany withdraw its forces within 24 hours, an ultimatum Hitler completely ignored. On September 3, both countries declared war on Germany, but were unable to aid Poland directly and ill-prepared militarily to open hostilities with Germany on its western border. Although Polish forces resisted bravely, within three weeks, overwhelming German military and air superiority and a **blitzkrieg** campaign forced the Polish government to surrender. In August 1939, the Soviet Union and Germany overcame their deep-rooted ideological antagonism to each other and signed a Non-Aggression Pact, whereby each country agreed not to attack the other. Secret protocols to this agreement envisaged the future division of Poland between Germany and the Soviet Union. While Poland fought German forces in the west, Soviet troops occupied the eastern portion of Poland, the territory that would remain part of the Soviet Union when World War II ended six years later.

As war began in Poland, Clare Hollingworth, a woman who found physical danger and fighting exhilarating, spent the next three weeks reporting on the course of the battle for Poland, before escaping to Britain through the Balkans. Within months, she published her first book, describing her adventures during this campaign. In 1940 she returned to southern Europe, first reporting from still neutral Romania, then covering the Greek campaign, and finally basing herself in Cairo, Egypt, attached to British forces as a military correspondent during the North African campaigns.

ASK YOURSELF

1. This account comes from a book published in London, a few months after the beginning of World War II, when censorship was already in place and paper was scarce. From spring 1940 onward, German forces swept across most of western Europe, and by late June 1940, Britain stood alone against Germany, without European allies. Do you think it likely that the British government saw some value for morale in publishing an adventurous young woman's story of her view of the war in Poland, and how she survived it?
2. Historians have recently argued that, although they did not turn against Hitler, the German people were far from enthusiastic for war with Britain and France in 1939, something the reaction of the ethnic German secretary at the consulate seems to confirm. If this picture is accurate, why did Germans continue to support or at least acquiesce in Hitler's war policies? Do you perceive any analogies with the feelings of the American public toward the war in Vietnam in the 1960s, or the wars against Afghanistan and Iraq in the 2000s?
3. Hollingworth was only one of a number of intrepid women journalists—others included the Americans Martha Gellhorn and Marguerite Higgins and the German Sigrid Schultz—who broke with career expectations by reporting on 20th-century wars. Military authorities often tried to ban them from combat situations. In what ways may the exploits and reporting of such women have helped to change popular images of what women could and could not accomplish?

TOPICS TO CONSIDER

1. Fifty years later, Hollingworth wrote an autobiography, *Front Line* (1990), in which she once again told this story, which differed significantly in detail from that of 1940. Whereas the 1940 version depicts a young woman fortunate—and enterprising—enough to be in the right place at the right time to report a major story, who feels some hesitation as to whether her belief that war has begun is correct, the second portrays a more self-assured, even intrepid, journalist-observer who remains throughout better informed and more au fait with events than any British diplomat in Poland. What do the differences between these two accounts suggest about the nature of memory, especially stories that the protagonist has told on numerous occasions for many years, in this case half a century?
2. No journalist or observer can report more than a small piece of the action taking place in any war. Is it possible—or indeed desirable—for historians to combine individual accounts and testimonies into a coherent story?

Further Information

Hollingworth, Clare. *Front Line*. London: Jonathan Cape, 1990. Updated with Neri Tenorio, and reissued as *Captain if Captured*. Hong Kong: Corporate Communications, 2003.

Hollingworth, Clare. *There's a German Just behind Me*. London: Secker and Warburg, 1942.

Hollingworth, Clare. *The Three Weeks' War in Poland*. London: Duckworth, 1940.

Sorel, Nancy Caldwell. *The Women who Wrote the War: The Compelling Story of the Path-Breaking Women War Correspondents of World War II.* New York: Arcade Publishers, 1999.
Wagner, Lilya. *Women War Correspondents of World War II.* New York: Greenwood Press, 1989.

Web Sites

Moore, Malcolm. "Second World War 70th Anniversary: The Scoop." *The Daily Telegraph*, http://www.telegraph.co.uk/comment/6111610/Second-World-War-70th-anniversary-The-Scoop.html.
Profile: "A Foreign Affair." *The Guardian,* http://www.guardian.co.uk/books/2004/jan/17/featuresreviews.guardianreview13.

3. W. H. AUDEN, "SEPTEMBER 1, 1939"

INTRODUCTION

As German tanks invaded Poland, the British poet W. H. (Wystan Hugh) Auden (1907–1973) wrote one of his most famous poems. At the beginning of 1939, Auden, together with his long-time friend, the British writer Christopher Isherwood, moved to the United States, where he would base himself for the next 33 years. During the 1930s Auden, like his Oxford University contemporaries Isherwood and the poets Stephen Spender, Louis MacNeice, and Cecil Day Lewis, had been a prominent figure on the intellectual and literary European left. He had lived in Germany and spoken at public meetings and rallies protesting against the brutal policies of the Fascist powers, both their internal repression of dissent and their attacks on other countries. During the Spanish Civil War of 1936–1939, when military Nationalist rebels led by General Francisco Franco sought to overturn the leftist Loyalist government, a conflict in which the rebels received substantial assistance from Nazi Germany and Fascist Italy while Soviet communists and leftist intellectuals from many countries fought for the government, Auden visited Spain and made propaganda broadcasts for the government. Paradoxically, the experience of visiting a country where leftists had closed the churches played its part in Auden's subsequent rejection of politics and his return to his once-lapsed strong Christian and Anglican faith. He spent most of the first six months of 1938 in China, unofficially at war with Japan since the summer of 1937, a conflict that would last until 1945, and returned to Britain by way of Japan, Canada, and the United States. By late 1938, Auden had become uncomfortable with political activism, and he moved permanently to the United States at the beginning of 1939.

KEEP IN MIND AS YOU READ

1. Auden was a highly educated, cosmopolitan figure, with a deep knowledge of both classical and more recent European literature and history, and was steeped in Freudian psychology. He was familiar with recent political events and their background, and had traveled extensively in Europe. His poetry contains many allusions to all these subjects, which he assumed his readers would be able to understand.

2. Auden originally considered dedicating this poem to the Nobel Prize winner Thomas Mann (1875–1955), a liberal German novelist and strongly anti-Nazi intellectual who fled to Switzerland when **Adolf Hitler** came to power in 1933. Two years later, in 1935, Auden, a homosexual, married Mann's eldest daughter, Erika, who had been declared an enemy of the German state and faced persecution and possibly death if she remained in Germany. The marriage was one of convenience, but Erika and Auden remained good friends for the rest of their lives. Like her father, she moved to the United States later in the 1930s. When Auden arrived in January 1939, she met him at the New York quayside.
3. The United States would remain formally neutral in World War II until December 1941, after the Japanese attacked Pearl Harbor and both Germany and Japan declared war on the United States. The poem suggests that the United States will not find it possible for very long to remain in its "euphoric dream" of neutrality.
4. At the beginning of World War I (1914–1918), many writers, for example, the British Rupert Brooke (1887–1915), hailed the coming of war with near exaltation, a sense that they were embarking on a noble conflict that would give their lives a higher purpose. Auden's poem, by contrast, treated the coming of war with weary resignation, as a measure that while possibly necessary and inevitable was likely to bring further suffering in its wake.
5. An excerpt from the diary of the famed dancer Vaslav Nijinsky apparently inspired Auden to write this poem. On June 27, 1940, Auden wrote to his friend E. R. Dodds: "The day war was declared I opened Nijinsky's diary at random (the one he wrote as he was going mad) and read 'I want to cry but God orders me to go on writing. He does not want me to be idle.' "

Fifty-second Street: An area of Manhattan (New York City) characterized by extremely high skyscraper buildings, well known as the home of many small bars and jazz clubs

"A low, dishonest decade": These words became a famous description of the 1930s, when many felt that the political leaders of the democratic nations and perhaps their peoples had miserably failed to meet the challenges facing them and the world

Luther: Martin Luther (1483–1546), German priest and professor of theology who launched the rebellion against the authority and teachings of the Roman Catholic church that led to the 16th-century Protestant reformation

Linz: The third-largest city in Austria, where **Adolf Hitler** spent most of his childhood, and which he always regarded as his home

W. H. Auden, "September 1, 1939"

I sit in one of the dives
On **Fifty-second Street**
Uncertain and unafraid
As the clever hopes expire
Of **a low dishonest decade**:
Waves of anger and fear
Circulate over the bright
And darkened lands of the earth,
Obsessing our private lives;
The unmentionable odour of death
Offends the September night.

Accurate scholarship can
Unearth the whole offence
From **Luther** until now
That has driven a culture mad,
Find what occurred at **Linz**,
What huge imago made

A psychopathic god;
I and the public know
What all schoolchildren learn,
Those to whom evil is done
Do evil in return.

Exiled **Thucydides** knew
All that a speech can say
About Democracy,
And what dictators do,
The elderly rubbish they talk
To an apathetic grave;
Analysed all in his book,
The enlightenment driven away,
The habit-forming pain,
Mismanagement and grief;
We must suffer them all again.

Into this neutral air
Where blind skyscrapers use
Their full height to proclaim
The strength of **Collective Man**,
Each language pours its vain
Competitive excuse;
But who can live for long
In an euphoric dream;
Out of the mirror they stare,
Imperialism's face
And the international wrong.

Faces along the bar
Cling to their average day;
The lights must never go out,
The music must always play,
All the conventions conspire
To make this fort assume
The furniture of home;
Lest we should see where we are,
Lost in a haunted wood,
Children afraid of the night
Who have never been happy or good.

The windiest militant trash
Important Persons shout
Is not so crude as our wish:
What mad **Nijinsky** wrote
About **Diaghilev**
Is true of the normal heart;

Thucydides: Athenian aristocrat (c. 460 to c. 395 BC) and historian of the Peloponnesian Wars, a conflict that took place during his life, and which demonstrated both the strengths and weaknesses of a political democracy. Held responsible for the surrender of the Athenian city of Amphipolis to Sparta, Thucydides was exiled for 20 years, during which time he gathered the material for his classic history of the war

Collective Man: Both Fascism and Communism were mass popular movements, whose leaders claimed that they were only carrying out the collective will. "Collective Man" was seen as more important and significant than the mere individual

Nijinsky and **Diaghilev:** The Russian ballet-dancer Vaslav Nijinsky (1890–1950) went mad in 1919, at the age of 31, and spent the remainder of his life in a lunatic asylum. Earlier in his career, he had been the lover of Serge Diaghilev (1872–1929), the patron and impresario of the Ballets Russes Company, of which Nijinsky was the star, but in 1913 Diaghilev dismissed Nijinsky when the latter married a female ballerina. In journals published in an expurgated version in the 1930s, Nijinsky complained of Diaghilev's jealousy and inability to tolerate rivals, stating: "Some politicians are hypocrites like Diaghilev, who does not want universal love, but to be loved alone. I want universal love."

For the error bred in the bone
Of each woman and each man
Craves what it cannot have,
Not universal love
But to be loved alone.

From the conservative dark
Into the ethical life
The dense commuters come,
Repeating their morning vow;
'I will be true to the wife,
I'll concentrate more on my work,'
And helpless governors wake
To resume their compulsory game:
Who can release them now,
Who can reach the dead,
Who can speak for the dumb?

All I have is a voice
To undo the folded lie,
The romantic lie in the brain
Of the sensual man-in-the-street
And the lie of Authority
Whose buildings grope the sky;
There is no such thing as the State
And no one exists alone;
Hunger allows no choice
To the citizen or the police;
We must love one another or die.

Defenseless under the night
Our world in stupor lies;
Yet, dotted everywhere,
Ironic points of light
Flash out wherever the Just
Exchange their messages:
May I, composed like them
Of **Eros** and of **dust**,
Beleaguered by the same
Negation and despair,
Show an affirming flame.

Eros: Physical love and desire
dust: According to the Bible, all humans were created out of dust, and to dust they shall return

Source: W. H. Auden, *Another Time* (London: Faber and Faber, 1940), 112.

AFTERMATH

This poem was published in the liberal American magazine *The New Republic* on October 18, 1939, and later included in the collection *Another Time,* published by Auden in 1940.

It was one of the most popular poems Auden ever produced, but was also considered controversial, inasmuch as the lines "Those to whom evil is done/Do evil in return" could be taken as exonerating Germany for the outbreak of war. Auden himself later claimed to dislike the poem and to consider it "the most dishonest poem I have ever written," even though or perhaps because the line "We must love one another or die" was probably the most famous he ever wrote. In later versions, Auden changed the line to "We must love one another and die" or omitted the entire stanza containing it. Eventually, he dropped "September 1, 1939," from editions of his collected poems, refused to allow it to be reprinted, and claimed to loathe it and consider it trash he was ashamed to have written.

ASK YOURSELF

1. Throughout the 1930s, as the international situation deteriorated, Auden had wrestled with the question of whether individuals or even groups were in some way responsible for the course of developing events, or whether they were at the mercy of broader historical forces sweeping them along. Does this poem suggest that he had reached any definite answer to that question that he found satisfying and convincing?
2. Two friends of Auden gave differing accounts of how and where he wrote this poem, one claiming that it was written in the Dizzy Club, the bar that is its supposed setting, and the other that he wrote it during the early days of World War II, while visiting friends in New Jersey. Another biographer claims that he wrote it over two days, September 1–2, 1939. What, if any, difference do these varying stories of its creation make to one's understanding of the poem?
3. In later years, critics of Auden often attacked him as a coward and deserter who had chosen to sit out the worst years of the war in relative comfort on the East Coast of the United States, rather than returning to his own country and perhaps fighting for it. Were these complaints justified?
4. This poem was not merely a comment on the coming of war, but clearly had personal and biographical as well as political implications for Auden. Does this invalidate its value as a historical document and, if so, why?
5. Auden originally wrote two additional stanzas to this poem, given below. The first was placed before the stanza beginning "All I have is a life" and the second before the final stanza. Can you suggest why he omitted these from the version published in October 1939?

First Omitted Stanza

No promises can stay
The ruling of the court
In session on an act
Nor magic wish away
Its summary effect;
What can I do but recall
What everyone knows in his heart,
One Law applies to us all;
In spite of terror and death
The continuum of truth
May not be torn apart.

Second Omitted Stanza

To testify my faith
That reason's roman path
And the trek of punishment
Lead both to a single g
Each pert philosopher's
Concupiscence or, worse,
Practical wisdom, all
Our public impatience can
Delay but may not prevent
The education of man.

TOPICS TO CONSIDER

1. After the events of September 11, 2001, when terrorist attacks destroyed two of the tallest skyscrapers in New York, Auden's poem resonated with many Americans, who e-mailed it to each other. Portions of the poem were often read aloud on National Public Radio, and many survivors found genuine and lasting emotional solace and comfort in its words. Auden wrote his poem in response to a specific event, the German invasion of Poland and the beginning of World War II. What does it tell us about a literary work written in a particular context, when it can be appropriated to help people understand and come to terms with another tragic public occurrence more than 60 years later?
2. Does the fact that a poet or writer later repudiates what he or she has written destroy that document's value as a historical text? Is it even possible to disavow a document one has produced at a certain time, in specific circumstances?
3. Given that there are several versions of this poem in existence, can any one version be considered more "genuine" than the others? If so, why?
4. Auden's poem was written in deliberate imitation of the Irish poet W. B. Yeats's "Easter 1916," on the unsuccessful Irish revolt against British rule that erupted in Dublin, Ireland, during World War I, a work in which Yeats described his torn emotions about this uprising, thanks to which, he concluded: "A terrible beauty is born." What can poetry or even fictional literature accomplish in enabling us to understand historical events, which is not possible through prose alone?

Further Information

Carpenter, Humphrey. *W. H. Auden: A Biography*. London: George Allen and Unwin, 1981.
Davenport-Hines, Richard. *Auden*. London: Heinemann, 1996.
Mendelson, Edward. *Early Auden*. New York: Viking Press, 1981.
Mendelson, Edward. *Later Auden*. New York: Farrar Straus and Giroux, 1999.

Web Site

The Auden Society Web site. http://audensociety.org.

Film and Television

The Addictions of Sin: W. H. Auden in His Own Words (2007). British Broadcasting Corporation.
The Habit of Art (2010), starring Richard Griffiths and Alex Jennings.

FROM POLAND TO PEARL HARBOR

4. Henry R. Luce, "The American Century," February 1941

Henry R. Luce (1898–1967) was one of the most influential journalists and publishers in U.S. media history. Born in 1898 in China to American missionary parents, he spent the first 14 years of his life there. After studying at Yale University in the United States and Oxford University in Britain, Luce ventured into journalism, and in 1923 cofounded *Time*, the first weekly news magazine in the United States. The new publication, of which Luce was initially business manager and from 1929 editor, proved to be enormously successful. Luce founded several other publications, most notably the business magazine *Fortune* in 1930, *Life* magazine in 1936, and *Sports Illustrated* in 1954. Luce remained editor-in-chief of all of them until 1964. By the late 1930s, Luce publications dominated the market for popular middle-brow news in the United States, and he had become immensely wealthy.

In February 1941, *Life* published Luce's essay, "The American Century." In this piece, whose title would be used as a cliché to describe the twentieth-century international role of the United States, Luce argued that his country was already effectively in the current war, and that it should in future play a far greater part in world affairs than before. Luce envisaged his country disseminating the American way of life and American ideals around the world.

KEEP IN MIND AS YOU READ

1. For much of the 1930s, Luce was sympathetic to the European Fascist powers, Germany and Italy, and his publications praised the **Munich Pact** of September 1938. A strong anti-Communist, Luce turned against Nazi Germany in August 1939, when **Adolf Hitler** concluded the **Nazi-Soviet Non-Aggression Pact** with Russia.
2. In fall 1940, Luce had supported the Republican presidential candidate Wendell Willkie, who ran unsuccessfully against the Democratic incumbent, **Franklin D. Roosevelt**. Luce expected to become secretary of state if Willkie won. This article therefore represented an alternative route whereby he might influence the making of American policy.
3. Luce's missionary background, which gave him a near messianic sense of his own destiny and that of his country, probably contributed to his broader ambitions.
4. Although Luce's publications strongly supported Willkie's candidacy in 1940, Willkie still lost the presidential election.

5. In 1940, Luce became a strong supporter of American assistance to British premier Winston Churchill's efforts to fight on against Germany, making Churchill *Time*'s Man of the Year for 1940.
6. At the time Luce wrote this essay, the United States was still officially neutral in World War II.

Henry R. Luce, "The American Century," February 1941

There is one fundamental issue which faces America as it faces no other nation. It is an issue peculiar to America and peculiar to America in the 20th Century—now. It is deeper even than the immediate issue of War. If America meets it correctly, then, despite hosts of dangers and difficulties, we can look forward and move forward to a future worthy of men, with peace in our hearts.

If we dodge the issue, we shall flounder for ten or 20 or 30 bitter years in a chartless and meaningless series of disasters. . . .

Where are we? We are in the war. All this talk about whether this or that might or might not get us into the war is wasted effort. We are, for a fact, in the war.

. . .

Furthermore—and this is an extraordinary and profoundly historical fact which deserves to be examined in detail—America and only America can effectively state the war aims of this war. . . .

The big, important point to be made here is simply that the complete opportunity of leadership is ours. . . .

In the field of national policy, the fundamental trouble with America has been, and is, that whereas their nation became in the 20th Century the most powerful and the most vital nation in the world, nevertheless Americans were unable to accommodate themselves spiritually and practically to their fate. Hence they have failed to play their part as a world power—a failure which has had disastrous consequences for themselves and for all mankind. And the cure is this: to accept wholeheartedly our duty and our opportunity as the most powerful and vital nation in the world and in consequence to exert upon the world the full impact of our influence, for such purposes as we see fit and by such means as we see fit.

. . .

Consider the 20th Century. It is ours not only in the sense that we happen to live in it but ours also because it is America's first century as a dominant power in the world. So far, this century of ours has been a profound and tragic disappointment. No other century has been so big with promise for human progress and happiness. And in no one century have so many men and women and children suffered such pain and anguish and bitter death.

. . .

What can we say about an American Century? It is meaningless merely to say that we reject **isolationism** and accept the logic of **internationalism**. What internationalism?

. . .

isolationism: belief that the United States should remain aloof from political and military entanglements outside the American (Western) hemisphere. Often used at this time to characterize the views of Americans who opposed U.S. intervention in World War II

internationalism: belief that the United States should be more actively involved in international affairs beyond the Americas. Often used at this time to characterize the views of Americans who supported U.S. intervention in World War II

Ours cannot come out of the vision of any one man. It must be the product of the imaginations of many men. It must be a sharing with all peoples of our **Bill of Rights**, our **Declaration of Independence**, our **Constitution**, our magnificent industrial products, our technical skills. It must be an internationalism of the people, by the people and for the people. . . .

Once we cease to distract ourselves with lifeless arguments about isolationism, we shall discover that there is already an immense American internationalism. American jazz, Hollywood movies, American slang, American machines and patented products, are in fact the only things that every community in the world, from **Zanzibar** to **Hamburg**, recognizes in common. Blindly, unintentionally, accidentally and really in spite of ourselves, we are already a world power in all the trivial ways—in very human ways. But there is a great deal more than that. America is already the intellectual, scientific and artistic capital of the world. Americans—**Midwestern Americans**—are today the least provincial people in the world. They have traveled the most and they know more about the world than the people of any other country. America's worldwide experience in commerce is also far greater than most of us realize.

Most important of all, we have that indefinable, unmistakable sign of leadership: prestige. And unlike the prestige of **Rome** or **Genghis Khan** or **19th Century England**, American prestige throughout the world is faith in the good intentions as well as in the ultimate intelligence and ultimate strength of the whole American people. We have lost some of that prestige in the last few years. But most of it is still there.

* * *

No narrow definition can be given to the American internationalism of the 20th Century. It will take shape, as all civilizations take shape, by the living of it, by work and effort, by trial and error, by enterprise and adventure and experience.

And by imagination!

As America enters dynamically upon the world scene, we need most of all to seek and to bring forth a vision of America as a world power which is authentically American and which can inspire us to live and work and fight with vigor and enthusiasm. And as we come now to the great test, it may yet turn out that in all of our trials and tribulations of spirit during the first part of this century we as a people have been painfully apprehending the meaning of our time and now in this moment of testing there may come clear at last the vision which will guide us to the authentic creation of the 20th Century—our Century.

* * *

America as the dynamic center of ever-widening spheres of enterprise, America as the training center of the skillful servants of mankind, America as the **Good Samaritan**, really believing again that it is more blessed to give than to receive, and America as the powerhouse

Bill of Rights, Constitution, and Declaration of Independence: seminal founding documents of the 18th-century United States, enunciating the basic principles of its political and juridical system

Zanzibar: group of islands off the coast of East Africa

Hamburg: leading German city on the Baltic Sea

Midwestern Americans: generally believed to be the most parochial and inward-looking section of the U.S. population

Rome: the most extensive empire of the classical world

Genghis Khan: Mongol ruler (1162–1227) who established the largest contiguous empire ever seen in history, extending through present-day China and much of Russia, the Middle East, and Eastern Europe

19th Century England: the century when Great Britain and its Empire dominated international affairs

Good Samaritan: biblical New Testament character who assisted a stranger whom thieves had robbed and left for dead

of the ideals of Freedom and Justice—out of these elements surely can be fashioned a vision of the 20th Century to which we can and will devote ourselves in joy and gladness and vigor and enthusiasm. . . .

It is in this spirit that all of us are called, each to his own measure of capacity, and each in the widest horizon of his vision, to create the first great American Century.

Source: Henry Luce, "The American Century," *Life,* v. 10 (February 1941).

AFTERMATH

Luce made Herculean efforts to publicize his views beyond *Life*'s 12 million readers. He reprinted the piece in full-page advertisements in newspapers throughout the country, and sent copies of a reprint pamphlet edition, bolstered by generally favorable commentary by several well-known journalists and pundits to hundreds of influential friends and associates. As he intended, Luce's article provoked wide-ranging discussion throughout the United States and beyond. Then and afterward, many on the left, Vice President Henry A. Wallace, for example, and socialist leader Norman Thomas, condemned Luce for envisaging a new international order run in the interests of American capitalism and business, a world system in which U.S. imperialism and militarism would replace those of the European colonial powers. If he had intended to set the terms of popular debate, Luce undoubtedly succeeded, indelibly and memorably labeling for posterity the growing world role of the United States.

HENRY R. LUCE AND CHINA

Given his background, Luce always took particular interest in China. He admired the Guomindang (GMD, Kuomintang, KMT, Nationalist) government of Jiang Jieshi (Chiang Kai-shek), who took power in the later 1920s and unified most of China under his own leadership. Luce used his magazines to promote the image of Jiang, together with his American-educated wife, Song Meiling (Soong May-ling), as the model of a Christian, modernizing Asian leader. Luce supported Jiang's efforts to eliminate what was by the mid-1930s his major political rival, the Chinese Communist Party (CCP), led by Mao Zedong (Mao Tse-tung). When the Sino-Japanese War began in summer 1937, Luce supported the Chinese cause, helped to raise substantial funding for war relief there, and supported American assistance to Jiang. At the end of 1937, *Time* named Jiang and his wife Man and Woman of the Year. Later in the war, Luce publications would become closely identified with continued assistance to Jiang and his wife, as an integral part of what would become the American China Lobby of Jiang supporters. When the CCP gained control of mainland China in 1949 and established the People's Republic of China (PRC), the Nationalists, still led by Jiang, fled to the offshore island of Taiwan, where they established a separate regime that claimed to be the legitimate government of China. Until his death, Luce continued to oppose U.S. governmental recognition of the PRC, and his publications routinely attacked American officials who sought to normalize U.S. relations with Communist China.

ASK YOURSELF

1. Luce referred to "the first great American century." How many American centuries did he expect to characterize the world's future history.
2. How were the governments and people of other nations likely to react to Luce's article?
3. Like many 20th-century press moguls, Lord Northcliffe and Lord Beaverbrook in Britain, for example, or the more recent Rupert Murdoch, Robert Maxwell, and Conrad Black, Luce sought to translate wealth into political clout, so that eventually he would be making the news rather than simply reporting it. He mounted a well-financed full-scale campaign to establish himself as someone whose foreign policy views deserved recognition and discussion, efforts which his personal wealth and media access greatly facilitated. Should wealthy communications magnates use their media outlets to promote their own favored causes and enhance their political influence? Is there any feasible way of preventing them from doing so?
4. Luce's article sounded many of the themes that would characterize postwar American internationalism. Implicit in it was the message that, if Americans did not rise to this challenge and become actively involved in the outside world, they would themselves suffer materially and psychologically. Rather than simply pursuing its own interests, the United States was also to propagate American political, economic, and cultural values, serving as a model to other countries. If you had read this article in 1941, would you have found its arguments convincing?

TOPICS TO CONSIDER

1. In its confident messianic sense of American international destiny, this essay drew not only on Luce's personal missionary heritage, but also on the long-standing broader sense of the United States as an exceptional chosen nation whose manifest destiny gave it a special mission to the world, an outlook epitomized earlier in the 20th century in the rhetoric of President **Woodrow Wilson** during World War I. In retrospect, "The American Century" would seem both prophetic and symptomatic, a seminal essay that both accurately predicted the nature of the future American international role during the Cold War and beyond, and in itself embodied the hubris and exaggerated sense of omnipotence that would on occasion be highly detrimental to the effective exercise of U.S. power. To what extent is a similar intellectual perspective discernible in the rhetoric of recent American political leaders from 2001 onwards?
2. The absence of any real humility in Luce's writing, his blunt insistence that his country was already the world's greatest power, was undoubtedly less than tactful and an example of the kind of triumphalist rhetoric that has so often repelled even nations friendly to the United States. Somewhat optimistically, but very much in the Wilsonian tradition, Luce affirmed that, whereas other great powers were distrusted, "throughout the world [there] is faith in the good intentions . . . of the whole American people." Do the governments and peoples of other nations feel this way about the present-day United States?

Further Information

Baughman, James L. *Henry R. Luce and the Rise of the American News Media.* Boston: Twayne, 1987.

Brinkley, Alan. *Henry Luce and His American Century.* New York: Alfred A. Knopf, 2010.

Elson, Robert T. *Time Inc.: The Intimate History of a Publishing Enterprise.* 3 vols. New York: Atheneum, 1968–1986.

Heidler, David Stephen, and Jeanne T. Heidler. *Manifest Destiny.* Westport, CT: Greenwood Press, 2003.

Herzstein, Robert E. *Henry R. Luce: A Political Portrait of the Man Who Created the American Century.* New York: Charles Scribner's Sons, 1994.

Herzstein, Robert E. *Henry R. Luce, Time, and the American Crusade in Asia.* New York: Cambridge University Press, 2005.

Hogan, Michael J., ed. *Ambiguous Legacy: American Foreign Relations in the "American Century."* New York: Cambridge University Press, 1999.

Mason, David S. *The End of the American Century.* Lanham, MD: Rowman and Littlefield, 2008.

Stephanson, Anders. *Manifest Destiny: American Expansionism and the Empire of Right.* New York: Hill and Wang, 1995.

Vanderlan, Robert. *Intellectuals Incorporated: Politics, Art, and Ideas Inside Henry Luce's Media Empire.* Philadelphia: University of Pennsylvania Press, 2010.

Television

American Masters: Luce (2004). Public Broadcasting Service.

5. "AMERICA FIRST": U.S. OPPOSITION TO INTERVENTION IN WORLD WAR II: CHARLES A. LINDBERGH, RADIO ADDRESS, APRIL 23, 1941

INTRODUCTION

While U.S. President **FRANKLIN D. ROOSEVELT** and his chief advisers were strongly interventionist in World War II, taking measures that effectively made American entry into the conflict more likely, opposition to the war also existed. The America First Committee was established in July 1940, as that year's presidential election campaign gained momentum, to organize those forces who believed that the best way the United States could meet the ever more serious international crisis was by building up American defenses while holding itself aloof from Europe. America First members argued that the European crisis, however deplorable, did not threaten U.S. security sufficiently to justify American intervention, while domestically American involvement in war would be highly detrimental to the United States. While usually supporting greater American defense spending and a strong military posture, America First members generally believed their country should confine its activities to the Western Hemisphere. Most opposed such administration-backed measures as the summer 1940 **Destroyers-for-Bases** deal, the passage and implementation of **Selective Service** legislation in September 1940, the **Lend-Lease Act** of spring 1941, and the various naval measures whereby the Roosevelt administration moved ever closer to war with Germany.

The best known member of America First was the famed aviator **CHARLES A. LINDBERGH** (1902–1974), who won international celebrity in 1927 when he became the first person to make a solo flight across the Atlantic. From late 1939, Lindbergh publicly opposed the pro-Allied policies of the Roosevelt administration, but only in April 1941 did he finally decide to join America First.

KEEP IN MIND AS YOU READ

1. Lindbergh delivered this address two months before Germany invaded the Soviet Union, embroiling itself in a lengthy and brutal conflict, which would ultimately be responsible for the bulk of German casualties in World War II.
2. Lindbergh delivered this speech very shortly after he had finally joined the America First Committee, and sought to explain this decision.
3. During the 1930s, Lindbergh frequently visited Germany, where he was welcomed as an honored guest and invited to inspect German military installations,

especially aviation facilities. In retrospect, it seems that German officials deliberately gave Lindbergh an inflated idea of their own aerial capabilities.

4. Lindbergh's celebrity status won his views very wide publicity in the American media. Ironically, Lindbergh normally disliked press attention, since he blamed intrusive newspaper and radio coverage of his family for the kidnapping and death in 1932 of his eldest son at the age of 20 months.
5. Lindbergh's role as one of the best-known antiwar spokesmen carried a personal price. His wife, Anne Morrow Lindbergh, daughter of a partner in J. P. Morgan and Company, a fervently pro-British New York private bank, loyally though perhaps rather unhappily supported him. Her sister, however, was married to Aubrey Morgan, a key official in the New York-based British Information Service, and her mother was also prominent in pro-Allied organizations. Both publicly attacked Lindbergh's stance.

Charles A. Lindbergh, Radio Address, 23 April 1941

I know I will be severely criticized by the interventionists in America when I say we should not enter a war unless we have a reasonable chance of winning. That, they will claim, is far too materialistic a viewpoint. . . . But I do not believe that our American ideals, and our way of life, will gain through an unsuccessful war. And I know that the United States is not prepared to wage war in Europe successfully at this time. . . .

I have said it before, and I will say it again, that I believe it will be a tragedy to the entire world if the British Empire collapses. That is one of the main reasons why I opposed this war before it was declared and why I have constantly advocated a negotiated peace. I did not feel that England and France had a reasonable chance of winning. France has now been defeated; and, despite the propaganda and confusion of recent months, it is now obvious that England is losing the war. I believe this is realized even by the British Government. But they have one last desperate plan remaining. They hope that they may be able to persuade us to send another American Expeditionary Force to Europe, and to share with England militarily, as well as financially, the fiasco of this war. . . .

In time of war, truth is always replaced by propaganda. I do not believe that we should be too quick to criticize the actions of a belligerent nation. There is always the question whether we, ourselves, would do better under similar circumstances. But we in this country have a right to think of the welfare of America first, just as the people in England thought first of their own country when they encouraged the smaller nations of Europe to fight against hopeless odds. When England asks us to enter this war, she is considering her own future and that of her Empire. In making our reply, I believe we should consider the future of the United States and that of the **Western Hemisphere**.

Western Hemisphere: the continents of North and South America

It is not only our right, but it is our obligation as American citizens, to look at this war objectively and to weigh our chances for success if we should enter it. I have attempted to do this, especially from the standpoint of aviation; and I have been forced to the conclusion that we cannot win this war for England, regardless of how much assistance we extend.

I ask you to look at the map of Europe today and see if you can suggest any way in which we could win this war if we entered it. Suppose we had a large army in America, trained and equipped. Where would we send it to fight? The campaigns of the war show only too clearly how difficult it is to force a landing, or to maintain an army, on a hostile coast.

Suppose we took our Navy from the Pacific and used it to convoy British shipping. That would not win the war for England. It would, at best, permit her to exist under the constant bombing of the German air fleet. Suppose we had an air force that we could send to Europe. Where could it operate? Some of our squadrons might be based in the British Isles, but it is physically impossible to base enough aircraft in the British Isles alone to equal in strength the aircraft that can be based on the continent of Europe.

I have asked these questions on the supposition that we had in existence an Army and an air force large enough and well enough equipped to send to Europe; and that we would dare to remove our Navy from the Pacific. Even on this basis, I do not see how we could invade the continent of Europe successfully as long as all of that continent and most of Asia is under Axis domination. But the fact is that none of these suppositions are correct. We have only a one-ocean Navy. Our Army is still untrained and inadequately equipped for foreign war. Our air force is deplorably lacking in modern fighting planes. . . .

I say it is the interventionists in America as it was in England and in France, who give aid and comfort to the enemy. I say it is they who are undermining the principles of democracy when they demand that we take a course to which more than 80 percent of our citizens are opposed. . . .

There is a policy open to this Nation that will lead to success—a policy that leaves us free to follow our own way of life and to develop our own civilization. It is not a new and untried idea. It was advocated by **Washington**. It was incorporated in the **Monroe Doctrine**. Under its guidance the United States became the greatest Nation in the world.

It is based upon the belief that the security of a nation lies in the strength and character of its own people. It recommends the maintenance of armed forces sufficient to defend this hemisphere from attack by any combination of foreign powers. It demands faith in an independent American destiny. This is the policy of the America First Committee today. It is a policy not of isolation, but of independence; not of defeat, but of courage. It is a policy that led this Nation to success during the most trying years of our history, and it is a policy that will lead us to success again. . . .

The United States is better situated from a military standpoint than any other nation in the world. Even in our present condition of unpreparedness no foreign power is in a position to invade us today. If we concentrate on our own defenses and build the strength that this Nation should maintain, no foreign army will ever attempt to land on American shores.

War is not inevitable for this country. Such a claim is defeatism in the true sense. No one can make us fight abroad unless we ourselves are willing to do so. No one will attempt to fight us here if we arm ourselves as a great nation should be armed. Over a hundred million people in this Nation are opposed to entering the war. If the principles of democracy mean anything at all, that is reason enough for us to stay out. If we are forced into a war against the wishes of an overwhelming majority of our people, we will have proved democracy such a failure at home that there will be little use fighting for it abroad.

Washington: George Washington (1732–1799), first president of the United States, who warned his countrymen against entering into a permanent alliance with any European country, on the grounds that this would involve the United States in conflicts that did not concern it, cause increased defense spending and higher taxes, and subvert American democracy

Monroe Doctrine: 1823 declaration by U.S. President James Monroe, warning European nations against seeking additional colonies anywhere in the Americas

Source: T.H. Breen, ed., *The Power of Words: Documents in American History, Vol. 2: From 1865* (New York: HarperCollins, 1996), 172–174.

AFTERMATH

Lindbergh's anti-interventionist stance soon brought allegations that he was a Fascist sympathizer and perhaps even in German pay, charges elaborated in a 28-page pamphlet, *Is Lindbergh a Nazi?,* which American interventionists published in September 1941. Such accusations were given added force later that month, when Lindbergh addressed a meeting in Des Moines, Iowa, and listed American Jews, "with their large ownership and influence in our motion pictures, our press, our radio, and our Government," among those groups who were promoting American intervention in the European war for their own ends. Naively at best, he warned that, if war came, American Jews might well face discrimination, even persecution at home. Lindbergh's ill-considered though undoubtedly sincere remarks, made against his wife's advice, immediately raised a storm of protest and denunciation from Jews, Protestants, and Catholics, newspapers, and politicians of every stripe, many of whom called upon America First—which split over his remarks—to repudiate Lindbergh. His reputation remained permanently tarnished by this episode, and his stated faith in eugenics, that is, selective breeding to improve the genetic quality of the human race, and the superiority of Western civilization lent charges of **anti-Semitism** additional credibility. At best, the speech revealed a near-foolhardy political insensitivity and imprudence that rebounded extremely detrimentally upon both Lindbergh himself and the cause he was representing.

ASK YOURSELF

1. After Germany invaded the Soviet Union in June 1941, Lindbergh warned that neither the United States nor Britain was justified in joining forces with a Communist power with whom they had nothing in common except their shared antagonism to Hitler. How valid was this position?
2. From 1939 to 1941, both opponents and supporters of American intervention in World War II felt so strongly on the rights and wrongs of the issue that they employed a wide range of smear tactics against their political adversaries. America First members faced widely disseminated accusations of accepting German funds to finance their activities, and of favoring the introduction of Fascist rule in the United States. Interventionists sustained comparable allegations that they were British puppets. However vital a public debate may be, are such tactics ever justified?
3. After the Pearl Harbor attack of December 1941, Lindbergh sought to reactivate his commission in the U.S. Army Air Force, but the War Department refused to allow this. Roosevelt particularly resented Lindbergh's past attacks on his own policies, and would not accept Lindbergh's services. Lindbergh therefore worked as a technical engineering consultant for several American aircraft production companies. In 1944, he eventually persuaded United Aircraft to assign him to the Pacific war theater, where he greatly enhanced the range, engine performance, and load-carrying capacity of American fighter-bombers. Attached as a civilian to a Marine squadron, Lindbergh flew around 50 combat missions against Japanese targets and aircraft. Marine and Army Air Force pilots who worked with him defended his patriotism and admired his courage. Was Roosevelt's wartime attitude toward Lindbergh justified, or did it merely represent a personal grudge or vendetta?

TOPICS TO CONSIDER

1. In a tactic more astute populist politicians would later emulate, in April 1941 Lindbergh claimed to be speaking for the majority of ordinary American people, "[o]ver a hundred million," who "[we]re opposed to entering the war" but had no real voice in politics. One irony was that Lindbergh himself, whether speaking on his own behalf and or for the pressure group America First, could not himself genuinely claim to represent the American people. He had not, as he might have done, made any effort to run for political office in the 1940 election. However unenthusiastic the American people were for war and however slippery the president might be, when Roosevelt won in November 1940 with a solid majority, few who supported him could have doubted that he was strongly pro-Allied in sympathy and ready to make considerable efforts to assist the British in their war against Germany. Why did Lindbergh and other America First members nonetheless make such claims?
2. In the novel *The Plot against America* (2004), the writer Philip Roth imagined an alternative America in which Lindbergh was elected U.S. president in 1940, allied his country with Nazi Germany, and emulated Hitler's anti-Semitic policies. An earlier novel, Eric Norden's *The Ultimate Solution* (1973), envisaged a scenario in which Lindbergh was puppet president of a Nazi-occupied United States. As early as 1942, the film *Keeper of the Flame* featured a dead national hero modeled on Lindbergh, who was posthumously revealed to be a secret Fascist, who planned to use his charismatic status with Americans, especially the young, to make his country a Fascist state and eradicate all inferior races from its population. Do such fictional treatments, based on popular perceptions of Lindbergh, have any historical value? Or do they merely perpetuate myths of little if any historical validity?
3. In the early 2000s, almost 30 years after Lindbergh's death, it was publicly revealed that for 17 years, from the late 1950s onward, he had secret love affairs with three German women, which produced seven children. Does this new information that he found German women attractive have any relevance to our understanding of Lindbergh's earlier views on Germany, or is it simply biographical data of no real historical significance?

Further Readings

Berg, A. Scott. *Lindbergh.* New York: G. P. Putnam's, 1998.

Cole, Wayne S. *Charles A. Lindbergh and the Battle against American Intervention in World War II.* New York: Harcourt Brace Jovanovich, 1974.

Cole, Wayne S. *Roosevelt and the Isolationists, 1932–45.* Lincoln: University of Nebraska Press, 1983.

Duffy, James P. *Lindbergh vs. Roosevelt: The Rivalry that Divided America.* Washington, DC: Regency Publishing, 2010.

Hixson, Walter L. *Charles A. Lindbergh: Lone Eagle.* New York: HarperCollins, 1996.

Kessner, Thomas. *The Flight of the Century: Charles Lindbergh and the Rise of American Aviation.* New York: Oxford University Press, 2010.

Lindbergh, Anne Morrow. *War Within and Without: Diaries and Letters of Anne Morrow Lindbergh, 1399–1944.* New York: Harcourt Brace Jovanovich, 1980.

Lindbergh, Charles. *The Wartime Journals of Charles Lindbergh.* Harcourt Brace Jovanovich, 1970.

Schneider, James C. *Should America Go to War?: The Debate Over Foreign Policy in Chicago, 1939–1941.* Chapel Hill: The University of North Carolina Press, 1989.
Wallace, Max. *The American Axis: Henry Ford, Charles Lindbergh, and the Rise of the Third Reich.* New York: St. Martin's Press, 2003.

Web Site

Charles Lindbergh: An American Aviator. http://www.charleslindbergh.com.

Films and Television

Declassified: Lindbergh (2010). A&E Home Video.
Lindbergh: Shocking Turbulent Life (1997). E1 Entertainment.
The Spirit of St. Louis (1957), starring James Stewart, Murray Hamilton, and Patricia Smith.

6. Mitsuo Fuchida's Recollections of Pearl Harbor, December 7, 1941

INTRODUCTION

On December 7, 1941, an unexpected Japanese attack on the U.S. naval base in Pearl Harbor, Hawaii, headquarters of the Pacific Fleet, marked the opening of the Pacific War. Skillfully planned by Admiral **Isoroku Yamamoto**, commander in chief of the Japanese Combined Fleet, the operation was designed to destroy the American fleet. Japanese leaders hoped thereby to gain a year's breathing space, during which they would take control of all Southeast Asia, and that afterwards the United States, faced with a fait accompli, would be prepared to reach a negotiated peace settlement leaving Japan with its gains intact. They failed to anticipate how swiftly American forces would recover and regain their strength in the Pacific. Although Japanese diplomats initially intended to hand American officials in Washington a declaration of war approximately an hour before the assault started, slow transcription of this message meant that it was not delivered until half an hour after the raid began. Popular resentment of what was generally considered an unheralded sneak attack contributed to American determination to fight Japan to the finish.

Operationally, Pearl Harbor was implemented with exceptional skill. As a Japanese task force under Admiral Chuichi Nagumo approached Pearl Harbor in late November, it maintained radio silence for several days, to prevent American and British scanners locating its position. On December 7, 1941, Nagumo dispatched 352 aircraft toward Pearl Harbor. Beginning at 7:55 A.M., Hawaiian time, the Japanese launched a two-wave air attack against shore installations and the U.S. Pacific fleet itself, then at anchorage in Pearl Harbor. Japanese Air Force Commander Mitsuo Fuchida (1902–1976) recalled in his memoirs how he led the first wave of the air attack on Pearl Harbor. Fuchida, who fought numerous air battles over China in the late 1930s and had accrued over 10,000 hours of flying time, was considered one of Japan's most able and experienced pilots, the reason he was given this assignment.

KEEP IN MIND AS YOU READ

1. Fuchida wrote this account of Pearl Harbor almost a decade after the event. Since the attack was one of the high points of his professional life as an aviator, he was likely still to remember it extremely vividly.

2. By August 1945, when Japan surrendered, Mitsuo Fuchida was the only pilot still living who had taken part in the Pearl Harbor attack. He was therefore speaking not just for himself but for all his fellows who had taken part in the raid.
3. After converting to Christianity in the early 1950s, Fuchida claimed that he deeply regretted taking part in the attack on Pearl Harbor.
4. Professional expertise was and is a bond that cuts across other loyalties. Pilots of all nationalities tended to respect particularly skilful and courageous exploits, even when performed by their enemies.

Mitsuo Fuchida's Recollections of Pearl Harbor

One hour and forty minutes after leaving the carriers I knew that we should be nearing our goal. Small openings in the thick cloud cover afforded occasional glimpses of the ocean, as I strained my eyes for the first sight of land. Suddenly a long white line of breaking surf appeared directly beneath my plane. It was the northern shore of **Oahu**.

Veering right toward the west coast of the island, we could see that the sky over Pearl Harbor was clear. Presently the harbor itself became visible across the central Oahu plain, a film of morning mist hovering over it. I peered intently through my binoculars at the ships riding peacefully at anchor. One by one I counted them. Yes, the battleships were there all right, eight of them! But our last lingering hope of finding any carriers present was now gone. Not one was to be seen.

It was 0749 when I ordered my radioman to send the command, 'Attack!' He immediately began tapping out the pre-arranged code signal: 'TO, TO, TO . . .'

Leading the whole group, **Lieutenant Commander Murata's** torpedo bombers headed downward to launch their torpedoes, while **Lieutenant Commander Itaya's** fighters raced forward to sweep enemy fighters from the air. **Takahashi's** dive-bomber group had climbed for altitude and was out of sight. My bombers, meanwhile, made a circuit toward **Barbers Point** to keep pace with the attack schedule. No enemy fighters were in the air, nor were there any gun flashes from the ground.

The effectiveness of our attack was now certain, and a message, 'Surprise attack successful!' was accordingly sent to *Akagi* (Flagship of the Japanese attack fleet) at 0753. The message was received by the carrier and duly relayed to the homeland. . . .

The attack was opened with the first bomb falling on **Wheeler Field**, followed shortly by dive-bombing attacks upon **Hickam Field** and the bases at **Ford Island**. Fearful that smoke from these attacks might obscure his targets, Lieutenant Commander Murata cut short his group's approach toward the battleships anchored east of Ford Island and released torpedoes. A series of white waterspouts soon rose in the harbor.

Lieutenant Commander Itaya's fighters, meanwhile, had full command of the air over Pearl Harbor. About four enemy fighters which took off were promptly shot down. By 0800 there were no enemy planes in the air, and our fighters began strafing the airfields.

Oahu or **O'ahu:** third largest Hawaiian island, site of Pearl Harbor
Lieutenant Commander Murata: Shigeharu Murata, leading four squadrons of torpedo bombers
Lieutenant Commander Itaya: Shigeru Itaya, leading three squadrons of fighters
Takahashi: Lieutenant Commander Kakuichi Takahashi, leading three squadrons of carrier-based dive bombers
Barbers Point: U.S. naval air station
Wheeler Field: U.S. Army Air Corps base
Hickam Field: principal U.S. air force base on Hawaii
Ford Island: U.S. naval air station

My level-bombing group had entered on its bombing run toward the battleships moored to the cast of Ford Island. On reaching an altitude of 3,000 meters, I had the sighting bomber take position in front of my plane.

As we closed in, enemy antiaircraft fire began to concentrate on us. Dark gray puffs burst all around. Most of them came from ships' batteries, but land batteries were also active. Suddenly my plane bounced as if struck by a club. When I looked back to see what had happened, the radioman said: 'The **fuselage** is holed and the **rudder** wire damaged.' We were fortunate that the plane was still under control, for it was imperative to fly a steady course as we approached the target. Now it was nearly time for 'Ready to release,' and I concentrated my attention on the lead plane to note the instant his bomb was dropped. Suddenly a cloud came between the bombsight and the target, and just as I was thinking that we had already overshot, the lead plane banked slightly and turned right toward **Honolulu**. We had missed the release point because of the cloud and would have to try again.

While my group circled for another attempt, others made their runs, some trying as many as three before succeeding. We were about to begin our second bombing run when there was a colossal explosion in battleship row. A huge column of dark red smoke rose to 1000 meters. It must have been the explosion of a ship's **powder magazine**. (This was the Battleship *Arizona*.) The shock wave was felt even in my plane, several miles away from the harbor.

fuselage: airplane hull
rudder: steering mechanism
Honolulu: state capital of Hawaii
powder magazine: explosive gunpowder store

We began our run and met with fierce antiaircraft concentrations. This time the lead bomber was successful, and the other planes of the group followed suit promptly upon seeing the leader's bombs fall. I immediately lay flat on the cockpit floor and slid open a peephole cover in order to observe the fall of the bombs. I watched four bombs plummet toward the earth. The target—two battleships moored side by side—lay ahead. The bombs became smaller and smaller and finally disappeared. I held my breath until two tiny puffs of smoke flashed suddenly on the ship to the left, and I shouted, 'Two hits!'

When an armor-piercing bomb with a time fuse hits the target, the result is almost unnoticeable from a great altitude. On the other hand, those which miss are quite obvious because they leave concentric waves to ripple out from the point of contact, and I saw two of these below. I presumed that it was battleship *Maryland* we had hit.

As the bombers completed their runs they headed north to return to the carriers. Pearl Harbor and the air bases had been pretty well wrecked by the fierce strafings and bombings. The imposing naval array of an hour before was gone. Antiaircraft fire had become greatly intensified, but in my continued observations I saw no enemy fighter planes. Our command of the air was unchallenged.

Source: Mitsuo Fuchida and Masatake Okumiya, *Midway, the Battle that Doomed Japan: The Japanese Navy's Story* (1955; reprinted. Annapolis, MD: Naval Institute Press, 1992), 51–54. Used by permission of Naval Institute Press.

AFTERMATH

Within two hours, Japanese aircraft had destroyed or seriously damaged 18 American vessels, including 8 battleships, 3 light cruisers, 3 destroyers, and 4 auxiliary craft. Some 73 aircraft were destroyed and 120 damaged, most of them on the ground at Hickam Field.

The raid, the worst foreign attack to occur on American soil until the September 11, 2001 destruction of the World Trade Center towers in New York City, left 2,403 Americans dead and a further 1,178 wounded. Japanese losses were 29 planes, 1 large and 5 midget submarines, and 64 men. The Japanese failed, however, to eliminate 2 aircraft carriers, which were then at sea, and also left unscathed the machine shops and oil storage tanks with 4.5 million barrels of fuel oil, all vitally important to the Pacific Fleet's subsequent ability to recover.

For three hours, Fuchida directed the operations of the 50 bombers under his direct command, after which he climbed to a higher altitude to assess the damage the raid had inflicted. Returning to base afterwards, he transmitted the famous radio message "Tora! Tora! Tora!" (Tiger, Tiger, Tiger), indicating his force's mission was accomplished. He became a national celebrity, and the Emperor Hirohito granted him an interview. In February 1942, he led the first wave of an aerial attack on Darwin, Australia. Badly wounded at the Battle of Midway in 1942, Fuchida thereafter held various naval staff positions.

ASK YOURSELF

1. Spending a week in Hiroshima on military talks in August 1945, Fuchida left the city one day before its destruction in an atomic attack. He returned the day after the bombing, as part of a team sent to assess the extent of the damage, and was the only one of the group who did not subsequently die of radiation poisoning. How did this double escape from death affect him?
2. Japan's defeat in August 1945 left Fuchida severely depressed, and for a while he became a reclusive peasant farmer. In 1952 he converted to Christianity and became a well-known traveling evangelist in the United States and Asia. He took American citizenship in 1960. How typical of former Japanese officers was his post-1945 career?
3. From 1951 onward, Fuchida published memoirs of Pearl Harbor and Midway and recorded extensive oral histories on his World War II military experiences, which became the basis of a biography of him by Gordon W. Prange and important source materials for many historians. Because he wrote so extensively, is it possible that histories of Japan's side of World War II overemphasize Fuchida's role and views? Is it possible to prevent historians relying too heavily on particular sources, when others may not be available, due to the death of participants or the failure of others to record or share their memories?

TOPICS TO CONSIDER

1. Fuchida was not the only well-known World War II flier who subsequently turned against war. Group Captain Leonard Cheshire (1917–1992), winner of the Victoria Cross, the highest British award for gallantry in battle, and an outstanding combat pilot with over 100 missions to his credit, was an official British observer at the nuclear bombing of Nagasaki. After the war Cheshire, a lapsed Christian, joined the Roman Catholic Church and spent the rest of his life organizing and running homes for the disabled. He also lectured extensively on conflict resolution. Cheshire ascribed his post-1945 epiphany to the long-term impact six years of war had upon him. How many veterans respond to their

experiences in war, once the conflict has ended, by turning to activities that will in some way make the world a better place?

2. Every war is ultimately fought by thousands, even millions, of individual combatants, each of whom usually sees only a small piece of the action taking place around him or herself. Since the mid-20th century, perhaps even before, oral history programs have made Herculean efforts to record the memories of ordinary people, not just the elite. Even such endeavors, however, tend to be disproportionately dominated by the more articulate, whose recollections will therefore be utilized by future historians. They also include only the reminiscences of those who are willing to discuss their past experiences. How representative or inclusive can even the best organized and most carefully thought out and run oral history programs ever be?

Further Information

Fuchida, Mitsuo. *From Pearl Harbor to Calvary*. 2nd ed. Denver, CO: Sky Pilots Press, 1958.

Fuchida, Mitsuo, and Masatake Okumiya. *Midway, The Battle That Doomed Japan: The Japanese Navy's Story.* Annapolis, MD: Naval Institute Press, 1992.

Prange, Gordon W. *At Dawn We Slept: The Untold Story of Pearl Harbor.* New York: McGraw Hill, 1981.

Prange, Gordon W., with Donald M. Goldstein and Katherine V. Dillon. *December 7, 1941: The Day the Japanese Attacked Pearl Harbor.* New York: McGraw Hill, 1988.

Prange, Gordon W., with Donald M. Goldstein and Katherine V. Dillon. *God's Samurai: Lead Pilot at Pearl Harbor.* Washington, DC: Brassey's, 1990.

Sakamaki, Kazuo. *I Attacked Pearl Harbor.* Trans. Toro Matsumoto. New York: Association Press, 1949.

Toland, John. *Infamy: Pearl Harbor and Its Aftermath.* Garden City, NY: Doubleday, 1982.

Weintraub, Stanley. *Long Day's Journey into War: December 7, 1941.* New York: Dutton, 1991.

Willmott, H. P., with Tohmatsu Haruo and W. Spencer Johnson. *Pearl Harbor.* New York: Cassell, 2001.

Zimm, Alan. *The Attack on Pearl Harbor: Strategy, Combat, Myths, Deceptions.* Havertown, PA: Casemate Publishers, 2011.

Web Sites

Pearl Harbor: Remembered. http://my.execpc.com/˜dschaaf/mainmenu.html.

Pearl Harbor.com. http://www.pearl-harbor.com.

Pearl Harbor.Org. http://www.pearlharbor.org.

Pearl Harbor Attacked. http://www.pearlharborattacked.com.

"Pearl Harbor Raid, 7 December 1941." Naval History & Heritage Command. http://www.history.navy.mil/photos/events/wwii-pac/pearlhbr/pearlhbr.htm.

Films

Pearl Harbor (2001), starring Ben Affleck, Kate Beckinsale, and Josh Hartnett.

Tora! Tora! Tora! (1970), starring Martin Balsam, Joseph Cotten, E. G. Marshall, and Jason Robards.

7. Franklin D. Roosevelt, "A Date Which Will Live in Infamy": December 7, 1941

INTRODUCTION

From President **Franklin D. Roosevelt** down, Pearl Harbor came as an overwhelming shock to virtually every American. Roosevelt immediately faced the task of requesting a declaration of war from Congress and of rallying the American people for what would inevitably be a long and almost certainly a difficult war. The day after Pearl Harbor, he asked both Houses of Congress formally to declare war on Japan, and with only one dissenting vote, they did so. When Roosevelt went to address Congress, Edith Bolling Wilson, widow of President **Woodrow Wilson**, the man who requested Congress to declare war on Germany in April 1917, accompanied him. It was estimated that 81 percent of American households listened to this speech, which was broadcast live by radio.

KEEP IN MIND AS YOU READ

1. The Pearl Harbor attack had a traumatic impact on most Americans, who remembered for the rest of their lives exactly where they were and what they were doing when they heard about it.
2. When Roosevelt addressed Congress, it was not yet clear whether Germany and Italy would join Japan in declaring war on the United States. He therefore spoke only about Japan. Germany and Italy declared war on the United States on December 11, 1941, four days after the Pearl Harbor raid, of which their governments had been forewarned.
3. Even though Japan had already attacked an American military installation and killed several thousand Americans, Roosevelt needed to obtain a formal declaration of war from Congress.
4. Roosevelt and his speechwriters prepared this address in 24 hours, which left little time for lengthy discussion or fine-tuning of the speech. The draft nonetheless underwent some significant modifications as the president worked on it. The first sentence originally read "a date which will live in world history," but Roosevelt replaced the last two words with "infamy," a change he believed would strengthen his statement.

DRAFT No. 1 December 7, 1941.

PROPOSED MESSAGE TO THE CONGRESS

Yesterday, December 7, 1941, a date which will live in ~~world history~~ [infamy], the United States of America was ~~simultaneously~~ [suddenly] and deliberately attacked by naval and air forces of the Empire of Japan.

The United States was at the moment at peace with that nation and was ~~continuing the~~ [still in] conversations with its Government and its Emperor looking toward the maintenance of peace in the Pacific. Indeed, one hour after Japanese air squadrons had commenced bombing in ~~Hawaii and the Philippines~~ [Oahu], the Japanese Ambassador to the United States and his colleague delivered to the Secretary of State a formal reply to a ~~former~~ [recent American] message ~~from the Secretary~~. [While] This reply ~~contained a statement~~ [stated] that [it seemed useless to continue the existing] diplomatic negotiations ~~must be considered at an end, but~~ [it] contained no threat ~~and no~~ [or] hint of ~~an~~ [war or] armed attack.

It will be recorded that the distance ~~of Manila, and especially~~ of Hawaii from Japan makes it obvious that the attack ~~were~~ [was] deliberately planned many days [or even weeks] ago. During the intervening time the Japanese Government has deliberately sought to deceive the United States by false statements and expressions of hope for continued peace.

DRAFT NO. 1

-2-

The attack yesterday on ~~Manila and on the Island of Oahu have~~ [the Hawaiian Islands has] caused severe damage to American naval and military forces. Very many American lives have been lost. In addition American ~~[illegible]~~ ships have been torpedoed on the high seas between San Francisco and Honolulu.

Yesterday the Japanese Government also launched an attack against Malaya.

[Last night Japanese forces attacked Guam.]

[The Philippine Islands]

Japan has, therefore, undertaken a surprise offensive extending throughout the Pacific area. The facts of yesterday speak for themselves. The people of the United States have already formed their opinions and well understand the implications ~~these attacks bear on~~ [to] the [very] safety of our nation.

As Commander-in-Chief of the Army and Navy I have, ~~of course,~~ directed that all measures be taken for our defense.

Long will we remember the character of the onslaught against us.

(A) [No matter how long it may take us to overcome this premeditated invasion the American people will in their righteous might win through to absolute victory.]

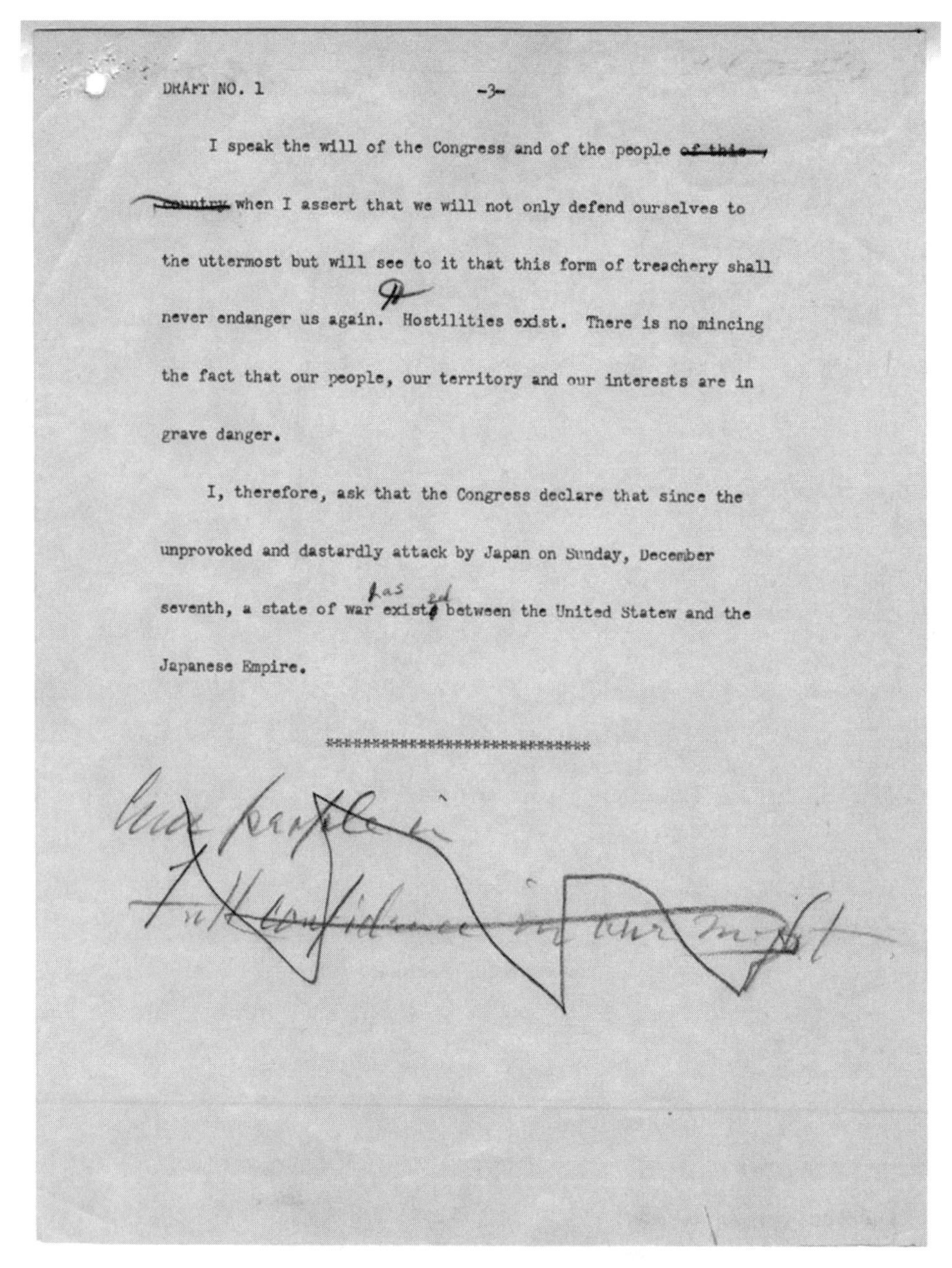
DRAFT NO. 1 -3-

I speak the will of the Congress and of the people ~~of this country~~ when I assert that we will not only defend ourselves to the uttermost but will see to it that this form of treachery shall never endanger us again. Hostilities exist. There is no mincing the fact that our people, our territory and our interests are in grave danger.

I, therefore, ask that the Congress declare that since the unprovoked and dastardly attack by Japan on Sunday, December seventh, a state of war has existed between the United Statew and the Japanese Empire.

****

Roosevelt, "A Date which Will Live in Infamy" speech, December 8, 1941, draft. On December 8, 1941, 81 percent of American homes switched on their radios to listen live as President Franklin D. Roosevelt addressed the U.S. Congress, seeking a formal declaration of war in response to the Japanese attack on the American fleet at the Pearl Harbor naval base in Hawaii the previous day. This was the largest audience in history for any American radio speech. Roosevelt was very conscious that he was addressing the American people in general, not simply a few hundred Senators and Congressmen. He drafted this speech in less than 36 hours following the Pearl Harbor raid. Roosevelt consulted his speech writers and the secretary of state, Cordell Hull, but rejected the latter's advice to give a detailed account of recent negotiations with Japan. Instead, he kept his message pithy, grim, and brief, a mere six-and-a-half minutes in all.

Although his aides helped to write this speech, the final decisions were Roosevelt's, as demonstrated by the president's handwritten amendments—including changing "a date which will live in world history" to "a date which will live in infamy"—to the typewritten draft his staff had produced, following his instructions. He wished this address to have a dramatic and emotional impact, placing the blame for the coming of war squarely on Japan, while rallying Americans—many of whom had previously opposed their country's intervention in the conflict—firmly in support of the war. In addition, he sought to give Americans confidence that, although the war might be lengthy, difficult, and demanding, ultimately their country would prevail. Overwhelmingly, Americans responded positively to Roosevelt's speech. Congress voted for war, with only one dissenter, while volunteers jammed recruiting stations. The successive drafts of Roosevelt's speech are among his official presidential papers at the Franklin D. Roosevelt Presidential Library in Hyde Park, New York. Recordings of the actual broadcast also allow us to reconstruct the experience of those millions of Americans who listened to it at the time.

Source: Franklin D. Roosevelt Presidential Library and Museum, Significant Documents Collection.

5. When Roosevelt made this speech, it remained uncertain whether Japan, Germany, or Italy would immediately attack American targets, shipping, or individuals, or where such moves might be expected. Security was tight and most Americans were likely to be extremely nervous.
6. Roosevelt deliberately kept this speech short—six-and-a-half minutes as delivered—because he felt brevity would make its impact more dramatic.

Franklin D. Roosevelt, Address to the United States Congress, 8 December 1941

Yesterday, December 7, 1941—a date which will live in infamy—the United States of America was suddenly and deliberately attacked by naval and air forces of the Empire of Japan.

The United States was at peace with that Nation and, at the solicitation of Japan, was still in conversation with its Government and its Emperor looking toward the maintenance of peace in the Pacific. Indeed, one hour after Japanese air squadrons had commenced bombing in Oahu, the **Japanese Ambassador to the United States** and his colleague delivered to the **Secretary of State** a formal reply to a recent American message. While this reply stated that it seemed useless to continue the existing diplomatic negotiations, it contained no threat or hint of war or armed attack.

It will be recorded that the distance of Hawaii from Japan makes it obvious that the attack was deliberately planned many days or even weeks ago. During the intervening time the Japanese Government has deliberately sought to deceive the United States by false statements and expressions of hope for continued peace.

The attack yesterday on the Hawaiian Islands has caused severe damage to American naval and military forces. Very many American lives have been lost. In addition American ships have been reported torpedoed on the high seas between San Francisco and Honolulu.

Yesterday the Japanese Government also launched an attack against **Malaya**.
Last night Japanese forces attacked **Hong Kong**.
Last night Japanese forces attacked **Guam**.
Last night Japanese forces attacked the Philippine Islands.
Last night the Japanese attacked **Wake Island**.
This morning the Japanese attacked **Midway Island**.

Japanese Ambassador to the United States: Kichisaburō Nomura
Secretary of State: Cordell Hull
Malaya and **Hong Kong:** British colonies; both fell to Japanese forces in the weeks after Pearl Harbor
Guam: Micronesian island, acquired by the United States in 1898, taken by Japanese forces on December 8, 1941
Wake Island: isolated coral atoll in the Pacific, annexed by the United States in 1899 as empty territory. In January 1941, U.S. troops constructed a military base on Wake Island, which Japanese forces overwhelmed on December 23, 1941, after fierce resistance from the American garrison
Midway Island: small coral atoll in the North Pacific, location of a major U.S. seaplane and submarine base, which Japanese forces failed to take

Japan has, therefore, undertaken a surprise offensive extending throughout the Pacific area. The facts of yesterday speak for themselves. The people of the United States have already formed their opinions and well understand the implications to the very life and safety of our Nation.

As Commander in Chief of the Army and Navy I have directed that all measures be taken for our defense.

Always will we remember the character of the onslaught against us.

No matter how long it may take us to overcome this premeditated invasion, the American people in their righteous might will win through to absolute victory. I believe I interpret the will of the Congress and of the people when I assert that we will not only defend ourselves to the uttermost but will make very certain that this form of treachery shall never endanger us again.

Hostilities exist. There is no blinking at the fact that our people, our territory, and our interests are in grave danger.

With confidence in our armed forces—with the unbounded determination of our people—we will gain the inevitable triumph—so help us God.

I ask that the Congress declare that since the unprovoked and dastardly attack by Japan on Sunday, December 7, a state of war has existed between the United States and the Japanese Empire.

Source: U.S. Department of State, *Peace and War: United States Foreign Policy, 1931–1941* (Washington, DC: Government Printing Office, 1943), 838–839.

AFTERMATH

Congress applauded Roosevelt's speech, and within an hour approved a declaration of war, with only one dissenting vote. Telegrams supporting Roosevelt's position poured into the White House, and thousands of young Americans immediately volunteered for the armed forces. The following day the president addressed the American people by radio on the national crisis, laying out at considerably more length what this war would mean for the United States and for average Americans. He warned that they must expect to "face a long war against crafty and powerful bandits" and that it would be "a hard war." Describing the enemies of the United States in apocalyptic terms, he proclaimed that: "Powerful and resourceful gangsters have banded together to make war upon the whole human race." Germany, Italy, and Japan were, he charged, following a coordinated strategy to dominate the world. Roosevelt recognized that the United States had now taken on a colossal task and, while reassuring Americans that they would eventually win through to victory, did not attempt to minimize the difficulties they must surmount. He warned that all would be required to make real sacrifices: to serve in the armed forces, work harder as civilians, pay heavy taxes, buy war bonds, and if necessary deprive themselves of unnecessary luxuries. Roosevelt bluntly stated that winning the war would require the economic mobilization of all his country's massive industrial strength on a yet unprecedented scale, envisaging the doubling or even quadrupling of production. He warned that it would be useless to defeat Japan if Italy and Germany retained control of much of Europe. He also anticipated that, once the war was won, the United States would have to remain involved in international affairs "to win the peace that follows."

ASK YOURSELF

1. What rhetorical means did Roosevelt use in this speech to rally Americans to unite in a collective effort against their enemy? The United States had been bitterly divided over whether or not to intervene in World War II. With the United States under attack, was he seeking to heal such divisions and unify the country?

FRANKLIN D. ROOSEVELT (1882–1945)

Democratic politician Franklin D. Roosevelt, elected president of the United States in 1933, an office he held until his death in 1945, was a distant cousin of former president **Theodore Roosevelt**. Both men believed that American security from attack ultimately depended upon the protection of the British fleet. From 1913 to early 1920, including all of World War I, Roosevelt served as assistant secretary of the navy in the administration of President **Woodrow Wilson**. While holding this position, he took an extremely pro-Allied and anti-German attitude, welcoming American intervention in April 1917. In 1920 Roosevelt ran as his party's vice presidential candidate and, though he lost, until the early 1930s, he remained one of the strongest American supporters of Wilson's League of Nations. Decidedly a politician, in the presidential campaign of 1932, Roosevelt jettisoned his support of the League of Nations in order to win the endorsement of influential anti-League Democrats. Even so, at heart he still believed that the United States should take on a far more substantial international role than that it had played between the wars. During the 1930s, Roosevelt acquiesced somewhat reluctantly in the passage of neutrality legislation, endorsed the Munich settlement of 1938, and hoped against hope that it might be possible to preserve European peace. Once war began in Europe in September 1939, his policies increasingly assisted the Allied powers, especially Great Britain, both economically and strategically, and the United States drew ever closer to war with Germany and Japan.

2. Roosevelt was a skilled orator, who frequently used the relatively new technology of radio to communicate directly and informally with the American people in what he termed "fireside chats." Radio gave the illusion of intimacy, since people listened to it in their homes or with their neighbors. Other politicians of all stripes, including **Winston Churchill, Adolf Hitler,** and **Benito Mussolini,** were likewise adept at using radio in the 1930s and 1940s. Why did radio become such an important political medium then?
3. Roosevelt addressed Congress at a time when Americans were still shocked by the Pearl Harbor attack. Besides asking Congress to declare war on Japan, he needed to reassure his countrymen that, however grave the immediate situation, the problems facing the United States were in no sense insuperable and that his administration could handle them. Even 30 or 40 years later, many Americans would still regard Roosevelt as the yardstick and standard against whom all American presidents should be judged. Does Roosevelt's speech give any insights into why they felt this way?
4. Roosevelt pointed out that Japan must have set preparations for the Pearl Harbor operation in motion several weeks earlier, when negotiations with the United States were still proceeding. Why did Americans find the secretive nature of Japanese planning for war with the United States particularly unacceptable? Does this speech deliberately juxtapose American innocence and virtue with Japanese duplicity and covert aggression? If so, why?
5. The journalist Edward R. Murrow, who was visiting the White House on the day of Pearl Harbor, revealed in 1945 that news of the Japanese raid left Roosevelt and all his senior advisers deeply shocked and surprised. Why did Murrow not make this information public in December 1941? Should he have done so earlier, to combat charges that the president knew in advance of the attack on Pearl Harbor?

TOPICS TO CONSIDER

1. From shortly after December 1941, Roosevelt's political opponents charged that he deliberately set out to provoke a war with Japan in order to enter the European war against Adolf Hitler's Germany through the back door of a war with Japan. Others subsequently alleged that the president and his top advisers received advance warning through intelligence intercepts that an attack was planned on Pearl Harbor, but deliberately forbore to warn the military officers in charge there because they sought an unassailable pretext for war. On close examination, none of these theories carries any great conviction. Had Germany and Italy not taken the initiative and declared war on the United States a few days after Pearl Harbor, the United States would in all probability have concentrated on winning the war in Asia, rather than focusing on the European war that Roosevelt considered the higher priority. Even if the U.S. government had been able to warn its forces at Pearl Harbor to expect a Japanese assault and they had been better prepared to resist it, the attack would still have led to war between the two countries. The fact that such allegations were made was nonetheless revealing. What do these charges suggest about the acrimony of the prevailing political climate in the United States in 1939 to 1941 and the bitter debate over issues of war and peace at that time? Are the controversies over Pearl Harbor in any way comparable to more recent debates over precisely which individuals or agencies within the American official bureaucracy failed to anticipate the events of September 11, 2001?
2. Speaking to Congress the day after Pearl Harbor, Roosevelt pledged to continue the war against Japan until the United States had achieved absolute victory over Japan. Expanding on this to the American people the following day, he implied that attaining this victory would also mean subjugating Germany and Italy. Did he at this stage envisage that accomplishing this objective would involve the total defeat of all three countries, the overthrow of their existing governments, and their occupation for several years by the forces of the United States and its allies?
3. During the October 1962 Cuban missile crisis, when top American military officials suggested that the United States launch an attack on missile bases in Cuba, Robert F. Kennedy, brother of President John F. Kennedy, argued strongly against this, on the grounds that he did not want his brother to go down in history as the president who authorized a Pearl Harbor-style attack on Cuban installations. What did Kennedy's analogy reveal about American popular understanding and memories of Pearl Harbor, two decades after that event? Do Americans today still view the attack in the same light?

Further Information

Best, Antony. *Britain, Japan, and Pearl Harbor: Avoiding War in East Asia, 1936–41.* New York: Routledge, 1995.

Borg, Dorothy, and Shumpei Okamoto, eds. *Pearl Harbor as History: Japanese-American Relations 1931–1941.* New York: Columbia University Press, 1973.

Clausen, Henry, and Bruce Lee. *Pearl Harbor: Final Judgment.* New York: Crown, 1992.

Gillon, Steven M. *Pearl Harbor: FDR Leads the Nation into War.* New York: Basic Books, 2011.

Heinrichs, Waldo H. *Threshold of War: Franklin D. Roosevelt and American Entry into World War II.* New York: Oxford University Press, 1988.
Mawdsley, Evan. *December 1941: Twelve Days That Began a World War.* New Haven, CT: Yale University Press, 2011.
Prange, Gordon W. *At Dawn We Slept: The Untold Story of Pearl Harbor.* New York: McGraw Hill, 1981.
Prange, Gordon W., with Donald M. Goldstein and Katherine V. Dillon. *December 7, 1941: The Day the Japanese Attacked Pearl Harbor.* New York: McGraw Hill, 1988.
Prange, Gordon W., with Donald M. Goldstein and Katherine V. Dillon. *Pearl Harbor: The Verdict of History.* New York: McGraw Hill, 1986.
Ryan, Halford R. *FDR's Rhetorical Presidency.* New York: Greenwood Press, 1988.
Weintraub, Stanley. *Long Day's Journey into War: December 7, 1941.* New York: Dutton, 1991.

Web Sites

"FDR's 'Day of Infamy' Speech: Crafting a Call to Arms." *National Archives: Prologue Magazine,* Vol. 33, no. 4 (Winter 2001), http://www.archives.gov/publications/prologue/2001/winter/crafting-day-of-infamy-speech.html.
Franklin D. Roosevelt Presidential Library and Museum. http://www.fdrlibrary.marist.edu/.

Film and Television

Betrayal from the East (1945), starring Lee Tracy and Nancy Kelly.
Prelude to War (1942), directed by Frank Capra.
Wake Island (1942), starring Brian Donlevy, Robert Preston, and Macdonald Carey.

FIGHTING THE WAR

8. The Siege of Leningrad: Diary of Anna Petrovna Ostroumova-Lebedeva, March–May 1942

INTRODUCTION

Anna Petrovna Ostroumova-Lebedeva (1871–1957) of Leningrad was a well-known artist, printmaker, and illustrator. During her lifetime, she published several volumes of edited *Autobiographical Notes,* in 1935, 1945, and 1951, which were based upon the diary and notebooks she kept for many years. She remained in Leningrad, which as St. Petersburg had been the Russian capital until 1918, during the protracted siege of the city by German and Finnish forces, which lasted from September 1941 to January 1944, 872 days in all. By exchanging her paintings for bread and wood, Ostroumova-Lebedeva, then in her 70s, managed to survive numerous privations. In November 1942, she was even named an Honored Artist of the Soviet Union, after she had helped to prepare a presentation album for the women of Scotland, who had sent a similar album to Leningrad to express their sympathy for the sufferings of that city. Many thousands of civilians, however, starved to death, as a combination of the evacuation of 1.2 million people and hunger reduced the city's population from its prewar 3.3 million to 575,900. There were well attested reports of cannibalism. It was estimated that at least one million Russian civilians and between 600,000 and one million soldiers died during the siege of Leningrad and the fighting around the city, which was repeatedly shelled and bombed.

KEEP IN MIND AS YOU READ

1. Ostroumova-Lebedeva was not able to publish these portions of her diary during her lifetime. Neither her complaints of inequitable distribution of food rations, looting, and profiteering, nor her implicit comparison of the grim honesty of Winston Churchill's speeches with the practices of Soviet leader **Josef Stalin**, would have been acceptable to the Russian censor.
2. Ostroumova-Lebedeva, who was in her late 40s when Russia became Communist, enjoyed a relatively privileged position in Soviet society as a respected artist who belonged to the cultural elite. She also demonstrated much of the intellectual freedom of thought and independence of the pre-1917 Russian intelligentsia, and remained very much in touch with artistic developments outside the Soviet Union.

3. The worst period of the siege of Leningrad, in terms of hunger and deaths through starvation and disease, came during 1942. From early 1943, some rail links with Russia had been restored, and trains began to bring food supplies into the city, while vegetable harvests within the city also improved.
4. Beginning in the 1920s, Josef Stalin was suspicious of Leningrad, Russia's westernmost city and unofficial second capital, fearing its cosmopolitan population, led by such rival Communist officials as Grigorii Zinoviev and Sergei Kirov, represented a threat to his own rule. In the 1930s he purged Zinoviev, while Kirov was assassinated. Although around 400 books on the siege were published in the Soviet Union, most of these appeared after Stalin's death.

8 March 1942

What an immense panorama of fire has engulfed the whole world! The whole world! No, it seems there is no country whose peoples would not writhe and die in the flame of this fire. Some kind of mad desire for mutual extermination has seized everyone.

And our Leningrad, its siege and we its inhabitants, perishing from hunger (20,000–25,000 per day) and from shells and bombs—we are only a tiny detail in this entire, horrible, nightmarish, but grandiose and amazing war.

And just think: among the nations of the entire world, especially among soldiers engaged in combat, how often have we seen manifested the ennobled feelings of heroism, self-sacrifice, courage, and resourcefulness. What tremendous mental anguish soldiers must experience when they are commanded to kill the enemy—people just like themselves. We might assume, and I think without error, that three-quarters of the combatants do not thirst for the blood of their enemies.

But simultaneously, along with the valorous actions of our warriors and of people in general, how often have they demonstrated brutality, cruelty, often completely unnecessary and senseless. And how much deception and baseness!

But there is nothing more vile and insidious than those who, preying on suffering and misfortune, bleeding people, stuff their pockets by means of speculation and stealing. And there are a good number of them!

Recently I came upon a speech by Churchill, published in our country, excerpted of course, in ***Pravda*** on 27 February. It amazed me. He conveys a stark picture of the madness that has gripped the whole world. And I would paint this picture thus: clouds of stinking black smoke have obscured the whole earth and sky. And tongues of fire, with sparks and steam, break through and dance about.

And below people swarm about. Fortresses fly into the air. Cities fall to the ground under the blows of artillery shells and falling bombs. People, like ants, perish under the debris of collapsing houses. Tens, hundreds of thousands of sailors cast themselves into the teeming waters from the fiery ships, all to perish in the sea. The African heat and sands incinerate entire divisions, and the desert is sown with the corpses of the unfortunate ones!

> ***Pravda:*** literally Truth, the official Soviet newspaper, heavily censored

Within a few days corpses are transformed into a pile of white bones under the scorching rays of the sun. In other arenas of the war, soldiers freeze to death in the bitter cold, which it is difficult to survive, especially for the wounded or unconscious.

In several hours they transform into ice-covered corpses. Then, later, it is difficult to find them, since the snow covers them with its white shroud, altering the relief of the terrain.

I return again to **Churchill's speech**. It was striking for the courage shown in admitting England's seemingly total powerlessness before Germany, Japan, and Italy. He had the courage himself to tell the whole nation and whole world about the surrender to Japan of 673,000 English soldiers, including their commanding officers.

In all this worldwide phantasmagoria, I feel some kind of satanic romanticism, and in addition, grandeur, a head-long irrepressible rush to death and destruction.

Some horrible and violent whirlwind has landed on earth, and everything has gotten mixed up and has started to spin in black smoke, fire, and snowstorm.

And we, we Leningraders, choking in the siege, are microscopic grains of sand in this whole, immense cyclone.

Churchill's speech: in widely reported public addresses, the British prime minister acknowledged that early 1942 was one of the worst periods of the war for Britain, as Japanese forces rapidly overran the British imperial possessions of Hong Kong, Malaya, Singapore, and Burma, threatened India, and bombed the Australian city of Darwin

Rubenesque: the 17th-century Flemish artist Peter Paul Rubens was famous for painting plump, well-fed women

22 May 1942

I write sluggishly and with difficulty. I haven't eaten well for the past ten days.

The academic ration I was allotted, and which I received for the first time on 8 April, wasn't distributed in May. And on what they give on the ration cards, it is impossible to survive, without starving, or losing the ability to work, or dying.

Anastasia Osipovna [professor of chemistry, Leningrad State University] came to see me. She had recently been to the public baths and was completely astounded by the large number of well-fed **Rubenesque** young women with radiant bodies and glowing physiognomies.

They are all workers in bakeries, cooperatives, soup kitchens, and children's centers.

In bakeries and cooperatives they cheat the unfortunate inhabitants. They divide the best food among themselves; for example, they leave the hind quarters for themselves.

In the soup kitchens and children's centers, they simply steal.

The same thing goes on, I think, at the highest level of the food-distribution system. What happened to two hundred cars of food, brought in as a gift to Leningrad from the collective farm workers? And many times we received gifts of food from various districts, and what did we see of them? Everything gets lost in the "apparatus."

The organization of the food-ration cards with three categories is very convenient for well-known goals, for example for the "unloading" [*razgruzka*] of Leningrad.

As it is now, the third category is a disgrace. It is the category of dependents, i.e., people who can't work, pensioners, i.e., old people, and that includes housewives (they work, but private).

All these old people, dependents, and pensioners are useless and represent superfluous mouths in Leningrad, and in order to get rid of them, the third-category ration is quite reduced, and if not reduced, then quite meager, and it is impossible to survive on it.

Then it remains for those persons in the third category either to die here from "emaciation," or to be evacuated, which for them also means death. In any case, the goal is achieved—people "leave," abandoning Leningrad.

Source: Excerpt from "Diary of Ann Petrovna Ostroumova-Lebedeva, artist" from *Writing the Siege of Leningrad: Women's Diaries, Memoirs, and Documentary Prose*, by Cynthia

Simmons and Nina Perlina, © 2003. (Pittsburgh: University of Pittsburgh Press, 2002), 30–32. Reprinted by permission of the University of Pittsburgh Press.

AFTERMATH

Ostroumova-Lebedeva died in 1957, aged 86, but the sufferings of the siege and its aftermath affected her health. Although one reason for her survival was that she could barter her paintings for vital food and firewood, she stopped making prints in 1946. She published two further volumes of *Autobiographical Notes* after the war, but these volumes were heavily expurgated, as material considered too politically sensitive was omitted. The full text of her diaries, which were donated to the Russian National Library in St. Petersburg after her death, remained unpublished until well after the Soviet Union had ceased to exist.

ASK YOURSELF

1. Ostroumova-Lebedeva was a highly cultivated and well-read woman, who speculated intensely on the meaning of the war and the different ways in which the conflict affected those caught up in it. How typical were her reflections?
2. Intellectuals and artists in Leningrad made great efforts to keep cultural life functioning during the siege, with libraries and academic institutes continuing open. The composer Dmitrii Shostakovich completed his Seventh Symphony during the siege, part of which he spent in Leningrad, and it was first performed there in August 1942. Did this reflect their loyalty to the Soviet government, Russia, or their own city, or some combination of all three?
3. The population of besieged Leningrad was disproportionately female, with one million women and children trapped in the city at the beginning of the siege. Until recently, however, histories of wartime Leningrad downplayed the role of women during the siege, as they took over many jobs once done by men, including heavy industrial work, and withstood the rigors and privations of the experience. By December 1942, 80 percent of all factory workers in the city were women. Why have historians tended to underrepresent women's experiences?
4. Surviving the siege of Leningrad depended in large part upon an individual's access to food. White-collar workers received higher rations than laborers, as did Communist Party members. How, if at all, might one recapture the experiences of those Leningraders who did not survive?

TOPICS TO CONSIDER

1. Even though in 1945 Leningrad was the first Russian city to be awarded the title Hero City, Stalin's hostility to the former St. Petersburg and its political elite continued after the war. In 1949 and 1950, he ordered the arrest and trial of around 200 Leningrad Communist leaders, on charges that they sought his overthrow. Many were executed. In 1953 the city's massive Museum of the Defense of Leningrad was closed, its 37,000 exhibits either dispersed to other museums or destroyed altogether, and its director shot. Soviet-era histories of World War II tended to de-emphasize the siege of Leningrad. In the 1980s and 1990s, within Leningrad/St. Petersburg the policies of greater openness (*glasnost*) brought a new pride in the city's record during the siege, together

with considerable resentment of the failure of Stalin's Moscow-based regime to do more to help the city during its sufferings. The museum reopened on a smaller scale in September 1989, with numerous artifacts, documents, and oral histories contributed by survivors of the blockade. What insights into the political role of historical memory can one gain from the history of the museum itself?

2. During World War II the civilian populations of many countries—Germany, the Soviet Union, Italy, Britain, Japan, China, to name only a few examples—endured often intense suffering as a result of war. This was particularly true of those in cities that became the targets of intensive bombing or sieges, or in areas where combat fighting or guerrilla warfare took place. Only rarely, though, did civilians on the home front turn against their governments, however brutal, or seek to replace totalitarian or incompetent political and military leaders. Why were so many people of all nationalities prepared to tolerate the sufferings that war inflicted on them, without seeking to overthrow the governments who might have been held responsible for these? Can you think of any comparable situations in earlier or later wars?
3. Since 2000, several substantial popular and critically well received historical novels, including the Russian American and Leningrad-born Paullina Simons's *The Bronze Horseman* (2000), the British Helen Dunmore's award-winning *The Siege* (2002), the American Elise Blackwell's *Hunger* (2003), the South African Gillian Slovo's *Ice Road* (2004), and the American Debra Dean's *The Madonnas of Leningrad* (2006), have centered upon the siege of Leningrad. Why should this lengthy episode of World War II appeal imaginatively to so many writers of fiction? What value do their recreations of the siege have either as sources, or as instances of historical memory at work? What, if anything, can one learn from a novel that one cannot obtain from nonfictionalized works of history?

Further Information

Barber, John, and Andrei Dzeniskevich, eds. *Life and Death in Besieged Leningrad, 1941–44.* New York: Palgrave Macmillan, 2005.

Glantz, David M. *The Battle for Leningrad, 1941–1944.* Lawrence: University Press of Kansas, 2002.

Jones, Michael. *Leningrad: State of Siege.* London: John Murray, 2008.

Kirchenbaum, Lisa A. *The Legacy of the Siege of Leningrad, 1941–1995: Myth, Memories, and Monuments.* Cambridge: Cambridge University Press, 2006.

Salisbury, Harrison. *The 900 Days: The Siege of Leningrad.* London: Macmillan, 1986.

Web Site

The 900-Day Siege of Leningrad. Saint.-Petersburg.com: History of St. Petersburg. http://www.saint-petersburg.com/history/siege.asp.

Films and Television

The Attack on Leningrad (2009), starring Mira Sorvino, Gabriel Byrne, and Armin Mueller-Stahl.

Battlefield: Russia: The Siege of Leningrad (2004). Pegasus.

The Siege of Leningrad (1943). Lenfilm Newsreel Studios, Leningrad, narrated by Edward R. Murrow.

9. A Russian "Night Witch": Reminiscences of Lieutenant Olga Lisikova, Pilot, Commander of Douglas C-47 Aircraft

INTRODUCTION

The country where women's contributions to the war effort were most prominent was the Soviet Union, where by 1945 women constituted 55 percent of the total civilian workforce, and over 80 percent of agricultural workers. Since its inception, the Soviet state had expected women to work, often in jobs traditionally considered male preserves, and during the war, this established tendency was reinforced by the shortage of able-bodied men outside the armed forces. The Soviet Union also made greatest use of women in the military, enlisting 800,000 in the Soviet armed forces, approximately half in the Air Defense Forces, the remainder in ground units. While other Allied armies generally restricted women's combat roles, the Soviet Union used them extensively. Women manned anti-aircraft batteries, barrage balloon units, and searchlights. Others served with combat units as tank and artillery crews, mechanics, cooks, and in medical and staff units. Almost 2,000 Russian women became snipers. Between 8,000 and 14,000 Polish women also served in national units under Russian command.

British and American women who served in their countries' armed forces were normally restricted to noncombatant jobs, with fliers, for example, working as ferry pilots, delivering airplanes or supplies. After the June 1941 German invasion, the Soviet Union, by contrast, raised three combat regiments of women fliers, most of them prewar pilots trained in civil aviation. Many of these units' ground crew also consisted of women. The much-publicized night witches flew both bomber and fighter missions throughout the war, over 30,000 combat sorties in all. The most prominent such pilot was Major Marina Raskova, who died in an aircrash.

Not all women fliers served in single-sex units. Olga Lisikova (1917–) was born in the Far East and daughter of a Leningrad intelligentsia family, entered flying school in 1937, and flew with the mostly male 1st Regiment. During the war, she soon became commander of an otherwise all-male crew.

KEEP IN MIND AS YOU READ

1. Lisikova's first husband was also a pilot, shot down in combat in October 1941. During the 1939–1940 Soviet-Finnish winter war, she flew a medical rescue plane while several months pregnant with their daughter.

2. As the only female pilot on her squadron, Lisikova was extremely conscious that any mistake she made would rebound on the reputation of all women fliers.
3. Lisikova refused to allow any of her crew or passengers to use bad language in her hearing.
4. Being a combat pilot did not exempt Lisikova from sexual harassment by superior officers.

A Russian "Night Witch": Reminiscences of Lieutenant Olga Lisikova, Pilot, Commander of Douglas C-47 aircraft

[After retraining in 1940] I was transferred to the Flying Division of Special Role, which was assigned to the State Committee of Soviet Defense. This organization completed missions on all fronts, from the Black Sea to the Barents Sea. The main base was at the Vnukovo airdrome, not far from Moscow. When we were fulfilling our combat missions, we flew out of auxiliary airfields closer to the front lines or to the location of our mission. The pilots were experienced airline pilots with many hours. Our missions were to bail out paratroopers, drop supplies for encircled troops, transport fuel and spare parts to advancing troops, fly to the **partisans** in the rear, drop intelligence officers to the enemy rear, and bring supplies to besieged Leningrad.

. . .

In a month I was appointed commander of the aircraft. But a few days later I was ordered to fly to Siberia to be assigned as a copilot ferrying aircraft from America. It turned out that the commander of my division learned that I, a woman, was flying in his division, and he was determined to get rid of me. But then he was ordered to another command, and my chief rescinded the order.

. . .

I actively took part in all the combat missions my division carried out. The new commander of the division summoned me and told me that I, being the only female pilot in the division, had a great responsibility, because all eyes were on me. Each flight, every landing was closely watched by the staff. And where the failure of a male pilot could pass unnoticed, mine would be always under surveillance. Any blunder, or worse—an accident—would not serve me well. He cautioned me to be demanding of myself. After that talk I changed drastically; I didn't look or act like myself. Everything congested inside; I became very strict with myself and my subordinates. Before, I would go to rest and relax after a mission; now, I went to the **navigators**' room and scrupulously studied the route of the next mission. When the crew went to see a movie, I went to the meteorological station and studied the weather reports. I would do everything better than the men.

partisans: civilian guerrilla fighters
navigator: officer responsible for plotting an aircraft's flight path

. . .

We were transferred to a division of the long-distance flights, closer to the front. After this redeployment, the commanding staff of the division invited me to a dinner with their major-general at the head of table. As the dinner came to an end, I noticed the general's staff were quietly sneaking out of the room. I tried to follow their example, but I was stopped by the commander of the division. I understood that the general wanted to bed me down. Yes, I was only a lieutenant, but apart from that I was Olga Lisikova, and it was impossible to bed me down. His pressure was persistent. I had to think very fast, because nobody would dare to come to my rescue. In desperation I said, "I fly with my husband in my crew!" and he was taken aback. He didn't expect to hear that. He released me; I immediately rushed out and found the radio operator and mechanic of my crew. I didn't make explanations. I, as commander of the crew, ordered that one of them was to be my fictitious husband and gave them my word of honor that nobody would ever learn the truth! Then I released them.

I couldn't sleep all night; I couldn't believe any commander would behave like that. I thought, Were generals allowed to do anything that came to mind? I couldn't justify his behavior. The only explanation that seemed appropriate was that I was really very attractive in my youth. Thank God we flew away early the next morning.

I already had 120 combat missions when our division began receiving the C-47 aircraft. It was a most sophisticated plane, beyond any expectations. We pilots didn't even have to master it—it was perfect and flew itself! Before I was assigned a mission in it, I made one check flight. My next flight was a combat mission, to drop paratroopers to liberate Kiev. Later, when Kiev had been liberated, I flew there again. There were few planes on the landing strip, and in the distance I saw an aircraft of unusual shape, like a cigar. I realized at once that it was an American B-29. I taxied and parked next to it. My radio operator, tail gunner, and I were invited aboard by the American crew. We spoke different languages, but my mechanic knew German and an American spoke it also; thus, the communication took place. The outside of the aircraft was no surprise, but when you got into it, touched it, and saw the most sophisticated equipment, you realized that it was the most perfect aircraft design. The Americans received us very warmly. The news that we flew the American C-47 made them respect us more. The most astonishing news for them was that I, a woman, was commander of the plane. They couldn't believe it. It was an instant reaction—I suggested that I would fly them in my plane to prove it! I put the crew in the navigator compartment and placed the copilot in the right seat beside me. The flight was short, six or seven minutes, but it was hilarious. After that I was strictly reprimanded by my commander.

By the time I had made 200 combat missions, I was entrusted at last to fly in the Intelligence Directorate of the General Staff of the Red Army. I will tell you about one of those flights. . . . I was assigned a mission to fly to the enemy rear and drop supplies to the partisans. I crossed the front line at 4,000 meters, and at the appointed place began a dive. The **altimeter** showed me to be lower and lower, but I could see nothing through the clouds. Finally the **altitude** read zero and then less than that. Judging by the meter I was to be deep in the soil, but still I held the dive. I couldn't return to base without completing my mission: I didn't want to be reproached after the flight that I hadn't fulfilled the risky mission only because I was a coward, because I was a woman. Then I glimpsed the ground, and below me was the target where we were to drop the cargo. The area was covered with dense, patchy fog. We dropped the supplies to the partisans and returned to base.

> **altimeter:** gauge that measures an aircraft's distance above the ground
> **altitude:** distance above the ground of aircraft

When we returned we learned that all the crews had turned back, not having managed to fulfill the mission. Everyone was astonished. How could I, a woman, do what other male pilots hadn't managed to accomplish? The division commander said he would promote me to be awarded the Gold Star of Hero of the Soviet Union, but I never received that award, because my crew consisted of males. If the crew had been female, it would have been awarded.

Source: Reprinted from Anne Noggle, *A Dance with Death: Soviet Airwomen in World War II* (College Station: Texas A & M University Press, 1994), 238–245 by permission of the Texas A&M University Press.

AFTERMATH

Lisikova flew 280 combat missions during the war, many of them ferrying supplies to her native Leningrad during the siege, and was considered one of Russia's flying aces, but "was never awarded a single order" for her later flying. Instead, she featured on a special poster praising her accomplishments. Friends believed this omission was partly because she was both beautiful and independent, qualities that annoyed male superiors. Moreover, her first husband was shot down in combat and seriously injured, incarcerated first as a German prisoner of war and then in Soviet detention, before returning to Leningrad in 1946. This sufficed to compromise Lisikova's own political bona fides and debar her from high honors and awards, even though she was a skilled aviator trusted to ferry top Soviet officials around. She ended the war a Guards Senior Lieutenant. In 1945 she met her second husband, Volf Plaksin, with whom she "lived in love . . . for forty-five happiest years" until his death. On the fiftieth anniversary of Russia's victory in World War II, her portrait was included among those of Russia's most celebrated wartime pilots in the Museum of the Great Patriotic War in Moscow. Lisikova "simply cried."

ASK YOURSELF

1. Lisikova was a notable athlete, twice the top skier in the Soviet Union, a good runner and tennis player, and a billiards champion. Did these skills make it easier for her to win acceptance in a largely male environment?
2. Women aviators generated good publicity for the Soviet Union. As early as 1937, Lisikova featured in a film, *Warriors of Our Motherland,* and was considered a star pilot, enabling her to pick any assignment she wanted. Did even a Russian woman need to be somewhat exceptional to make a success of a flying career, especially in a masculine unit?
3. Lisikova came from the liberal-minded, independent Leningrad intelligentsia, a cultivated musical and literary household of six families and 11 children in one large apartment, whose residents included at least one novelist. What advantages and disadvantages did this background give her in Communist Soviet society?
4. Why were American fliers so surprised to meet a female Russian flight commander?

TOPICS TO CONSIDER

1. German troops first christened the Russian women fliers *Nachthexen* (night witches) when the all-female 586th, 587th, and 588th Squadrons flew thousands of night bombing sorties against them on the Eastern Front, using rickety trainer biplanes. Why did the women adopt this derogatory term as a label of pride?
2. Can you think of any particular advantages or disadvantages in having single-sex (all-male or all-female) military combat units, as opposed to mixed-sex units?

Further Information

Cottam, Kazimiera Janina. *Women and Resistance: Selected Biographies of Soviet Women Soldiers.* Nepean, ON: New Military Publishers, 1998.

Cottam, Kazimiera Janina, ed. *Women in Air War: The Eastern Front of World War II.* Rev. ed. Nepean, ON: New Military Publishers, 1997.

Myles, Bruce. *Night Witches: The Untold Story of Women in Combat.* Chicago: Academy Chicago Press, 1990.
Noggle, Anne. *A Dance with Death: Soviet Airwomen in World War II.* College Station: Texas A & M University Press, 1994.
Pennington, Reina. *Wings, Women, and War: Soviet Airwomen in World War II Combat.* Lawrence: University Press of Kansas, 2001.

Web Sites

Interview with Olga Mikhaylovna Lisikova. http://lend-lease.airforce.ru/english/articles/lisikova/index.htm.
Lisikova, Olga: Photo, Biography. Celebrities. http://www.persona.rin.ru/eng/view/f/0/18249/lisikova-olga.

Film

"Only Girls Go to Battle." "Night Witches"! Female Combat Pilots on Eastern Front! http://www.youtube.com/watch?v=fSEro1gVbOY.

10. The Eastern Front: Recollections of Hans Heinrich Herwarth von Bittenfeld on the German Occupation

INTRODUCTION

In Russia, many inhabitants of the Baltic states, the Ukraine, and the Crimea, who had suffered particularly harshly during the purges of the 1930s, initially welcomed the German invaders as liberators, until the harshness of German occupation, together with rousing appeals by Soviet leader **Josef Stalin** to patriotism, disabused most of the belief that German rule would be any improvement. German atrocities against not just Jews and Muslims, but also the Russian population of the occupied zones in general, soon turned the inhabitants against them.

The well-born Hans Heinrich Herwarth von Bittenfeld (1904–1999) came from a Prussian noble family whose members traditionally served in the army or as diplomats. In 1930 he joined the German Foreign Service, spending most of the 1930s as a junior diplomat in Moscow. Sociable, intelligent, and charming, Herwarth was on excellent terms with many British, French, and American diplomats, who referred to him as Johnny. Immediately the **Nazi-Soviet Non-Aggression Pact** was signed, Herwarth joined the aristocratic German First Cavalry, and with his regiment took part in the 1939 invasion of Poland, the 1940 Western **blitzkrieg** across of the Low Countries and France, and the 1941 attack on the Soviet Union. Herwarth was particularly active in efforts to recruit discontented Soviet soldiers for the Nazi war effort.

KEEP IN MIND AS YOU READ

1. Hans Herwarth von Bittenfeld recorded these reminiscences in the early 1990s, almost 50 years after the events had taken place, when he was in his 80s.
2. At the time that Herwarth was speaking, Germany had for over 40 years been part of a Cold War alliance against the Soviet Union with the United States, Britain, and other West European powers.
3. The appalling conditions Russian prisoners of war faced often impelled them to volunteer for the German army simply as a way to obtain enough to eat.
4. Although some German military officers welcomed the idea of recruiting disaffected volunteers—some Russian, some of Cossack, or other ethnic origin—to fight against Stalin, **Hitler** was unenthusiastic. Only in 1944 did Germany

authorize the creation of an independent Russian Liberation Army, headed by General Andrey Andreyevich Vlasov, former commander of the Thirty-Seventh and Twentieth Soviet Armies, whom German troops captured in 1942.

Recollections of Hans Herwarth von Bittenfeld

We soldiers already had an eerie feeling when we first marched into the Soviet Union. I was with a regiment that was half East Prussian and half Bavarian. Prussians and Bavarians alike were in awe of the size of Russia; it reached all the way to the Pacific Ocean. The troops were not at all enthusiastic about the prospects of fighting in the Soviet Union.

Once, a representative from the Propaganda Ministry visited us and gave a speech that was, in fact, quite excellent. In an attempt to prepare us for what lay ahead, he reminded us that in the Middle Ages **German knights** had also ridden east. We listened silently, and there was no applause. Afterwards we stood around, and the speaker said to my divisional commander, "I am actually rather disappointed. I don't see any enthusiasm here." A captain responded, "Sir, enthusiasm is not the point. But when we are ordered to fight, we do it extremely well." In a sense, this explains the tragic situation of the German front officer. We did our damned duty, but we never believed in ultimate victory over the Soviet Union.

When we marched into the Soviet Union we were initially looked upon as liberators and greeted with **bread and salt**. The farmers shared the little they had with us. They hoped finally to be treated as Europeans and as human beings. They expected the end of **collective farming**. Hitler, on the other hand, claimed this to be the best system for requisitioning grain. Thus Hitler thought the same as Stalin on the subject of collectivization. That was the disaster. The [Nazi] party functionaries succeeded in driving people who were willing to cooperate with us back into the arms of Stalin.

They managed to achieve this through a reign of terror and the behavior of the **SS**. The SS dealt with the minorities first by murdering Jews and many Muslims. Because Muslims were circumcized [*sic*], they were thought to be Jews, considered subhuman. Naturally this stupid, inhuman treatment of the population slowly eroded the good will of the people.

Interestingly enough, it was different in the southern part of the Soviet Union. There, because the **North Caucasus** region was under military administration, people were treated properly. The troops were ordered to behave as if they were on maneuvers in their own country. General [Ernst] von Köstring, the former military attaché in Moscow who was half German and half Russian, was sent to the region to ensure that a situation similar to the one in the **Ukraine**—where the people were driven back to Stalin—did not arise. In the North Caucasus, the collective farms were dissolved, and the troops behaved properly. The result: no **partisans** whatever.

We realized that the idea of transforming the war against the Soviet Union into a civil war could only succeed without Hitler. That was a tragedy. After all, at the end of the war we had 800,000 Soviet volunteers in the German army. Sometimes people maintained that

German knights: the Teutonic knights, a monastic military order that fought against Polish, Lithuanian, and Russian power in the Baltic area from the 13th to 15th centuries
bread and salt: traditional Russian welcome offering to visitors
collective farming: communal agricultural cultivation, introduced by Stalin in the 1930s to replace individual peasant plots
SS: *Schutzstaffeln* or Protection Police. The much-feared German security force responsible for internal and subsequently external security
North Caucasus: area of European Russia between the Black Sea and the Caspian Sea, including portions of Georgia and Azerbaijan
Ukraine: then one of the largest republics within the western Soviet Union, bordering on the Black Sea; now an independent state
partisans: civilian guerrilla fighters

all these volunteers were pressed into service. That, of course, is incorrect. Granted, there were surely a few who enlisted because they wanted out of the **POW** camps. But I myself saw how Russian soldiers deserted, came over to us, and said they wanted to fight on our side. Once, a Russian captain we had captured asked me where our artillery positions were. Since I can speak Russian I told him: "That is none of your business." "It is," he answered, "because your artillery has consistently been off target. I want to show your gunners how to aim the guns better." This best illustrates how much hatred there was toward the Soviet Union, and it was justified hatred. There was no family in the Soviet Union which had not suffered under Stalin.

POW: prisoner of war

Source: From the book *Voices from the Third Reich: An Oral History* by Johannes Steinhoff, Peter Pechel, and Dennis Showalter, eds. (Washington, DC: Regnery Gateway, 1989), 129–131.

AFTERMATH

In 1944 Herwarth was among those German officers who unsuccessfully attempted to assassinate German dictator Adolf Hitler. Herwarth's wife was a cousin of Count Claus von Stauffenberg, who headed the plot. More fortunate than most of the conspirators, Herwarth escaped with his life, as those arrested did not betray him. When the war ended soon after, Herwarth's efforts stood him in good stead, as former American friends of his debriefed him and then recruited him to work on Austrian reconstruction for them. Eventually Herwarth returned to the diplomatic service. In 1955 he became the first postwar German ambassador to Britain, a post he held for six years, and subsequently served as German ambassador to Italy. He ended his diplomatic career as head of the West German foreign office. From 1971 to 1977, he was president of the German Goethe Institut, responsible for Germany's cultural relations with other states.

ASK YOURSELF

1. According to Herwarth, the German military, though lacking enthusiasm for the war against the Soviet Union, took pride in fighting well when ordered to do so. Is this kind of attitude common among military men, whatever their nationality?
2. Herwarth had genuinely strong anti-Nazi credentials. As a young diplomat in Germany's Moscow embassy, he joined his ambassador in urging Britain, France, and the United States to withstand Germany's territorial demands. In August 1939, he informed British and American diplomats in Moscow of the details of the Nazi-Soviet Non-Aggression Pact, just one day after that agreement had been signed. He warned the Allies in advance of Hitler's decision to launch Operation Barbarossa, the invasion of the Soviet Union. He also passed on information on Nazi atrocities against the Jews and other civilians on the Eastern front. Herwarth nonetheless remained a German diplomat and military officer and fought doggedly against the Soviet Union for several years. Do you think his efforts to work against the Nazis from within the regime, rather than outside, were the most effective course of behavior available to him?

3. One of Herwarth's grandmothers was Jewish, a fact that, had it become known to the Nazi regime during the 1930s and 1940s, might easily have rendered him liable to persecution, discrimination, and even death. Were his anti-Nazi activities the product merely of an aristocratic distaste for Hitler's government, or did they also reflect a level of Jewish loyalty and identification on his part?
4. Within a few years of the ending of World War II, the new Federal Republic of Germany (West Germany) dramatically changed its relationship with the United States and Britain, metamorphosing from a defeated enemy into a valued Cold War ally against the Soviet Union. As one of West Germany's top diplomats, Herwarth had every reason to stress his country's—and his own—past anti-Soviet credentials, and to indulge in speculation that, but for Hitler's folly in terrorizing the Russian populace, in the early 1940s the German military might have succeeded in backing a Russian civil war, which would have destabilized Stalin's hold on power and overthrown Communist rule in the Soviet Union. Simple logic might, of course, suggest that without Hitler, German forces would not have been on Russian soil in the first place, but Herwarth did not allow such minor caveats to overturn his fascinating exercise in speculation! How far and in what ways were Herwarth's memories of his support for these anti-Soviet groups affected by Cold War considerations, and his wish to suggest that Germany, the United States, and other West European powers should have formed an anti-Soviet alliance much sooner?

TOPICS TO CONSIDER

1. About 250,000 Cossack and 102,300 Caucasian peasants and soldiers, who sought independence from Soviet and Russian rule, together with several hundred thousand ex-Soviet troops, served under German command during World War II. Their loyalties to Germany were sometimes questionable. In May 1945, units of the Russian National Liberation Army, led by General Vlasov, even assisted Czech resistance groups in a bloody uprising against German occupying forces in Prague, the Czech capital, a contest in which advancing Soviet troops stood aside and refused to aid the Czechs. At the end of the war, in 1945 and 1946, the United States and Britain repatriated most of the renegade Cossack, Russian, and other soldiers to the Soviet Union, where the majority of them were executed. Why did the Western allies acquiesce in sending these men back to almost certain death in Stalin's Russia, instead of allowing them to become exiles in the West?
2. Herwarth, who disliked Hitler and the **Nazi Party**, remained in Germany and tried to undermine their rule from within, serving in mid-level civilian and military positions while maintaining contact with sympathetic American and British diplomats. Other Germans went into exile or joined the German resistance. Significant numbers of Cossacks, Ukrainians, members of other minorities, and anti-Communist Russians decided to fight against the Soviet Union in World War II, seeking either national independence or the overthrow of Stalin's rule. Why did individuals, all of whom had great reservations about their own country's existing government, make such diverse choices? How great a choice did many of them, especially starving prisoners, genuinely have? What would you do, if you were in their circumstances? What does patriotism mean, when one is alienated from the rulers or policies of one's own country?

THE KATYŃ MASSACRE, 1940

The Germans were not alone in using mass murder to eliminate political opponents and other undesirables. In the course of World War II, Poland suffered at both German and Russian hands. In September 1939, German forces invaded Poland from the west, while Russian troops moved in from the east, and the two attackers divided Poland's territory between themselves. On Josef Stalin's orders, in April and May 1940, the Soviet military and secret police rounded up and killed almost 22,000 Poles, including 8,000 captured military officers, plus members of the intelligentsia and professional classes who had been deported to Russia. The best known such mass execution took place at a camp for Polish prisoners of war in the Katyń Forest in Russia, where German troops in 1943 discovered 4,243 bodies of Polish military officers; this was one of seven or eight sites of similar murders. Already planning to maintain postwar political control of Poland, Soviet leaders sought to eliminate potential nationalist opponents. Unwilling to offend their Soviet partner, Allied leaders looked the other way. In 1944 and 1945, President **Franklin D. Roosevelt** and U.S. Army chief of staff **George C. Marshall** suppressed American reports that held Stalin responsible for the Polish deaths. British prime minister **Winston Churchill** privately believed Russian officials had carried out the massacres, but was likewise unwilling to disrupt Britain's relationship with its Soviet ally. Not until 1990 did Russian officials admit that Stalin—rather than Nazi Germany—instigated these killings.

3. Herwarth was aware that his behavior in passing information to Allied diplomats might have exposed him to charges of "treason." He defended his actions as "an attempt to protect Germany from being entangled in another two-front world war which we would surely lose," arguing that Hitler was "obviously insane" and "a menace to Germany." Depending on one's point of view, Herwarth and the Soviet troops who fought against Stalin might all have been termed patriots, collaborators, or traitors. Can you define the differences between these three terms?

Further Information

Andreyev, Catherine. *Vlasov and the Russian Liberation Movement, 1941–1945: Soviet Reality and Émigré Theories.* New York: Cambridge University Press, 1987.

Baigent, Michael, and Richard Leigh. *Secret Germany: Stauffenberg and the True Story of Operation Valkyrie.* London: Jonathan Cape, 1994.

Dallin, Alexander. *German Rule in Russia, 1941–1945: A Study of Occupation Policies.* 2nd rev. ed. Boulder, CO: Westview, 1981.

Herwarth, Hans von, with S. Frederick Starr. *Against Two Evils.* New York: Rawson Wade, 1981.

Jones, Nigel. *Countdown to Valkyrie: The July Plot to Assassinate Hitler.* Barnsley, UK: Frontline Books, 2009.

Lucas, James. *War on the Eastern Front, 1941–1945: The German Soldier in Russia.* New York: Bonanza Books, 1979.

Mawdsley, Evan. *Thunder in the East: The Nazi-Soviet War 1941–1945.* New York: Bloomsbury, 2007.

Mazower, Mark. *Hitler's Empire: How the Nazis Ruled Europe.* New York: Penguin Press, 2008.

Mulligan, Timothy Patrick. *The Politics of Illusion and Empire: German Occupation Policy in the Soviet Union, 1942–1943.* New York: Praeger, 1988.

Rees, Laurence. *World War Two: Behind Closed Doors—Stalin, the Nazis and the West.* London: BBC Books, 2009.
Stahel, David. *Operation Barbarossa and Germany's Defeat in the East.* New York: Cambridge University Press, 2009.
Steenberg, Sven. *Vlasov.* Trans. Abe Farbstein. New York: Alfred A. Knopf, 1970.
Strik-Strikfeldt, Wilfried. *Against Stalin and Hitler: Memoir of the Russian Liberation Movement, 1941–1945.* Trans. David Footman. New York: John Day, 1970.
Thorwald, Jurgen. *The Illusion: Soviet Soldiers In Hitler's Armies.* Trans. Richard and Clara Winston. New York: Harcourt, Brace, Jovanovich, 1975.

Web Sites

Anders, Lt. Gen. Wladyslaw, and Antonio Munoz. "Russian Volunteers in the German Wehrmacht in WWII." Feldgrau.com—Research on the German Armed Forces 1918–1945. http://www.feldgrau.com.
"Vlasov and the Russian Liberation Army." A Journey Through Slavic Culture. http://russianculture.wordpress.com/.

Film and Television

Mein Krieg: My Private War (1993), directed by Harriet Eder and Thomas Kufus. Kino Video.
World War Two behind Closed Doors: Stalin, the Nazis and the West (2009). BBC/PBS.

11. The Eastern Front: Reminiscences of General Aleksey Kirillovich Gorlinskiy on the Soviet Advance, 1944–1945

INTRODUCTION

German forces ruthlessly exploited and abused conquered or subject peoples, undercutting **Hitler's** claims to establish a New Order in Europe, which would benefit areas under German domination. Even in Western Europe, where German occupation policies were relatively mild, this was the case, but these practices were far more pronounced in Polish and Russian territories. Nazi doctrine considered Slavs, native Poles, Russians, Ukrainians, and the like, intrinsically inferior races, suitable only for forced labor, exploitation, and eventual deportation as far east as possible, perhaps to Siberia, unless they conveniently died in the process.

In June 1941, Aleksey Gorlinskiy, the son of a Soviet career military officer, obtained a degree in chemistry from Kiev University and planned a career as a scientist. He joined the Russian artillery as a lieutenant on June 22, 1941, the first day of Russia's war with Germany, and fought through the entire war, beginning in the western Ukraine. He took part in the battles of Kiev, Stalingrad, and the Kursk Salient, crossed the River Dnieper, and helped to liberate the Ukraine, Romania, Poland, eastern Germany, and Czechoslovakia, finishing the war as a major. As a junior officer, Gorlinskiy was present on April 25, 1945, when American and Soviet troops met at Torgau on the Elbe.

KEEP IN MIND AS YOU READ

1. General Gorlinskiy is recalling events that took place about 40 years earlier.
2. Over 8 million Soviet soldiers died during World War II, and by some estimates close to 20 million Russian civilians. While some of these deaths were due to **Stalin's** scorched earth policies and the harsh retribution he exacted on any troops suspected of disloyalty, the majority were directly caused by German action.
3. The mortality rate among Soviet prisoners of war (POWs) in German hands was 57 percent, far higher than that for French, British, or Americans, though Germans captured by the Soviets faced equally dismal survival prospects. The Germans shot Jewish prisoners and political officers among the POWs out of hand, and many Soviet prisoners died of starvation, exposure, or overwork.

4. In 1945 and afterwards, invading Soviet troops treated the German population in areas they occupied far more brutally than British or American soldiers did, and Stalin did little to stop this. Most Russians felt that the German people deserved to experience such retribution.

Reminiscences of General Aleksey Kirillovich Gorlinskiy on the Soviet Advance, 1944–1945

This was in the Ukraine. The Germans were retreating; we were driving them out, and I remember seeing rows of gallows, the bodies of our people still hanging from them. All were in civilian clothes. Maybe they were **partisans**, and maybe they didn't have any resistance connections at all but were simply the first people to get caught. I have seen even worse scenes. When we took the village of Reshetilovka, not far from the town of Poltava, it was terribly hot and we were thirsty. So we looked for a well. And we found it . . . completely filled with children's corpses. The **fascists** had conducted a **scorched-earth** policy there. All the houses were burned. When we entered villages, we generally found only chimneys standing. And then it fell upon me to liberate prisoners from concentration camps. The first such death camp was near Shepitovka. Most of the prisoners were French. Things were not so bad there. The Germans treated the French better; I certainly didn't see in this camp what I saw later in camps with our own people. In short, the first concentration camp didn't leave an especially strong impression on me. The concentration camp on Slavut left a considerably stronger impression. It was close to Shepitovka, and it was for our people. When we got there, most prisoners were dead; the Germans had machine-gunned them before retreating. Then, the camp at Terezin [Theresienstadt] in Czechoslovakia. The Germans used it as a showcase; they had even brought the Red Cross there. . . .

partisans: civilian guerrilla fighters, liable to be killed on the spot if captured
fascists: Germans
scorched-earth: destruction of everything valuable, so that nothing is left for the enemy
oxen: cattle

And before Terezin, I remember, was Lignitz, in Polish territory. There were also many Frenchmen there, but there were a great many of ours. When we entered the camp, how these people did meet us! It was impossible to describe. They could barely stand on their legs, merely skin and bones, and from them I also discovered that conditions for the prisoners were unequal. They were especially terrible for the Russians, the Soviets.

You can imagine what kind of hatred our soldiers felt. And it was not simply hatred for an inhuman, sadistic enemy, it was a hatred which rallied the people and helped us fight.

I recall coming across the body of a German officer. He had a wallet, and, of course, you always checked such things for documents or papers. I found a photograph in that wallet. Apparently, this photo came from home. It showed six Soviets harnessed like **oxen** to a cart, and two German boys, about twelve years of age, were driving them with whips. Beside them stood adult Germans, making sure the poor bastards couldn't do anything. I gave this photograph to a correspondent who published it in a newspaper. How could such a thing not evoke hatred? Yes, we took it out on the Germans; we made them pay for what they did to us.

. . .

I was then in command of the detachment at the artillery headquarters of the 5th Guards Army. . . . Officers were busy fending off the German counterattack; they sent a group of junior officers, myself included, along with the corps that went to the Elbe River. We were instructed not to cross it. A short while earlier, it was decided that a predetermined line for the meeting with the Americans was going to be at the Elbe. For this reason, only a small scout unit of several people were to cross to the other side.

On the 25th of April [1945], at about 1:30 in the afternoon, I found myself at the observation post of one of the commander's batteries. It was six hundred meters from the Elbe. The river wasn't big, about 100–120 meters wide. I was looking at the other bank—there was the village of Torgau, until then an unknown little Saxon village. Suddenly, I noticed a flicker of light—it came from one of the towers of a small castle on the other bank. I immediately realized this could be sunlight reflected off an enemy helmet or gunsight. Germans? I began to look more carefully and discovered that there were soldiers there, not in uniforms of that mouse-gray color we hated so much but of a color unfamiliar and new to us, something quite different. We had this preliminary agreement with the Allies: for mutual recognition, in order not to shoot each other, we would fire a red flare, and they would answer, in turn, with a green one; or the other way around, they would fire a green one, and we would answer in red.

We fired the red flare—no answer. Well, you know . . . could it be that the Germans had changed uniforms? Was this a trick? Then I saw three people run from the tower toward the shore. It then became clear they were Americans. They began to shout at the top of their lungs, "Russians! Washington! Moscow! Hitler **kaput**!" At that point I realized I was witnessing history. There was, as I have said, six hundred meters to the shore. I was already a captain then, and I was young. I sprinted toward the river bank, followed by the rest. The bridge spanning the Elbe here had been blown up by the Germans, and only the supports could be seen sticking up out of the water. One American, not waiting for either a boat or a raft, started to cross, climbing along the supports with acrobatic dexterity. One of ours also started along the trusses. Thus did our meeting occur . . . "on the bridge," right in the middle of the river. That was our first contact. And then a boat appeared from somewhere, and the Americans started to cross over to our side.

Of course, that feeling would stay with me for my entire lifetime. We didn't know English, and the Americans didn't know Russian. But nothing could have been more eloquent than the soldiers' language: the embraces, the back-slapping, the photographs—when you knew without words that this was his wife and kids. . . . We spread our waterproof capes on the grass, and we shared our simple fare. I tasted whisky then for the first time in my life, and the Americans discovered Russian vodka for the first time; in our **canteens** we never carried water. I have never forgotten this and never will—neither that linkup nor those men, many of whom I have seen since then.

We made an oath there. . . . [T]there was no official text; we never wrote anything down. We raised a toast to victory and to never having another war, and we swore that neither we nor our children nor our grandchildren would ever know war again. That was the oath. . . . you know, now when we meet with those who are still alive—and we meet every year—I always ask—we always ask each other; "Do you remember the oath on the Elbe?" And always the answer is, "I remember."

kaput: destroyed
canteens: drinking flasks

Source: Helene Keyssar and Vladimir Pozner, *Remembering War: A U.S.-Soviet Dialogue* (New York: Oxford University Press, 1990), 71–73, 205–207. Used by permission.

AFTERMATH

Gorlinskiy remained in the army for many years, reaching the rank of major general before he retired. He then served on the Soviet Veterans' Committee and on the Soviet Peace Committee of Generals for Peace. In 1986 he was one of a group of Soviet war veterans who visited the United States, traveling to Washington, DC, Chicago, Detroit, and Dallas, and meeting many Americans.

ASK YOURSELF

1. Gorlinskiy prepared his remarks in connection with a televised spacebridge dialogue, using technology to bring together participants in both the United States and the Soviet Union to discuss and contrast their wartime experiences, a program later edited and aired in May 1985 to mark the 40th anniversary of the ending of World War II in Europe. At this time, Soviet president Mikhail Gorbachev was in power and had instituted domestic policies of *glasnost* (openness), while seeking a dramatic improvement in Soviet relations with the United States. How might the particular circumstances in which he was speaking have affected the memories that Gorlinskiy highlighted for the occasion?
2. Despite the Cold War, it seems that Soviet and American veterans from the April 1945 meeting at Torgau managed to hold regular reunions and remain on friendly terms. In November 1983, they even came together on the banks of the Elbe to inter the body of Joseph Polowski, an American soldier from Chicago who had been present at the original meeting and wished to be buried at its site. At that time those attending renewed their pledge to do all they could for peace. How significant is it that, notwithstanding official Soviet-American hostility, the military personnel involved maintained their contacts for many decades?
3. In the late 1990s, Galina Oreschkina, a Russian schoolteacher, established a Reconciliation Memorial at Rossoschka, part of the battlefield around Stalingrad, the south Russian city that from August 1942 until February 1943 withstood German assaults, in a confrontation that marked the turning point of World War II in Europe. Oreschkina collects the remains of German and Russian soldiers and gives both alike respectful burial in peaceful surroundings. What do such symbolic gestures accomplish?

TOPICS TO CONSIDER

1. German occupation forces in World War II exploited conquered territories and treated their inhabitants with great brutality, killing those who were considered politically or racially suspect, enslaving many others, and exacting savage retribution on the civilian population for any hostile activities. Why did German officials adopt harsh policies that were likely to turn the bulk of the subject population against their rule? What did this reveal about Nazi visions of the future German empire?
2. After World War II, Germany was divided into two states, in the west the German Federal Republic, a liberal capitalist democracy aligned with the United States in the Cold War, and in the east the German Democratic Republic, a

Communist satellite of the Soviet Union. In 1989, the East German Communist government lost power and a year later the two Germanies were reunited. Soviet, British, and French political leaders all expressed strong misgivings about this development. How far were their views affected by their memories of German behavior during World War II?

Further Information

Bellamy, Chris. *Absolute War: Soviet Russia in the Second World War.* New York: Alfred A. Knopf, 2007.

Cottam, Kazimiera J. *Defending Leningrad: Women Behind Enemy Lines.* Nepean, ON: New Military Publishers, 1998.

Dallin, Alexander. *German Rule in Russia, 1941–1945: A Study of Occupation Policies.* 2nd rev. ed. Boulder, CO: Westview, 1981.

Fritz, Stephen G. *Ostkrieg: Hitler's War of Extermination in the East.* Lexington: University Press of Kentucky, 2011.

Keyssar, Helene, and Vladimir Pozner, eds. *Remembering War: A U.S.-Soviet Dialogue.* New York: Oxford University Press, 1990.

Mawdsley, Evan. *Thunder in the East: The Nazi-Soviet War 1941–1945.* New York: Bloomsbury, 2007.

Rees, Laurence. *War of the Century: When Hitler Fought Stalin.* New York: New Press, 1999.

Rees, Laurence. *World War Two: Behind Closed Doors—Stalin, the Nazis and the West.* London: BBC Books, 2008.

Schulte, Theo J. *The German Army and Nazi Policies in Occupied Russia.* New York: Berg, 1989.

Werth, Alexander. *Russia at War, 1941–1945.* 2nd ed. New York: Carroll and Graf, 2000.

Web Sites

"Invasion of the Soviet Union June 1941." Holocaust Encyclopedia: United States Holocaust Memorial Museum. http://www.ushmm.org.

Rees, Laurence. "Hitler's Invasion of Russia in World War Two." BBC: World Wars in-depth. http://www.bbc.co.uk/history/worldwars/wwtwo/hitler_russia_invasion_01.shtml.

Films and Television

Come and See (1985), starring Aleksey Kravchenko and Olga Mironova.

My Name is Ivan (1963), starring Nikolay Burlyaev and Valentin Zubkov.

The Rainbow (1944), starring Nina Alisova, Natalya Uzhviy, Versa Ivashova, Yelena Tyapkina, and Hans Klering.

World War Two Behind Closed Doors: Stalin, the Nazis and the West (2009). BBC/PBS.

12. D-Day: Diaries of Forrest C. Pogue

INTRODUCTION

On June 6, 1944 2,727 ships, part of an armada of more than 5,000, landed a combined United States, British, and Canadian invasion force, five infantry divisions of 156,000 men, on five Normandy beaches over a 30-mile front, the greatest and best equipped such operation ever undertaken in history. Three airborne divisions totaling 23,000 troops, two-thirds of them American, also parachuted in the night before, taking heavy casualties of more than one-third. In the following two days, another 156,000 troops landed, and within a month, a total of more than one million Allied men had come ashore. Ten thousand Allied aircraft provided air cover, and immediately before the invasion began had bombarded all German communications in the surrounding area, destroying almost every bridge across the Seine. This was the opening of Operation Overlord, the long-awaited Allied Second Front against Germany, the full-scale invasion of Western Europe, aimed at the center of German power, which Soviet leader **Josef Stalin** had demanded ever since Pearl Harbor. Conscious that failure would be disastrous, United States leaders had waited until they had assembled an invasion force sufficiently large and well-equipped to maximize their chances of victory.

Forrest C. Pogue (1912–1996), then a young official combat historian in the U.S. Army, was present at the **D-Day** landings. He accompanied American units as they fought their way through France and into Germany, an assignment during which he became well-known for taking risks while pursuing historical truth. His group of five combat historians was attached to part of the 175th Infantry, who were supposed to land on the afternoon of June 6, 1944, D-Day itself. Congestion on the invasion beaches meant the 175th did not land until June 7, 1944, while the historical personnel remained on board ship until the following day. Pogue described what he was able to observe of the day's fighting on June 7, and the picture he pieced together of the landings on D-Day itself.

KEEP IN MIND AS YOU READ

1. Much of Pogue's account is a composite picture, put together from interviews with dozens of soldiers in the days and weeks following D-Day.
2. Pogue interviewed soldiers very shortly after the events they were describing, when the fighting they had been through was very fresh in their minds.

3. Pogue was consciously trying to construct a coherent picture of exactly what had happened during the Allied landings on D-Day, cross-checking one account against another where possible.
4. Many of the Allied soldiers who took part in the D-Day landings had not seen combat before, and were experiencing real battlefield fighting, as opposed to training exercises, for the first time.

Forrest C. Pogue Describes the D-Day Landings

Naval craft off the beaches fired sporadically. Everyone seemed pleased that the French ships were joining in the attack on shore positions. Destroyers lay near the shore and fired on shore positions several miles in. The Germans replied occasionally to the fire, but without effect, and as for German air, we saw only one enemy plane, a reconnaissance aircraft, during the day. British and American planes were over in force all day. In one fifteen-minute period we counted five flights of eighteen Marauders each.

After three o'clock the skies cleared except for a few clouds over the fighting area and it turned hot, to our great discomfort. We wanted to go ashore, but orders came out that only people with rifles, who were prepared to use them, were to go in. So we parasites, armed for the most part with pistols, stayed aboard as spectators of the second act. Standing on jeeps and trucks, we watched developments off **Omaha Beach** as if we were at a fair. Actually, we could make out very little on the shore. Signs of movement were obscured by smoke from the firing, fires that had been started by shells, and by the demolition of mines. I did not see how it was possible for troops to have recognized any landmarks, nor have I been able to understand how **correspondents**, who watched the D-Day attack from ten miles out, ever got such vivid pictures of the shore. . . .

My own picture of D-Day was gleaned from dozens of interviews with officers and men who went in during the morning of 6 June. Some I talked to shortly after they were wounded, others I interviewed as they rested near the front lines, and some gave their stories weeks later. A short outline of that morning is given below.

The ships that took the assault elements to Normandy had been loaded, much like ours, in many coves and inlets in Wales, southern England, and the eastern counties. On the evening of 5 June they had proceeded from the rendezvous area near the Isle of Wight southward toward France. Shortly after midnight, **minesweepers** of the Allied fleet began to clear channels through the minefields for the ships. British and American airborne units took off from English fields and flew overhead to drop over their objectives—the British east of the Orne [river] and the Americans in the Cotentin Peninsula. The British reached their bridgehead early and secured it, while the American forces, scattered to a considerable degree, had a tough job of assembling for concerted action.

Toward daylight the planes and ships took up their task of softening up the enemy, the chief change in plan being that . . . the air force struck a few miles inland instead of at the beaches. On the western limit of Omaha Beach, the Rangers scrambled ashore to find that the six guns they were to knock out were pulled back out of their way.

By daylight, ship channels had been cleared to the beaches and the small landing craft had been filled with men from the **LSTs** and larger transports and were on their way in from

Omaha Beach: D-Day landing site
correspondents: journalists
minesweepers: specialized ships with equipment to collect, move, or neutralize explosive mines
LSTs: landing ship tanks, large ships that could transport tanks and other heavy equipment

rendezvous points some ten miles out. The floating tanks were started in, as were guns in small craft. Only five out of thirty-two **DDs** survived of those that tried to float in under their own power, while most of those in the other tank battalion, sent in at the last minute by boat, got in safely. In one field artillery battalion all but one gun was lost when the craft carrying them capsized.

The accounts of the early landings tend to follow the same pattern. Heavy seas threatened to swamp the smaller craft and made many of the soldiers seasick. Enemy fire struck numerous craft or forced navy crews to unload in deep water. Poor visibility, obstacles, and inexperience led other navy crews to land on the wrong beaches. Many of the soldiers in the first waves had to wade ashore carrying heavy equipment, which they often disposed of in deep water. At the extreme ends of the beaches, the cliffs interfered to some extent with the enemy fire and gave our troops some protection. In front of Vierville, the men hid behind the seawall that ran along the beach, and near Saint-Laurent-sur-Mer they found mounds of shingles to use as cover. Accounts of the first hours on the beaches speak of efforts of officers and **noncoms** to organize their units and get them off the beaches, but often those who tried to direct the attack fell as soon as they exposed themselves to the enemy. In some cases, platoons stuck together, but in others sections landed some distance apart—and there were instances where dispersed elements attached themselves to entirely different regiments and divisions and did not return to their parent organization for two or three days.

The first real effort to give direction to the attack came after the regimental commanders landed. The command group of the 116th Regimental Combat Team, which included Brigadier General Norman D. Cota, the assistant division commander, and Colonel C. D. W. Canham, the regimental commander, came in at about 7.30 a.m. The **S-4** of the regiment was killed near the water's edge and other members of the command group were hit. Colonel Canham was wounded as he tried to organize the attack, but after receiving first aid he returned to his task. One of the most active commanders was General Cota, who, according to the accounts of the soldiers, was apparently everywhere that morning. Some spoke of his handling the **bangalore torpedo** that breached the wire at one of the exits, and others had him handling a Browning automatic rifle. His activities in the first weeks ashore made him almost a legendary figure. Noncoms were also called on to give leadership, as heavy casualties were inflicted on the junior officers. In one case, a private who had worked until a short time before in the regimental Post Exchange rallied the men of his unit by calling them by name and persuading them to follow him over the seawall.

On the 16th Infantry's beaches, Colonel George Taylor, the **RCT** commander, gained lasting fame by saying to his officers and men: "The only people on the beach are the dead and those who are going to die—now let's get the hell out of here." In a short time he had the men in his sector moving. He and Colonel Canham were promoted to the rank of brigadier general for their work on D-Day.

The manner of the advance up the **bluffs** differed somewhat among the various units. Some stayed behind the seawall until units in the second and third waves came in through them and went up the cliffs. Others, after being reorganized, pressed forward and by noon were on top of the bluffs.

DD tanks: duplex drive tanks (also known as Donald Duck tanks), amphibious tanks that could float on water
noncoms: lower-ranking or noncommissioned officers, either sergeants, sergeant majors, or warrant officers
S-4: regimental logistics officer
bangalore torpedo: explosive charge on the end of a long, extensible metal tube
RCT: regimental combat team
bluffs: cliffs

By midnight on 6 June all of the regiments in the 1st Division (the 16th, the 18th, and 26th) and two from the 29th (the 116th and 115th) had been landed on Omaha Beach. The 2d and 5th Ranger Battalions were in position to their right. Heavy seas, landings on the wrong beaches, intense fire from well-entrenched positions, the foundering of DD tanks and artillery pieces, abnormally high casualties among officers, failure to open all the beach exits, beach congestion, the slowness of some of the assault waves to move forward from the seawall, the difficulty of using the full force of naval gunfire because of the fear of inflicting losses on the infantrymen, the lack of sufficient gaps in underwater obstacles and beach obstacles, and the failure, for various reasons, of air bombardment to take out beach fortifications all placed V Corps a considerable distance from its D-Day objectives, and, as a result of the presence of the German 352d Division in the area, in danger of a counterattack before the time estimated. In the face of this situation, the regiments were reorganized, defenses were set up for the night, and preparations made for a vigorous offensive to attain the D-Day objectives as quickly as possible.

Source: Forrest C. Pogue, *Pogue's War: Diaries of a WWII Combat Historian* (Lexington: University of Kentucky Press, 2001), 51–54. Used by permission.

AFTERMATH

After the war, Forrest Pogue wrote the official history of the U.S. Supreme Command during World War II. He was later selected as the official biographer of General George C. Marshall, chief of staff of the U.S. Army throughout the war and subsequently both secretary of state and secretary of defense, on whom Pogue produced a massive four-volume work. He also became famed for the generous encouragement he gave to younger scholars just beginning their careers. Pogue always intended to publish a book based on his diaries and notes of interviews taken while he was on wartime service in Europe, but many other projects intervened, and in his final years poor eyesight prevented him from doing so. After Pogue's death, his nephew took the battered volumes of his pocket diary, transcribed them, and completed the manuscript on his uncle's behalf.

ASK YOURSELF

1. Pogue pioneered the use and techniques of oral history, conducting extensive interviews with personnel in the armed forces, and later with General George Marshall and many of his associates. Did these experiences make him more sensitive than many interviewers not just to the benefits but also to the potential pitfalls of oral history?
2. Pogue became renowned for his courage and the risks he took in the cause of historical research when accompanying combat troops. According to the historian Stephen E. Ambrose, "He was shelled, he ducked machine-gun and rifle fire, and he was bombed. He seldom got a chance to change clothes, had only cold water sponge baths, ate C rations, carried his weapons along with his briefcase and writing instruments, slept on the ground, and suffered from the cold and the almost constant rain." In what ways were his readiness to share the hardships and dangers of the men he was interviewing advantageous to him as a historian?
3. Pogue was a highly knowledgeable and cultured man, according to Ambrose "one of the best-educated sergeants in the U.S. Army" as well as "one of the smartest." He completed a bachelor's degree at the age of 18, earned a master's

degree in European history from the University of Kentucky at 19, and was 24 when he completed his Ph.D. in European history at Clark University in Worcester, Massachusetts. He spent 1937–1938 studying at the University of Paris, becoming fluent in French, and then went on to Germany as World War II loomed. When he left the country in the late 1930s, he risked attracting unwelcome attention from German customs officials and secret police by carrying out with him a suitcase full of both Nazi and anti-Nazi propaganda he had collected during his months there. As the Allied forces fought their way through France and Germany, what were his feelings likely to be on revisiting countries he had known in happier times?

TOPICS TO CONSIDER

1. Pogue was primarily interested in providing an accurate overview of the Normandy invasion, and did not attempt to minimize any blunders that had occurred, such as the dispersion of units, losses of equipment, "land[ings] on the wrong beaches," or confusion once the troops were ashore. He cited a long list of difficulties encountered on Omaha Beach in particular, some at least probably avoidable. His diaries also contain illuminating discussions of such unsavory subjects as corruption and peculation, especially the unauthorized appropriation of scarce supplies, within the U.S. armed forces; racism and race relations in the military; and the effectiveness of German infiltration of American units once these reached German soil. Journalists and historians embedded in military units often feel some pressure to minimize or ignore such matters, with the interests of public morale and security considerations often cited as reasons for official or self-censorship. Is it ethical or even sensible for historians and journalists to conceal the less attractive aspects of military campaigns and personnel?
2. If one is writing an official history, how independent a viewpoint should one expect to be able to take? Should there be any constraints at all upon the judgment and interpretation of the individual in such circumstances?

Further Information

Ambrose, Stephen E. *D-Day, June 6, 1944: The Climactic Battle of World War II.* New York: Simon & Schuster, 1994.

Astor, Gerald, comp. *June 6, 1944: The Voices of D-Day.* New York: St. Martin's Press, 1994.

Balkoski, Joseph. *Omaha Beach: D-Day, June 6, 1944.* Mechanicsburg, PA: Stackpole Books, 2004.

Beevor, Antony. *D-Day: The Battle for Normandy.* New York: Penguin, 2010.

Hastings, Max. *Overlord: D-Day and the Battle for Normandy.* New York: Simon and Schuster, 1984.

Lewis, Adrian R. *Omaha Beach: A Flawed Victory.* Chapel Hill: University of North Press, 2001.

Ryan, Cornelius. *The Longest Day: June 6, 1944.* New York: Simon & Schuster, 1959.

Web Sites

The Battle of Normandy. http://www.dday-overlord.com/eng/index.htm.

D-Day Museum and Overlord Embroidery. http://www.ddaymuseum.co.uk.

Films and Television

Band of Brothers (2002). HBO Home Video.
The Longest Day (1962), starring John Wayne, Robert Ryan, Richard Burton, and Henry Fonda.
Saving Private Ryan (1998), starring Tom Hanks, Matt Damon, and Tom Sizemore.

13. German Infantryman Robert Vogt Describes the D-Day Landings and the Normandy Campaign

INTRODUCTION

By early June 1944, when the **D-Day** invasion of Western Europe began, Soviet forces were advancing into Eastern Europe, and Stalin coordinated a major Soviet military offensive with the operation, to give the Allied offensive the best chance of success. Germany now faced assaults by huge armies from both the west and the east, who would eventually meet at the Elbe River in Germany itself in late April 1945. Field Marshal **Erwin Rommel**, the charismatic commander of the 50 German divisions facing the Allied invasion, begged German Führer **Adolf Hitler** for as much additional support as possible, especially German panzer tank reserves. The only German chance of resisting defeat, he believed, was to repel the Allied invasion force on the landing beaches, since once they broke through the highly mechanized North American and British units, who faced far less well-equipped and therefore less mobile German troops, would be able to range throughout France.

Despite continuing German reverses on the eastern front, Hitler himself welcomed the Allied invasion, which would finally give German troops the opportunity to meet the main bulk of the Anglo-American armies. Allied disinformation, moreover, had convinced Hitler—and initially Rommel too—that that the Normandy invasion was only a feint, with the main thrust to come elsewhere, and additional German units and equipment were slow in arriving, in part due to Allied air supremacy. Hitler did order the reinforcement of Normandy's defenses in late April 1944, believing that the Allies would land airborne forces there as part of a broader invasion concentrated on the Pas de Calais, but the new fortifications, mines, and other defensive preparations were patchy and incomplete. German airplane production could not match that of the United States and the Soviet Union, while gasoline shortages caused cutbacks in pilot training time, so that German fliers were increasingly inexperienced and accident-prone, with their craft no longer of the highest quality. The **Luftwaffe** had virtually no planes in reserve in France, and though 10 wings were supposedly transferred from Germany to meet the invasion, in practice, only a few arrived, and between 50 and 150 German aircraft faced 10,000 Allied counterparts.

Robert Vogt was a 19-year-old German infantryman who took part in 10 days of fighting, from the actual invasion until June 16, 1944, when he was wounded and captured.

KEEP IN MIND AS YOU READ

1. Vogt's reminiscences, published more than 40 years after D-Day as part of a book of oral history recollections of the Third Reich, give one rather young soldier's individual view of his small part in a vast operation.
2. By 1944 many of the more battle-hardened German soldiers had died on the Eastern front, and new recruits, of whom Vogt was one of the oldest, were increasingly young and obviously inexperienced.
3. These 10 days in Normandy were Vogt's only experience of combat fighting.
4. Infantry privates, such as Vogt, were the basic fighting men who had to carry out the orders of those above them and do the bulk of usually rather unglamorous ground combat, often facing the heaviest casualties and the greatest danger.

Recollections of Robert Vogt

Before June 6, 1944, the day of the D-Day landings, we were directly on the coast near **Arromanches**, planting "**Rommel Asparagus**." . . .

All this construction went on under great pressure, because there were virtually no **bunkers** at our location, only **dugouts**. This was the time when Field Marshal Rommel said the famous words, "You must stop them here on the first day. If you don't stop them here, it's over."

We worked in shifts around the clock. I caught some shut-eye that night. We had built two- and three-story bunk beds in a farmhouse about 500 yards from the beach. It must have been around 2:30 A.M. when I jumped out of bed at the sound of a huge crash. At first I had absolutely no idea what was going on. Of course we had been expecting something, but we didn't have a clue as to where and when. We didn't know that this was the invasion. In the distance, we heard bomb carpets falling all along the coast and in the rear areas. There were intermittent pauses which lasted anywhere from half an hour to an hour, but the area we were in was a terrible mess.

All at once we were under alarm condition three, the highest level. By then we guessed it must be the invasion, but since it was still dark outside and we couldn't see any ships or anything, we still weren't sure.

In the morning, my **platoon** leader told me to go to the coast to try and make contact with the other platoons in our **company**. On the way, I ran into a bomber attack, but I managed to get to our position on the Arromanches cliffs. Guns and machine guns were already firing. Then a voice called, "Enemy landing boats approaching!" I had a good view from the top of the cliffs and looked out at that ocean. What I saw scared the devil out of me. Even though the weather was so bad, we could see a huge number of ships. Ships as far as the eye could see, an entire fleet, and I thought, "Oh God, we're finished! We're done for now!"

Arromanches: small Normandy village
Rommel Asparagus: wooden frames used as bases for mines, intended to destroy any invasion craft. Vogt described the process of constructing them: "We put in a wooden beam and then, at a distance of, I'd say, five yards, another beam. On top of these, we attached a third beam with clamps—all of it done by hand—and secured more clamps. We attached land mines to the tips of the beams, all such that at high tide, the mines were so close to the water surface that even a flat-bottomed boat would touch them and be destroyed."
bunkers: deep fortified shelters
dugouts: shallow trenches intended to provide limited protection against bombs and artillery attack
platoon: smallest fighting unit, usually between 25 and 50 men
company: larger fighting unit, usually comprising three platoons

During the following days, we were stuck in **foxholes** along the front. And when these foxholes were shot up—if the Americans were stalled for long enough—other troops came and we were pulled out again.

I last saw action on July 16, 1944. We only had infantry weapons; we didn't even have a **bazooka**. And to top it off, we were even short of small-arms **ammo**. The supply columns had not taken the Allies' total air superiority into account. They got caught in heavy fire and were terribly shot up, so we didn't get any supplies. Our company commander sent several men to the shot-up supply units at night to pick up ammunition and bring it back to us at the front. And the Americans were right. They dropped leaflets in German which read, "Attacked from the front, Cut off from behind, Written off by Hitler."

Every day we told ourselves, "Now, finally, the Luftwaffe squadrons are going to come and whip them good." They didn't come. I didn't see a single German tank the entire time, either. We only had some light machine guns and the ammunition we had scrounged up, no heavy weapons or anything else. Well, we dug ourselves in at the edge of some woods, and when the Yanks came over the next hedgerow, we shot at them with our machine guns, trying to use our ammunition sparingly. After two or three bursts it usually got quiet, but it didn't take long until mortar and artillery fire set in. What was really bad were the heavy battleship guns. And then came the **Marauders**, the **Lightnings**, and the **Thunderbolts**—that was the worst.

I think we were used as cannon fodder. You know, it was the fifth year of the war, and we just didn't have the means. The Allies could afford to spare their troops, what with their superiority in equipment. They said, "Why should we sacrifice a single **GI** against German infantry fire; the Germans outdo us there anyway. No, we'll just carpet-bomb them. We'll just use our fliers to drop the sky on their heads. We'll just make use of our superior artillery."

At the time, we had to rely on little apple trees for cover. I could still hug those trees today. The pilots flew 100 feet over our heads and if they saw anything, they didn't only drop bombs, they sent their Thunderbolts to fire rockets at us. It was pretty bad. We made use of every blade of grass and every little tree when we heard the planes coming.

I was scared stiff the entire time, but at the same time, I was incredibly angry that we were being used against such odds. Still, we wanted to hold the front under any circumstances, and hoped from day to day that the German tanks would finally show up, that some artillery would arrive, and, above all, that the German Luftwaffe would fly in. One single time I saw two German fighter planes, and that was at Arromanches on the morning of June 6. Two Messerschmitts. When we saw them, we all shouted hurrah, but they were the only ones. That was it. It was so terribly depressing.

On the morning of June 16, between 11:00 and 11:30, we came under heavy machine gun fire. And then the monsters came: tanks. They approached our positions through the brush and fired at us. At this point we were in a large meadow surrounded by hedges. I would guess that the tanks were about 250 yards away. I counted 15 of them. They didn't come directly at us. They stopped, practically taunting us. And whenever they spotted any of us, they let loose a **barrage** of **shells**. It was horrible.

I looked right and I looked left, and I told myself that shooting any more with a machine gun was pointless. We didn't have any bazookas. They must have thought we did, though, otherwise they would have advanced more quickly. As it was, they stopped at a distance

foxholes: small temporary shelters dug into the ground on a battlefield
bazooka: portable rocket anti-tank weapon
ammo: ammunition
Luftwaffe: German air force
Marauders, **Lightnings**, and **Thunderbolts:** American and British warplanes
GI: American soldier
barrage: constant flow
shells: explosive artillery missiles

slightly out of bazooka range. Then they came forward very slowly. We got tank fright and I saw German ***Landser*** moving back to my left and right. My comrades and I took off too. We only took our weapons along with us. We left all of our personal belongings—there wasn't much—back in the foxholes.

About 400 yards from the positions we had just left, we came upon a great miracle: an 88 mm **ack-ack gun**. We reported to the commanding officer that tanks were coming up. At nineteen, I was one of the oldest. The officer pulled out his machine pistol and said, "If you don't advance and reinforce our position in a half-circle of at least 200 yards, I'll shoot you!" To say the least, we suddenly got our courage back!

> ***landser:*** short for ***landsknecht,*** low-ranking German soldier
> **ack-ack gun:** anti-aircraft gun

I had advanced about 150 yards when I came under heavy fire again. I hit the dirt behind a tree and then, oh God, I heard our flak gun shooting. I can't tell you what a tremendous lift that gave me! The next moment I saw a tank coming toward me, crushing the shrubbery in its path, and I did exactly what I shouldn't have done: I jumped up and ran away because I thought it was going to crush me flat. I hadn't gone three or four steps when I was hit above the left knee with what felt like a sledgehammer. It hurt, and then again, it didn't. I tried to stand up two or three times, but my leg just wouldn't participate. Uh-oh, I thought, now they've got you. And then my only thought was the hope that I wouldn't be run over by that tank.

Later I heard that the attack was stopped by the German flak gun, and that the Americans drew back again. The unwounded German soldiers were able to hold the position for a few more days.

Source: From the book *Voices from the Third Reich: An Oral History* by Johannes Steinhoff, Peter Pechel, and Dennis Showalter, eds. (Washington, DC: Regnery Gateway, 1989), 253–256.

AFTERMATH

Despite the absence of air support and tanks, German troops put up fierce resistance, inflicting 2,500 casualties on the American forces that landed at Omaha Beach on D-Day itself. During the Normandy campaign, the casualty rate among Allied troops was 50 percent higher than that they inflicted on German soldiers, who fought highly efficiently in desperate circumstances. Over the first three days, the invasion force took 10,300 casualties, and not until the end of July did the Allies break out of their Normandy bridgehead into France proper.

On June 16, as his unit tried to withstand an attack by 15 Allied tanks, Vogt was shot in the leg and taken prisoner. He ended up in Rouen, after spending time in several prison camps, where his weight had dwindled to 98 pounds. As a prisoner, he was impressed by the kindness of black American soldiers, who saw to it that he and other starving captured Germans received enough to eat, and he came to regard the African Americans as his "protectors." The discrepancy between their behavior and Nazi teaching that black Americans were "subhuman, barbarians" who would savagely mistreat the Germans led Vogt to question other Third Reich propaganda. Vogt later became a salesman.

ASK YOURSELF

1. How typical were Vogt's experiences among German troops fighting on the Western front in 1944?
2. The war in Western Europe continued for almost a year after D-Day, until Germany's final defeat in April 1945. This was a great contrast with the very swift campaigns of a few weeks in France, Belgium, the Netherlands, and Scandinavia four years earlier, in 1940. Why did Vogt and other German troops fight on so bravely and doggedly for so long in defense of Germany?
3. The chaos and confusion Vogt describes characterize almost every war, especially when an army is on the receiving end of an offensive attack. It is worth remembering that Allied forces nonetheless took six weeks to break out of Normandy. Did German forces in fact fight rather well, despite all their shortages of equipment?
4. Vogt graphically described the Allied superiority in military equipment of every kind. How much is victory in modern warfare not primarily a question of personal courage or fighting ability, but simply a question of having the advantage over the enemy in terms of firepower and technology?

TOPICS TO CONSIDER

1. Six weeks after the Normandy invasion began, Field Marshal Erwin Rommel (1891–1944), the charismatic and much respected commander of German forces in France, sent Hitler a teletype message warning that Germany faced defeat by the Allies and should withdraw from France. Ignoring this advice, Hitler ordered what became a disastrous German counterattack against advancing Allied units around Caen. On July 17, 1944, Rommel—often known as the Desert Fox since his earlier campaigns in Africa—was severely injured when British fighter planes strafed his car. In company with other like-minded German generals, Rommel had intended that, if Hitler ignored his advice, he would open negotiations with Allied commanders in France for an armistice and a separate peace in the West, a move he hoped would spare Germany from invasion by Russian forces from the east. Rommel had also met with a representative of another group of German military officers who intended to assassinate Hitler, though he himself apparently knew nothing of these plans. He had, however, stated that he believed Hitler should be removed from power, albeit without bloodshed, and put on trial. On July 20, the planned coup failed, and the conspirators, who were arrested and tortured, eventually implicated Rommel. In order not to embarrass the German government and damage popular morale, he was given the opportunity to commit suicide, which he accepted. After his death, he received a hero's funeral, with full military honors. Were Rommel's actions in disobeying Hitler's orders justified? When should a military commander ignore the instructions of his civilian superior(s), or even attempt to remove civilian leaders?
2. Rommel has become something of a German folk hero since World War II, due not simply to his outstanding military and leadership abilities, but also because of his chivalry to defeated enemies, and his refusal to carry out orders

to kill prisoners of war, civilians, and Jews in territories he had conquered. Until 1944 Rommel nonetheless served the Nazi state loyally and with distinction, undertaking military campaigns that enhanced German power at the expense of other nations in Europe and beyond. Only when Germany came close to military defeat did he seriously consider removing Hitler from power. Even though Rommel may have been personally admirable, especially in declining to countenance Nazi atrocities and terror in areas under his jurisdiction, did his willingness to work for the Nazi regime for many years in practice make him complicit in its behavior? Or was he simply a patriotic German?

Further Information

Fraser, David. *Knight's Cross: A Life of Field Marshall Erwin Rommel.* New York: HarperCollins, 1993.

Fritz, Stephen G. *Frontsoldaten: The German Soldier in World War II.* Lexington: University Press of Kentucky, 1995.

Hart, Russell A. *Clash of Arms: How the Allies Won in Normandy.* Boulder, CO: Lynne Riener, 2001.

Isby, David C., ed. *Fighting the Invasion: The German Army at D-Day.* London: Greenhill Books, 2000.

Lewis, John E., ed. *Eye-Witness D-Day: The Story of the Battle by Those Who Were There.* New York: Carroll and Graf, 1994.

Mitcham, Samuel W., Jr. *The Desert Fox in Normandy: Rommel's Defense of Fortress Europe.* Westport, CT: Praeger, 1997.

Web Site

D-Day Museum Arromanches. http://www.musee-arromanches.fr/accueil/index.php?lang=uk.

Films and Television

D-Day: The Total Story (1994). A & E Home Video.

The Desert Fox (1951), starring James Mason, Cedric Hardwicke, and Jessica Tandy.

14. David K. E. Bruce Describes the Liberation of Paris, August 24–25, 1944

INTRODUCTION

Like its fall to German forces in June 1940, the liberation of Paris, the French capital city, by Allied troops was one of the war's great symbolic moments. Free French military units forces under the command of General **Charles de Gaulle** insisted on taking the lead when entering the city. Two Americans did, however, succeed in joining them. From their first landings on **D-Day** Colonel David K. E. Bruce, the European head of the Office of Strategic Services (OSS), the wartime U.S. overseas intelligence agency, accompanied the invading Allied forces. He and his compatriot, the novelist and foreign correspondent Ernest Hemingway, were the first two Americans to enter Paris, in the vanguard of the liberating forces. By the afternoon of August 24, 1944, their unit was on the outskirts of the city, whose center Allied troops entered the next day.

KEEP IN MIND AS YOU READ

1. Bruce, a cosmopolitan American whose father-in-law had been U.S. ambassador in London, knew Paris extremely well, as did Hemingway, who had spent several years there as a newspaperman. There is an almost sensuous relish in the way Bruce recounts seeing its famous landmarks once more after several years of German occupation.
2. By mid-August 1944, French resistance units were undertaking extensive anti-German sabotage and military operations against the occupation forces that had controlled Paris since June 1940. The city was almost at a standstill, as railroad, transport, and postal workers, the police, and other vital services all went on strike. Although many of the German occupiers withdrew on August 19, when liberating forces entered, sporadic skirmishes were still in progress.
3. Members of the Vichy government, which had accepted German dominance, and other Frenchmen and women who had collaborated with the German occupiers now faced brutal retribution from their compatriots.
4. A political struggle over just who would rule liberated France had already begun. Not all the resistance forces supported de Gaulle, a nationalist military man.

Leftist French resistance units sought to install a Socialist or Communist postwar government.

5. As European head of the Office of Strategic Services, between 1941 and 1944 Bruce sent numerous secret agents into occupied France. The Germans captured, tortured, and killed quite a number of these operatives. For the rest of his life, Bruce had no great liking for Germans.

David K. E. Bruce, Diary Entry, 24 August 1944

We got up at six o'clock, and waited around for a couple of hours before joining one of **Le Clerc's** columns. . . .

As we went down the hill toward the Seine about five o'clock in the afternoon, the streets were lined with people. All houses were gay with flags, and the population was almost hysterical with joy. Our progress was extremely slow, and there were many long halts as road blocks were cleared, or small pockets of enemy resistance eliminated. During these stops we were mobbed by the bystanders. They gave us fruit and flowers, they kissed us on both cheeks, men, women, and children throwing their arms around us and saying, **"Merci, Messieurs"** (often adding: "We have waited for you four years.") When they knew we were Americans that often seemed to increase their enthusiasm. Although we were passing through a tenement district, the people, on the whole, appeared to be moderately well dressed and fed. The French flag was everywhere—often it had the **Cross of Lorraine** imprinted on it. There were a good many American and British flags, and a few Russian, in evidence. We yelled ourselves hoarse, shouting **"Vive la France"** as we passed through the crowds. Everyone thrust drinks at us that they had been hoarding for this occasion. It was impossible to refuse them, but the combination was enough to wreck one's constitution. In the course of the afternoon, we had beer, cider, white and red Bordeaux, white and red Burgundy, champagne, rum, whiskey, cognac, armagnac, and Calvados.

As night fell, we were still a mile short of the Pont de Sèvres, and there was determined resistance in a factory below the bridge at which our tanks were cutting loose. The vehicles were drawn up along the sidewalks. Mouthard found a house in which we distributed ourselves, and we had our rations there. . . .

LeClerc: Free French General Jacques LeClerc, commander of the French Second Armored Division, which spearheaded the French advance into Paris
Merci, Messieurs: Thank you, gentlemen
Cross of Lorraine: emblem of the Free French forces, who broke with the Vichy government in 1940 and fought on against Germany
Vive la France: Long live France
tricolor: the French national flag, striped red, white, and blue

David K. E. Bruce, Diary Entry, 25 August 1944

There had been some fighting during the night and this morning. We did not get under way until 12:30 p.m. when we crossed the bridge. . . . As we drove into a large square near the Bois de Boulogne, we were suddenly halted in front of a café, and it was said that snipers were firing with machine guns from some of the upstairs windows of a larger apartment house. . . . Finally, a tank sent a few shells into the unfortunate house, and we were told to move on. From that point forward, we were surrounded continually by surging masses of cheering people. Kissing and shouting were general and indiscriminate. It was a wonderful sunny day and a wonderful scene. The women were dressed in their best clothes, and all wore somewhere the **tricolor**—on their blouses, in their hair, and even as earrings.

We stopped once when three German tanks were signalled ahead. We then turned off and, under the guidance of a **Spahis** lieutenant raced through the side streets until we emerged, just behind the Arc de Triomphe, on Avenue Foch where we parked the cars. The Majestic Hotel, which had been German headquarters, was on fire. At the end of the Champs Elysées a vehicle was burning in the Place de la Concorde, and behind, in the Tuileries Gardens, it looked as if a tank was on fire. Smoke was issuing from the Crillon Hotel, and across the river, from the Chamber of Deputies. Snipers were firing steadily into the area around the Arc de Triomphe, and the French were firing back at them.

We walked across to the Tomb of the Unknown Soldier. It was being guarded by six veterans, standing at attention, and a mutilated ex-soldier, seated in a wheel chair. They had been there all during the fracas at the Majestic. The French Captain in charge asked us if we wanted to ascend to the roof of the Arc. We did so and were greeted by a squadron of Pompiers standing at attention. For some reason, their Commander presented me with a pompier's medal. The view was breathtaking. One saw the golden dome of the Invalides, the green roof of the Madeleine, Sacré-Coeur, and other familiar landmarks. Tanks were firing in various streets. Part of the Arc was under fire from snipers. A shell from a German 88 nicked one of its sides.

When we descended, Mouthard led us back toward our car. Seven or eight German soldiers lay dead in a heap on the street. As we made our way forward there was a burst of fire. We found the head of the street, where our car stood, barricaded, while shots were interchanged with a Gestapo headquarters there. . . . As we started down Avenue Foch, firing became general again. Every side street seemed enfiladed. There was enthusiastic confusion. Almost every civilian had a weapon and wanted to shoot it. People on roofs were being shot at, and in many of the top stories of buildings. Some of them were, no doubt, German snipers dressed in civilian clothes, and some of them the hated **French Milice**. . . .

Hemingway, Red (Hemingway's driver) and myself, finding the Champs Elysées absolutely bare of traffic, passed down it at racing speed to the Travellers Club. When we entered, we found the rooms all closed with the exception of the bar. There a number of the Old Guard had collected, including the President of the Club. We were the first outsiders to come there since the taking of Paris. They celebrated by opening champagne. In the midst of this festivity a sniper began to fire from an adjoining roof. Red shouldered his musket and made for the roof, but was balked.

We next collected our gang and not knowing what was ahead except for the usual indiscriminate popping of small arms, dashed to the Café de la Paix. The Place de l'Opéra was a solid mass of cheering people, and, after kissing several thousand men, women, and babies, and losing a carbine by theft, we escaped to the **Ritz**. Except for the manager, the imperturbable [Claude] **Auzello**, the Ritz was completely deserted, so we arranged to quarter there as well as to take lodging for the Private Army. This was done. Auzello asked what he could immediately do for us, and we answered we would like fifty martini cocktails. They were not very good, as the bartender had disappeared, but they were followed by a superb

Spahis: French light cavalry, usually North African in origin

French Milice: Collaborationist French militia, known for their brutality, who had worked closely with the German occupiers

Ritz: a famous and exclusive Paris hotel, founded in 1898, used as an administrative base by top-ranking German officers during the occupation of France

Claude Auzello: Manager or Managing Director of the Ritz Hotel from 1925–1969. In June 1944 the Gestapo had arrested his wife Blanche, who had concealed her Jewish origins and worked covertly for the French Resistance during the war; she was released a few days before Allied forces entered Paris.

dinner. During the night, there was almost incessant shooting. The French Forces of the Interior are well out of hand, and draw on anybody whom they consider suspicious.

Source: Nelson Lankford, ed., *OSS against the Reich: The World War II Diaries of Colonel David K. E. Bruce* (Kent, OH: Kent State University Press, 1991), 170–174. Used by permission of the Virginia Historical Society and the Bruce family.

AFTERMATH

Bruce remained in Paris until August 29, when he flew back to OSS headquarters in London. He noted how sporadic fighting and attacks by German and French Milice snipers continued in Paris for several days, even dramatically disrupting the official service of Thanksgiving at Notre Dame Cathedral on August 26, which de Gaulle attended. He also visited the nearby countryside, some of it devastated by heavy fighting. Many of the French Resistance fighters with whom the OSS and its British counterpart, the Special Operations Executive, had worked during the war came from this area. Reflecting on the French Resistance or Maquis just before he left France, after several days when they had taken part in unpredictable fighting in Paris, "cleansing it of the enemy," Bruce described its members as "ill-organized and unused to weapons" and "a dangerous nuisance in some respects." Even so, he continued, "it is they who, throughout France, have raised the standard of revolt, . . . have accounted for thousands of Germans, and even freed whole districts and large cities unaided." These accomplishments, he felt, justified all he and others in OSS had done to work with the resistance over the previous four years.

ASK YOURSELF

1. The revenge that French resistance and vigilante groups wreaked on compatriots accused of collaboration with the German occupiers was often harsh, swift, and extra-legal. Charges of assisting the Germans could also be used to settle other scores, pursue personal grudges, or even to eliminate political rivals. Given the prevailing disorder in Paris and France at this time, was there any way that justice could have been less rough?
2. The Free French units constituted a relatively small portion of the Allied forces that invaded Western Europe in June 1944. Ten weeks later, their leaders nonetheless successfully ignored the orders of American generals, and made the liberation of Paris their next objective. A few sympathetic, high-ranking American officers, such as Bruce, even travelled with them, with no apparent fear of the consequences. What does the episode reveal about the nature of coalition warfare in World War II, at least among the Western Allies?

TOPICS TO CONSIDER

1. **Dwight D. Eisenhower**, American supreme commander of the Allied invasion forces, had wished to defer the liberation of Paris until later. He feared that German troops would destroy the city before surrendering it, and that taking Paris would represent an expensive and unnecessary diversion from other, more strategically important, military objectives. De Gaulle, however, insisted on

sending French units to take Paris, and General LeClerc disobeyed a direct order from his American superior and commanded the French Second Armored Division to advance on Paris. De Gaulle had both symbolic and political considerations in mind: he wished to end the German occupation of the French capital as soon as possible, and he did not wish to strengthen leftist French forces by leaving the liberation of the city and possibly its ultimate control to them. Is it always possible, in such situations, to make clear distinctions between military, strategic, political, and symbolic motives?

2. The Allied invasion forces included a substantial contingent of Free French troops, who had escaped from France in 1940 in order to continue fighting Germany, under de Gaulle's leadership. Once France had been liberated, it escaped further Allied occupation and within a few months was regarded as one of the Western Allies, to the point where it was allocated an occupation zone within defeated Germany. Did this rapid rehabilitation of France make it easier or more difficult for the French to confront the legacy of the Vichy government's cooperation with Germany between 1940 and 1944?

Further Information

Beevor, Antony, and Artemis Cooper. *Paris after the Liberation 1944–1949*. Rev. ed. New York: Penguin, 2004.

Blumenson, Martin. *The Duel for France 1944: The Men and Battles that Changed the Fate of Europe*. New York: Da Capo Press, 2000 (reprint of 1963 ed.).

Gildea, Roberts. *Marianne in Chains: Daily Life in the Heart of France during the German Occupation*. New York: Metropolitan Books, 2003.

Lankford, Nelson W. *The Last American Aristocrat: The Biography of David K. E. Bruce, 1898–1977*. Boston: Little, Brown, 1996.

Reynolds, Michael S. *Hemingway: The Final Years*. New York: Norton, 2000.

Willis, Thornton. *The Liberation of Paris*. New York: Harcourt, Brace, 1962.

Web Sites

"Charles de Gaulle, le site de reference." Web site of the Charles de Gaulle Foundation. http://www.charles-de-gaulle.org/.

The Liberation of Paris (1944), with General de Gaulle and General Bradley. American 16mm Kodachrome film. Romano-Archives: "Unknown World War 2 in Color–WW2 Europe" section. http://www.webalice.it/romanoarchives/.

Films

Is Paris Burning? (1966), starring Kirk Douglas, Glenn Ford, Gert Fröbe, and Yves Montand.

La Libération de Paris (1944). Contemporary documentary shot by le Comité de Libération du Cinéma Français.

TECHNOLOGY AND AIR POWER

15. Letter from an American Bomber Pilot: Robert S. Raymond to Betty Raymond, January 27, 1943

INTRODUCTION

When war began in Europe, Robert S. Raymond (1912–2002), whose ancestors left Somerset, England, in the 1650s to settle in Massachusetts, was a young furniture salesman in Kansas City, where his father ensured that he "worked ten hours a day six days a week and went to church on Sundays." In spring 1940, he volunteered to serve in the French army. During the fall of France he was evacuated to Great Britain, where he joined the Royal Air Force and trained as a bomber pilot, flying 30 missions on Lancaster bombers. Although other Americans served as fighter pilots in the British forces, Raymond was the only American bomber pilot in the Royal Air Force. In early 1943, he wrote to Betty Raymond, a distant cousin whom he married in December 1943, describing a major bombing raid over the German Rhineland city of Düsseldorf from which he had just returned. Written at midnight, when Raymond, though tired, was still too keyed up to sleep, it has an immediacy rarely present in accounts written at a greater distance in time on the events they describe.

KEEP IN MIND AS YOU READ

1. In every country, fliers ranked high among the elite of the fighting forces. Although service in the air forces was extremely dangerous, with casualty rates of close to 10 percent among aircrew on some of the major Allied raids over Germany in 1943–1944, aviators had perhaps the most glamorous image of any in the armed forces. At the time Raymond was writing, his chances of surviving an operational tour of 30 missions were only one in three.
2. Raymond was probably writing in part to release his tensions after a rather draining and wearing experience in which he and his crew had come uncomfortably close to death.
3. Whereas fighter pilots often flew alone, a bomber crew consisted of several men, including pilot, copilot, navigator, radio operator, and one or more gunners and bomb-aimers, all of whom had to work closely together in hazardous conditions, putting a premium on coordinated teamwork. Their job demanded considerable training, skill, and technical ability.

4. Most fliers were young men in their 20s; anyone aged 30 or above, as Raymond was by the time he wrote this letter, was considered comparatively elderly.
5. Raymond's crew thought so highly of his flying abilities that they refused to fly with any other pilot.

Robert S. Raymond to Betty Raymond, 27 January 1943

Have just returned from Düsseldorf, and sitting here in my quiet room, with **Griffiths** sleeping peacefully, it seems incredible that I was there only 4 hours ago. Griffith's curly blonde head is little troubled by the experience of another bombing raid, but I am not yet sleepy and shall tell you about it, for memory, particularly mine, is a transient thing, and inevitably softens the clear-cut lines of any experience, however impressive.

Düsseldorf is a great industrial city situated in the **Ruhr** on the Rhine River, producing great quantities of vital war materials so badly needed by the **Wehrmacht** on all fronts. It is vulnerable in that the great river is an outstanding landmark, enabling easy identification, and because it is less than 400 miles from England, making it possible for us to carry a much greater weight of bombs than, for instance, to Italy.

We took off under low cloud with the promise of better weather over the target and on our return. Climbed up through several cloud layers just as the sun was tinting them with the last red colours of the day, and so up over the North Sea with **George** flying. Some **flak** over the Dutch coast was sent up to our height through a solid layer of cloud, and from then on we were never entirely free from it until we had arrived within a few minutes of the target, when I remarked to **Watt** that, although we were quite sure of our position, it looked too quiet to be entirely healthy. But we were evidently the first to arrive, and the defenses were lying **doggo** in the hope that we would either pass over and not bother them or, being uncertain of our position, fail to locate the city. Neither happened; being quite sure of where we were even above the scattered cloud, we ran straight in and planted our **cookie** and incendiaries (more than 1000 of them) and, since, the scattered cloud below made a good photo of the result improbable, I turned away immediately.

Watt said, "Bombs gone."

Immediately after the cookie blossomed into a great red mushroom glow and the string of incendiaries began to sprinkle on the ground, more than 50 searchlights concentrated on the place where we should have been after dropping that load, and the flak was bursting right at the apex of the searchlight cone. The ground defenses had been quietly plotting our track all the while, and now that they knew they were to be the "Target for tonight," they threw up everything they had. I'm afraid we left our companions a hard row to hoe, but we have faced the same situation elsewhere.

Griffiths: Bert Griffiths, the flight engineer, "a 19-year-old, blonde, curly-headed cherub," who "entered the R.A.F. as a boy apprentice at the age of 16, was trained for two years as an engine mechanic, and . . . has acquired the rank of Sgt. [Sergeant] only very recently after completing a six-week course studying every part of this particular plane and knows it much better than I do."
Ruhr: Germany's foremost industrial area, subjected to intense Allied bombing raids from 1943 onward
Wehrmacht: the German military
George: the autopilot
flak: ground-based anti-aircraft artillery fire
Watt: the bombardier or bomb-aimer, from County Down, Ireland, "30 years old, unmarried, slim, athletic, 5'7" tall, light brown wavy hair and blue eyes, was an architectural draftsman in civil life and worked for ten different firms in as many years, is generally against everything and is outspoken in his dislike for the present political system."
doggo: quiet
cookie: huge blockbuster bomb, weighing 4,000 pounds, containing over 3,000 pounds of explosives

Flak all the way to the coast, and finally the blessed emptiness of the lonely North Sea, where we found ice forming on our wings when we attempted to descend through the cloud, and so stayed upstairs at lower temperatures until we were over England and **Price** could get us the latest weather report from our Base.

An hour before we arrived the cloud ceiling was 4,000 feet and closing down rapidly. By the time we got there, it was down to 800 feet with rain falling and the air gusty and full of pockets (air currents) that tossed us around like peas in an empty sack between 300 and 1200 feet. Having just [censored] just before setting course from Base earlier in the evening, we were even more cautious than usual. Discipline in the air is absolutely essential, for only the **W.A.A.F.** in the **control tower** knows where everyone is. Reviewing the situation now, I know that six months ago under such conditions I would most certainly have been listed as missing with my Crew from this night's operations. But somewhere during my training I learned to fly confidently by instruments alone, and only that accuracy enabled me to maintain contact and land on the **flarepath** as smoothly and easily in darkness as it is possible to do during the day. All members of air-crew are trained, not born, for their jobs, and only hard work and practice enable any crew to live through an Operational tour. I've known so many who trusted to instinct, luck and fortune to carry them through. Each serves in more or less marginal situations, but eventually there can be no substitute. For that reason an Operational Crew of proven ability is a premium product and a valuable unit. They can be developed from average material, but somehow the sum of their abilities must be so integrated that the whole is something greater than the sum of its parts. And that is one of the reasons why I still enjoy flying a bomber.

Price: Stanley Price, the wireless operator, "20 years old, unmarried, a happy-go-lucky Canadian but plenty tough, fair-haired, 5'8", with a pleasant personality."

W.A.A.F.: A member of the British Women's Auxiliary Air Force, which provided support services for aircrew, including controllers who plotted the whereabouts of each aircraft

control tower: radar control center directing air operations

flarepath: the trail of lights guiding returning aircraft back to the runway on an airfield

Primarily, I suppose, it's based on vanity. We live a life of comparative ease and leisure, are fed, clothed, housed and paid more than others, but when the chips are down, it's up to small units of 7 men each, to do in a few hours what would otherwise cost the lives of many thousands to accomplish. Our capacity for destruction is tremendous. God grant that in the days of peace to come we shall work as hard and be as zealous to rebuild and recreate the brave new world.

Several bursts of flak were so near tonight that the Gunners still think we were hit, since we could not examine the plane adequately in the dark when we had parked it at the dispersal point, but we shall see tomorrow. . . .

My letters inevitably taper off to unconnected inconsequentials. Just remembered some sounds I would like to hear—the long, hollow whistle of a train—you, singing—birds on a spring morning—frogs at midnight—traffic on Main Street—the smooth patter of a salesman (with the goods)—wind in a pine forest—the K.C. [Kansas City] Philharmonic—a church choir—the clatter of a mowing machine—the rustle of tall corn—the drowsy hum of bees around a hive—the crackle of a wood fire—carpenters sawing and hammering—and many others, but most of all your voice.

Source: Robert S. Raymond, *A Yank in Bomber Command*, rev. ed. (Pacifica, CA: Pacifica Press, 1998), 158–160. Original from "Diary (4)" File, World War II Participants and Contemporaries Collection, Dwight D. Eisenhower Presidential Library, Abilene, Kansas.

AFTERMATH

Raymond survived his operational tour. Somewhat reluctantly, in April 1943, he transferred to the U.S. Air Force and returned to the United States. He switched to flying American Liberators (B-24s) and Flying Fortresses (B-17s), and spent the remainder of the war as an instructor in U.S. Technical Training Command. In December 1943, he married Betty. The following March, the British government awarded him the Distinguished Flying Cross. In later life, Raymond took pride in having seen military service in the armed forces of three different countries during the same war. After the war, Raymond spent two years working in his father's furniture store, and then studied at the London School of Economics in 1947–1948. He earned an MBA degree from the University of Kansas in 1951 and a doctorate from Ohio State University in 1953. From 1948 onward, Raymond was a professor of marketing, spending the years 1960 to 1982 at the University of Athens in Ohio, where he retired as a professor emeritus. In 1977, he wrote a memoir describing his time in British bomber command, a work based in considerable part on his letters and diaries; an expanded and revised version appeared in 1998. Eventually, Raymond donated his typescript of these documents to the Dwight D. Eisenhower Presidential Library in Abilene, Kansas.

ASK YOURSELF

1. Raymond appeared unconcerned by the damage his crew and the other bombers accompanying him had wrought upon Düsseldorf or other German cities. Indeed, he took some pride in being part of a small and in some ways pampered elite force that could inflict such disproportionately heavy destruction upon its enemies, thereby saving many Allied soldiers' lives. He did, however, express the hope that once the war was over, the United States would turn its enormous energies and capacities from devastation to reconstruction. Did other Allied fliers of the time share Raymond's outlook?

AIR CREWS OF WORLD WAR II

For both bombers and fighters, flying combat missions was a highly stressful enterprise. American aircrews were normally supposed to be rotated home after flying a tour of 24 missions, and to receive a week off after every five missions. During the major Allied bombing raids of 1943–1944, however, the attrition rate was such that on average bomber crews could expect to fly only 15 missions before being shot down. American losses in the air war in Europe were 9,949 bombers, 8,500 fighters, and 64,000 airmen killed, while the British Bomber Command lost 57,000 men. The most experienced crews generally had the best chances of survival, while newly trained pilots were most at risk. While fighter airplanes were highly maneuverable, bombers, though well armed with machine guns, flew in tight formation and were vulnerable to attacks from enemy fighters and anti-aircraft fire (flak) from the ground. Freezing subzero cold and loss of oxygen, as well as enemy gunfire, could both kill aircrew. Nervous breakdowns were fairly common among overstrained fliers, especially those piloting transport planes navigating the dangerous hump route over the Himalayas ferrying supplies from India to China.

2. Even though he was writing to a woman who might well be concerned for his safety, Raymond did not attempt to minimize the dangers to which he was exposed on a fairly routine basis. Why not?
3. Like many men away at war, Raymond used his memories of home to anchor and orient himself in a very different life of combat. He finished his letter by recalling some of the everyday sounds of Kansas City, where he hoped to and indeed did return once the war was over. Did the experience of having escaped death fairly narrowly only a few hours earlier make him more reflective than might otherwise have been the case?

TOPICS TO CONSIDER

1. Airmen who took part in the massive raids on enemy targets often took considerable pride in their flying skills and ability to complete their destructive missions, which were frequently aimed at civilian targets. Raymond himself later admitted that he had little idea of the broad lines of Allied air strategy, but simply flew on raids as and when instructed. Should one consider this attitude an example of the dehumanizing effect of highly technological warfare?
2. The atmosphere on a wartime airfield was usually one of intense camaraderie, with ground personnel waiting anxiously every time airplanes set off on a raid, to see how many of them would return and how many would be missing in action. The life expectancy of flying crew was often low, especially as the war continued and more young men with only basic training were taken into the air force. Fliers were often eager to begin romantic relationships with the young women working in support roles on the air bases, or with civilians from neighboring communities, but many such women tried to avoid emotional entanglements with men whose chance of surviving for more than a few months was poor. How great a psychological toll did the uncertainties of war inflict, not just on those men at risk of dying or serious injury, but also on wives, families, and friends?
3. Raymond wrote this letter knowing that it would probably take several weeks to reach his cousin, and there was a possibility it would be lost in transit due to enemy action. Soldiers today can communicate almost instantaneously by e-mail and other electronic means with friends and families and expect a very rapid response. Does this make a difference to how and why they keep in touch with those at home?

Further Information

Ambrose, Stephen E. *The Wild Blue: The Men and Boys Who Flew the B-24s over Germany.* New York: Simon & Schuster, 2001.

Hynes, Samuel. *Flights of Passage: Reflections of a World War II Aviator.* Annapolis, MD: Naval Institute Press, 1988.

Raymond, Robert S. *A Yank in Bomber Command.* Newton Abbot: David and Charles, 1977; revised and expanded edition, Pacifica, CA: Pacifica Press, 1998.

Schaffer, Ronald. *Wings of Judgment: American Bombing in World War II.* New York: Oxford University Press, 1985.

Steinbeck, John. *Bombs Away: The Story of a Bomber Team.* New York: Viking, 1942.

Web Site

"Aviation During World War II: The Bombing Raids of World War II." A Century of Flight. http://www.century-of-flight.net/Aviation%20history/WW2/bombing%20raids.htm.

Films

The Dam Busters (1955), starring Michael Redgrave and Richard Todd.
Dresden (2006), starring Felicitas Woll, John Light, and Benjamin Sadler. teamWorx.
The Memphis Belle (1990), starring Matthew Modine, Eric Stoltz, and Tate Donovan.

16. Will of Kamikaze Pilot Ryōji Uehara, Late 1944 or Early 1945

INTRODUCTION

As defeat came ever closer, the Japanese fought with a ferocity that dismayed and astonished their Western opponents. Specially trained Japanese pilots undertook kamikaze (literally, divine wind) suicide missions in which they deliberately sacrificed themselves and crashed an airplane into an enemy ship or other major target. Although the majority of kamikazes were shot down before reaching their objective, they were especially dreaded by American troops and sailors; perhaps they seemed to epitomize the fanatical Japanese determination to fight to the death.

The bloodiest Pacific battle of World War II took place on the island of Okinawa, where from April to June 1945, Japanese defenders fought ferociously and suicidally against invading American forces. American casualties numbered 12,000 dead, 38,000 wounded, and 26,000 losses due to battle stress, while 107,539 Japanese soldiers were killed, 23,764 sealed in caves or buried by the Japanese themselves, and a mere 10,755 were captured or surrendered. Okinawan civilians numbering 100,000 or more also died during the fighting. During the campaign, hundreds of Japanese kamikaze airplanes flying in mass formation repeatedly attacked the 1,600 American naval vessels assembled for the Okinawa assault, sinking 30 and damaging a further 164. The Japanese lost about 8,000 aircraft over Okinawa, half in combat and half due to other causes, while U.S. naval aircraft losses totaled 763. At the beginning of April, the Japanese naval command also dispatched the *Yamato,* the largest battleship in the world, to assist the embattled forces on Okinawa; with insufficient fuel for a return journey, its instructions were simply to inflict as much damage as possible on the enemy before it was destroyed. On April 7, massed American and British carrier airplanes launched repeated bomb and torpedo attacks on the *Yamato,* and eventually it sank well before it reached the battle area.

Among the kamikaze pilots who took part in the Battle of Okinawa was army captain Uehara Ryōji, a student from Keio University in Tokyo who was called up for military service in December 1943, and chosen for what was termed the Special Attack Unit. He died in action at the age of 22 on May 11, 1945, when he attacked an American mechanized unit in Kadena Bay, Okinawa. Before doing so, Uehara wrote a last will and testament to his parents.

KEEP IN MIND AS YOU READ

1. Most soldiers and aviators recognized that there was a real possibility they would be killed in action. A kamikaze pilot, however, knew that if he followed his orders, it was virtually certain that he would die while fulfilling his mission.
2. Uehara was a member of the well-educated Japanese elite of university students.
3. Uehara was a political liberal who had little sympathy with his country's wartime policies and the politicians and military men directing them. He nonetheless felt obliged to die in defense of them.
4. Uehara was trying to give some comfort to his parents, who had already lost one son, and would, he suspected, find his own death emotionally devastating.
5. Uehara knew that his own life would be extremely short. When writing his will, he sought to make some sense for himself of this fact, and also of his own experiences.

Will of Ryōji Uehara

To my dear Father and Mother:

I was so lucky ever since I was given my life some twenty years ago that I was brought up never deprived of anything. Under the love and affection of my loving parents, and with constant encouragement from my wonderful elder brothers and younger sister, I was so fortunate to spend such happy days. I say this in face of the fact that at times I had a tendency to act in a spoiled and selfish manner. Throughout, of all of us siblings, I was the one who caused you, Father and Mother, the most worry. It pains my heart that my time will come before I can return, or try to return, any of these favors I received. But in Japan, where loyalty to the **Emperor** and **filial piety** are considered one and the same thing, and total loyalty to the nation is a fulfillment of filial piety. I am confident of your forgiveness.

> **Emperor:** the head of the Japanese state, whom most Japanese still believed to be a god
>
> **filial piety:** respect for one's parents, a particularly strong virtue in Confucian Asian societies such as Japan

As a member of the flying staff, I spent each and every day with death as the premise. Every letter and each word I wrote constituted my last will and testament. In the sky so high above, death is never a focus of fear. Will I in fact die when I hit the target? No, I cannot believe that I am going to die, and there was even a time when I felt a sudden urge somehow to dive into a target. The fact of the matter is that I am never afraid of death, and, to the contrary, I even welcome it. The reason for this is my deep belief that, through death, I'll be able to get together again with my beloved older brother, Tatsu. To be reunited with him in heaven is what I desire the most. I did not have any specific attitude toward life and death. My reasoning was that the cultivation of a specific attitude toward life and death would amount to an attempt to give a meaning and value to death, something that would have to stem from a person's utter fear of an uncertain death. My belief is that death is a passage leading to reunion with my loved ones in heaven. I am not afraid to die. Death is nothing to be afraid of when you look at it as just a stage in the process of ascending to heaven.

Succinctly speaking, I have always admired liberalism, mainly because I felt that this political philosophy was the only one to follow were Japan really to survive eternally. Perhaps this sort of thinking seems foolish, but it is only because Japan is currently drowned in totalitarianism. Nevertheless, and this state of affairs notwithstanding, it will be clear to any human being who sees clearly and is willing to reflect on the very nature of his or her humanity that liberalism is the most logical ideology.

It seems to me that a nation's probable success in the prosecution of a war would, on the very basis of that nation's ideology, be clearly evident even before the war was fought. It would in fact be so obvious that eventual victory would clearly be seen to belong to the nation that holds a natural ideology, i.e., an ideology which in its way is constitutive of human nature itself.

My hope of making Japan like the British Empire of the past has been utterly defeated. At this point, therefore, I gladly give up my life for Japan's liberty and independence.

While the rise and fall of one nation is indeed a matter of immense importance for any human being, the same shift dwindles to relative insignificance if and when that same human being places it within the context of the universe as a whole. Exactly as the saying has it, "Pride goeth before a fall (or, those who savor victory will soon find themselves in the camp of the defeated)," and even if America and Great Britain turn out to be victorious against us, they will eventually learn that the day of their own defeat is imminent. It pleases me to think that, even if they are not to be defeated in the near future, they may be turned to dust anyway through an explosion of the globe itself. Not only that, but the people who are getting the most fun out of life now are most certainly doomed to die in the end. The only difference is whether it comes sooner or later.

In the drawer, right side of my bookcase, in the annex of the house, you will find the book I am leaving behind. If the drawer does not open, please open the left drawer and pull out a nail—then try the right drawer again.

Well, then, I pray that you will take good care of yourselves.
My very best to my big brother, sister Kiyoko, and to everyone.
Well, then. Good-bye. Farewell. Good-bye forever.
FROM RYŌJI

Source: Kike Wadatsumi no Koe, *Listen to the Voices from the Sea*, trans. Midori Yamanouchi and Joseph L. Quinn, S.J. (Scranton: The University of Scranton Press, 2000), 236–238. Used by permission of the University of Scranton.

AFTERMATH

When Uehara's parents looked for the book that he mentioned at the end of his will, they found a copy of a study of the Italian philosopher Benedetto Croce. On the back page of that volume, Uehara had written another will. He had also circled some characters in the book, and together these constituted a message to a young woman with whom he had fallen in love, who was, however, happily engaged to marry another man. Uehara told her that, even though he had given up "the idea of whispering the words of love to you," he would nonetheless always love her.

The ferocity with which Japanese soldiers and aviators fought at Okinawa did not bring them victory. It was, however, a major factor in persuading American leaders that the Japanese were prepared to fight to the bitter end in defense of their homeland and in doing so would inflict massive casualties upon U.S. troops, in a war that was likely to continue well into 1946. This in turn was one significant reason why the U.S. government decided to use atomic weapons against Japan in August 1945.

ASK YOURSELF

1. Many soldiers wrote letters to be given to their closest relatives, wives, or parents, in case they were killed in action, but few of them could be as certain as Uehara that they would die. What differences does this make to our understanding of Uehara's last will?
2. Were Uehara's parents likely to find any comfort when they read his will and knew what he had written?
3. By the spring of 1945, Japanese leaders knew that their country was facing ultimate defeat by the United States and Britain, and that the most they could achieve by fighting desperately on was to inflict heavy casualties on the enemy, at great cost to their own people, and thereby postpone the Allied victory. Were Japanese officials justified in expecting their countrymen to fight on in these circumstances?

TOPICS TO CONSIDER

1. Uehara's will was part of a larger collection of writing—mostly diaries and letters—produced by Japanese university students who died in World War II, which Japanese academics in the late 1940s compiled in an effort to deter their countrymen, especially young people, from ever embarking on war again. After some debate, the editors and publishers decided to exclude writings glorifying war or expressing ultranationalist sentiments. Their reasons for doing so were that those young students who had "even momentarily" stated such views were in reality victims of "that dark and extremely hideous national structure, the military, and its principal members," and "such occasional *pitiful and painful* writings must actually be viewed as the voices, recorded in print, of the tormented spirits of young people who were driven to the utmost limits of sanity itself, and might be read more realistically as cries for help." Were the editors justified in selecting only material that represented a viewpoint they found sympathetic? Or could they be accused of producing propaganda, albeit propaganda against war, and distorting the historical record?
2. Uehara was far from alone among Japanese students in having great doubts about the justice of the war his country was fighting and in which he was serving, but when called up he nonetheless enlisted, trained, and died. Were any alternative courses of action open to him? What course should a soldier of any nationality follow when he believes that he is fighting for a cause that lacks moral justification?

Further Information

Adams, Andrew, ed. *The Cherry Blossom Squadrons: Born to Die.* Trans. Nobuo Asahi and the Japan Tech Co. Los Angeles: Ohara Publications, 1973.

Axell, Albert and Hideaki Kase. *Kamikaze: Japan's Suicide Gods.* New York: Longman, 2002.
Brouwer, Sigmund. *Terror on Kamikaze Run.* Wheaton, IL: Victor Books, 1994.
Brown, Raymond Lamont. *Kamikaze: Japan's Suicide Samurai.* London: Arms and Armour, 1997.
Feifer, George. *Tennozan: The Battle of Okinawa and the Atomic Bomb.* New York: Ticknor and Fields, 1992.
Foster, Simon. *Okinawa, 1945: Final Assault on the Empire.* London: Arms and Armour, 1994.
Hamer, David. *Bombers Versus Battleships: The Struggle Between Ships and Aircraft for the Control of the Surface of the Sea.* Annapolis, MD: Naval Institute Press, 1998.
Hoyt, Edwin P. *The Kamikazes.* New York: Arbor House, 1983.
Inoguchi, Rikihei and Tadashi Nakajima with Roger Pineau. *The Divine Wind: Japan's Kamikaze Force in World War II.* New York: Bantam Books, 1958.
Kuwahara, Yasuo and Gordon Allred. *Kamikaze.* New York: Ballantine Books, 1957.
Nagatsuka, Ryuji. *I Was a Kamikaze: The Knights of the Divine Wind.* Trans. Nina Rootes. New York: Macmillan, 1973.
Ohnuki-Tierney, Emiko. *Kamikaze, Cherry Blossoms, and Nationalisms: The Militarization of Aesthetics in Japanese History.* Chicago: University of Chicago Press, 2002.
Ohnuki-Tierney, Emiko. *Kamikaze Diaries: Reflections of Japanese Student Soldiers.* Chicago: University of Chicago Press, 2006.
Rice, Earle, Jr. *Kamikazes.* San Diego, CA: Lucent Books, 2000.
Warner, Dennis, and Peggy Warner with Sadao Seno. *The Sacred Warriors: Japan's Suicide Legions.* New York: Van Nostrand Reinhold, 1982.
Yagara, Hiromichi. *The Battle for Okinawa.* Trans. Roger Pineau and Masatoshi Uehara. New York: Wiley, 1995.

Web Site

Kamikaze Images. http://wgordon.web.wesleyan.edu/kamikaze/index.htm.

Films and Television

Gekkou no Natsu (*Summer of the Moonlight Sonata*) (1993).
Hotaru (*Firefly*) (2001), starring Ken Takakura, Yuko Tanaka, Tomoko Naraoka, and Isashi Igawa.
Nijuuroku ya mairi (A Moon Twenty-Six Days Old) (1998), starring Emi Wakui. TBS.
Ningen no Tsubasa (Wings of a Man) (1995), starring Toshihide Tonesaku, Mayumi Yamaguchi, and Kazuyoshi Sakai.

17. Father Johannes A. Siemes Recalls the Atomic Attack on Hiroshima of August 6, 1945

INTRODUCTION

In an often brutal war where civilians frequently suffered equally with military personnel, the use of atomic bombs on the Japanese cities of Hiroshima and Nagasaki was still unique in terms of the scale of destruction one single bomb could wreak on an entire city. On August 6, 1945, a B-29 bomber dropped an atomic bomb fueled by uranium-235 on the city of Hiroshima, which at the time probably housed about 350,000 people. By November 1945, approximately 130,000 of these were dead, either in the blast itself or in its aftermath, and in subsequent years many more would succumb to radiation sickness. Three days later a second, plutonium bomb fell on Nagasaki, whose population was then around 270,000. Encircling hills limited this weapon's effects, but even so by November 1945 somewhere between 60,000 and 70,000 people had lost their lives.

In September 1945, Jesuit Father Johannes A. Siemes, a German Catholic missionary priest and philosophy professor at Catholic University in Tokyo who had been evacuated to a mission on the outskirts of Hiroshima, recorded his impressions of the city immediately after the bomb had been dropped. He gave a careful, often gruesome description of the bomb's effect upon those victims beyond the center of impact where all were immediately destroyed, and then tried to assess its overall consequences.

KEEP IN MIND AS YOU READ

1. Father Siemes was interviewed by representatives of the **Manhattan Project**, those responsible for developing atomic weapons, as they collected data for an official report on the impact of the nuclear attacks on Hiroshima and Nagasaki eventually issued in June 1946.
2. The interviewers filmed Father Siemes as he spoke to them. Portions of this footage were later included in a film *The Atom Strikes,* issued by the U.S. Army Signal Corps in 1945.
3. Since atomic weapons had never been used before, in summer 1945 no one knew exactly what their impact, both short- and long-term, would be. Siemes was unfamiliar with the aftereffects of radiation poisoning from nuclear explosions.

Hiroshima—August 6th, 1945, Interview of Father Johannes A. Siemes, recorded in September 1945

August 6th began in a bright, clear, summer morning. About seven o'clock, there was an air raid alarm which we had heard almost every day and a few planes appeared over the city. No one paid any attention and at about eight o'clock, the all-clear was sounded. I am sitting in my room at the **Novitiate** of the Society of Jesus in Nagatsuke; during the past half year, the philosophical and theological section of our Mission had been evacuated to this place from Tokyo. The Novitiate is situated approximately two kilometers from Hiroshima, half-way up the sides of a broad valley which stretches from the town at sea level into this mountainous hinterland, and through which courses a river. From my window, I have a wonderful view down the valley to the edge of the city.

Novitiate: the house for novices (i.e., clergy still undergoing an initial period of probation)

Suddenly—the time is approximately 8:14—the whole valley is filled by a garish light which resembles the magnesium light used in photography, and I am conscious of a wave of heat. I jump to the window to find out the cause of this remarkable phenomenon, but I see nothing more than that brilliant yellow light. As I make for the door, it doesn't occur to me that the light might have something to do with enemy planes. On the way from the window, I hear a moderately loud explosion which seems to come from a distance and, at the same time, the windows are broken in with a loud crash. There has been an interval of perhaps ten seconds since the flash of light. I am sprayed by fragments of glass. The entire window frame has been forced into the room. I realize now that a bomb has burst and I am under the impression that it exploded directly over our house or in the immediate vicinity.

I am bleeding from cuts about the hands and head. I attempt to get out of the door. It has been forced outwards by the air pressure and has become jammed. I force an opening in the door by means of repeated blows with my hands and feet and come to a broad hallway from which open the various rooms. Everything is in a state of confusion. All windows are broken and all the doors are forced inwards. The bookshelves in the hallway have tumbled down. I do not note a second explosion and the fliers seem to have gone on. Most of my colleagues have been injured by fragments of glass. A few are bleeding but none has been seriously injured. All of us have been fortunate since it is now apparent that the wall of my room opposite the window has been lacerated by long fragments of glass.

We proceed to the front of the house to see where the bomb has landed. There is no evidence, however, of a bomb crater; but the southeast section of the house is very severely damaged. Not a door nor a window remains. The blast of air had penetrated the entire house from the southeast, but the house still stands. It is constructed in a Japanese style with a wooden framework, but has been greatly strengthened by the labor of our Brother Gropper as is frequently done in Japanese homes. Only along the front of the chapel which adjoins the house, three supports have given way (it has been made in the manner of a Japanese temple, entirely out of wood.)

Down in the valley, perhaps one kilometer toward the city from us, several peasant homes are on fire and the woods on the opposite side of the valley are aflame. A few of us go over to help control the flames. While we are attempting to put things in order, a storm comes up and it begins to rain. Over the city, clouds of smoke are rising and I hear a few slight explosions. I come to the conclusion that an incendiary bomb with an especially strong explosive action has gone off down in the valley. A few of us saw three planes at great altitude over the city at the time of the explosion. I, myself, saw no aircraft whatsoever.

Perhaps a half-hour after the explosion, a procession of people begins to stream up the valley from the city. The crowd thickens continuously. A few come up the road to our house. We give them first aid and bring them into the chapel, which we have in the meantime cleaned and cleared of wreckage, and put them to rest on the straw mats which constitute the floor of Japanese houses. A few display horrible wounds of the extremities and back. The small quantity of fat which we possessed during this time of war was soon used up in the care of the burns. Father Rektor who, before taking holy orders, had studied medicine, ministers to the injured, but our bandages and drugs are soon gone. We must be content with cleansing the wounds.

More and more of the injured come to us. The least injured drag the more seriously wounded. There are wounded soldiers, and mothers carrying burned children in their arms. From the houses of the farmers in the valley comes word: "Our houses are full of wounded and dying. Can you help, at least by taking the worst cases?" The wounded come from the sections at the edge of the city. They saw the bright light, their houses collapsed and buried the inmates in their rooms. Those that were in the open suffered instantaneous burns, particularly on the lightly clothed or unclothed parts of the body. Numerous fires sprang up which soon consumed the entire district. We now conclude that the epicenter of the explosion was at the edge of the city near the Jokogawa Station, three kilometers away from us. . . .

Soon comes news that the entire city has been destroyed by the explosion and that it is on fire. . . .

[In the late afternoon, the fathers went into the city to try to assist other members of their mission who were injured.] Hurriedly, we get together two stretchers and seven of us rush toward the city. Father Rektor comes along with food and medicine. The closer we get to the city, the greater is the evidence of destruction and the more difficult it is to make our way. The houses at the edge of the city are all severely damaged. Many have collapsed or burned down. Further in, almost all of the dwellings have been damaged by fire. Where the city stood, there is a gigantic burned-out scar. We make our way along the street on the river bank among the burning and smoking ruins. Twice we are forced into the river itself by the heat and smoke at the level of the street.

Frightfully burned people beckon to us. Along the way, there are many dead and dying. On the Misasi Bridge, which leads into the inner city we are met by a long procession of soldiers who have suffered burns. They drag themselves along with the help of staves or are carried by their less severely injured comrades . . . an endless procession of the unfortunate. . . .

Finally we reach the entrance of the park. A large proportion of the populace has taken refuge there, but even the trees of the park are on fire in several places. Paths and bridges are blocked by the trunks of fallen trees and are almost impassable. We are told that a high wind, which may well have resulted from the heat of the burning city, has uprooted the large trees. It is now quite dark. Only the fires, which are still raging in some places at a distance, give out a little light.

[That night, the fathers brought back some of their own wounded to the mission house, returning to the city the next day.]

We take off again with the hand cart. The bright day now reveals the frightful picture which last night's darkness had partly concealed. Where the city stood everything, as far as the eye could reach, is a waste of ashes and ruin. Only several skeletons of buildings completely burned out in the interior remain. The banks of the river are covered with dead and wounded, and the rising waters have here and there covered some of the corpses. . . .

We took under our care fifty refugees who had lost everything. The majority of them were wounded and not a few had dangerous burns. Father Rektor treated the wounds as well as he could with the few medicaments that we could, with effort, gather up. He had to confine himself in general to cleansing the wounds of **purulent** material. Even those with the smaller burns are very weak and all suffered from diarrhea. In the farm houses in the vicinity, almost everywhere, there are also wounded. Father Rektor made daily rounds and acted in the capacity of a painstaking physician and was a great **Samaritan**. Our work was, in the eyes of the people, a greater boost for Christianity than all our work during the preceding long years. . . .

purulent: suppurating, septic, or infected
Samaritan: biblical New Testament character who helped a stranger whom thieves had robbed and left for dead

The magnitude of the disaster that befell Hiroshima on August 6th was only slowly pieced together in my mind. I lived through the catastrophe and saw it only in flashes, which only gradually were merged to give me a total picture. What actually happened simultaneously in the city as a whole is as follows: As a result of the explosion of the bomb at 8:15, almost the entire city was destroyed at a single blow. Only small outlying districts in the southern and eastern parts of the town escaped complete destruction. The bomb exploded over the center of the city. As a result of the blast, the small Japanese houses in a diameter of five kilometers, which compressed 99% of the city, collapsed or were blown up. Those who were in the houses were buried in the ruins. Those who were in the open sustained burns resulting from contact with the substance or rays emitted by the bomb. Where the substance struck in quantity, fires sprang up. These spread rapidly.

The heat which rose from the center created a whirlwind which was effective in spreading fire throughout the whole city. Those who had been caught beneath the ruins and who could not be freed rapidly, and those who had been caught by the flames, became casualties. As much as six kilometers from the center of the explosion, all houses were damaged and many collapsed and caught fire. Even fifteen kilometers away, windows were broken. It was rumored that the enemy fliers had spread an explosive and incendiary material over the city and then had created the explosion and ignition. A few maintained that they saw the planes drop a parachute which had carried something that exploded at a height of 1,000 meters. The newspapers called the bomb an "atomic bomb" and noted that the force of the blast had resulted from the explosion of uranium atoms, and that gamma rays had been sent out as a result of this, but no one knew anything for certain concerning the nature of the bomb.

How many people were a sacrifice to this bomb? Those who had lived through the catastrophe placed the number of dead at least 100,000. Hiroshima had a population of 400,000. Official statistics place the number who had died at 70,000 up to September 1st, not counting the missing . . . and 130,000 wounded, among them 43,500 severely wounded. Estimates made by ourselves on the basis of groups known to us show that the number of 100,000 dead is not too high. Near us there are two barracks, in each of which forty Korean workers lived. On the day of the explosion, they were laboring on the streets of Hiroshima. Four returned alive to one barracks and sixteen to the other. 600 students of the Protestant girls' school worked in a factory, from which only thirty to forty returned. Most of the peasant families in the neighborhood lost one or more of their members who had worked at factories in the city. Our next door neighbor, Tamura, lost two children and himself suffered a large wound since, as it happened, he had been in the city on that day. The family of our reader suffered two dead, father and son; thus a family of five members suffered at least two losses, counting only the dead and severely wounded. There died the Mayor, the President of the central Japan district, the Commander of the city, a Korean prince who had been stationed in Hiroshima in the capacity of an officer, and many other high ranking officers. Of the professors of the University, thirty-two were killed or severely injured. Especially hard hit were the soldiers. The Pioneer Regiment was almost entirely wiped out. The barracks were near the center of the explosion.

Thousands of wounded who died later could doubtless have been rescued had they received proper treatment and care, but rescue work in a catastrophe of this magnitude had not been envisioned; since the whole city had been knocked out at a blow, everything which had been prepared for emergency work was lost, and no preparation had been made for rescue work in the outlying districts. Many of the wounded also died because they had been weakened by under-nourishment and consequently lacked in strength to recover. Those who had their normal strength and who received good care slowly healed the burns which had been occasioned by the bomb. There were also cases, however, whose prognosis seemed good who died suddenly. There were also some who had only small external wounds who died within a week or later, after an inflammation of the **pharynx** and oral cavity had taken place. We thought at first that this was the result of inhalation of the substance of the bomb. Later, a commission established the thesis that gamma rays had been given out at the time of the explosion, following which the internal organs had been injured in a manner resembling that consequent upon **Roentgen irradiation**. This produces a diminution in the numbers of the white **corpuscles**.

Only several cases are known to me personally where individuals who did not have external burns later died. **Father Kleinsorge** and **Father Cieslik**, who were near the center of the explosion, but who did not suffer burns became quite weak some fourteen days after the explosion. Up to this time small incised wounds had healed normally, but thereafter the wounds which were still unhealed became worse and are to date [in September 1945] still incompletely healed. The attending physician diagnosed it as **leucopenia**. There thus seems to be some truth in the statement that the radiation had some effect on the blood. I am of the opinion, however, that their generally undernourished and weakened condition was partly responsible for these findings. It was noised about that the ruins of the city emitted deadly rays and that workers who went there to aid in the clearing died, and that the central district would be uninhabitable for some time to come. I have my doubts as to whether such talk is true and myself and others who worked in the ruined area for some hours shortly after the explosion suffered no such ill effects.

None of us in those days heard a single outburst against the Americans on the part of the Japanese, nor was there any evidence of a vengeful spirit. The Japanese suffered this terrible blow as part of the fortunes of war . . . something to be borne without complaint. During this, war, I have noted relatively little hatred toward the allies on the part of the people themselves, although the press has taken occasion to stir up such feelings. After the victories at the beginning of the war, the enemy was rather looked down upon, but when allied offensive gathered momentum and especially after the advent of the majestic **B-29s**, the technical skill of America became an object of wonder and admiration. . . .

pharynx: back of the mouth and throat

Roentgen irradiation: X-rays, excessive exposure to which can cause organ damage in humans

corpuscles: blood cells

Father Kleinsorge: Wilhelm Kleinsorge (1907–1977)

Father Cieslik: Hubert Cieslik (1914–1988), a highly respected historian of Japanese Christianity

leucopenia: illness due to decreased numbers of white blood cells

B-29s: B-29 Superfortress four-engined bombers, responsible for numerous highly destructive bombing raids on Japanese cities in late 1944 and 1945, as well as the mining of shipping routes and harbor approaches

We have discussed among ourselves the ethics of the use of the bomb. Some consider it in the same category as poison gas and were against its use on a civil population. Others were of the view that in total war, as carried on in Japan, there was no difference between civilians and soldiers, and that the bomb itself was an effective force tending to end the bloodshed, warning Japan to surrender and thus to avoid total destruction. It seems logical to me that he who supports total war in principle cannot complain of war against civilians. The crux of the matter is whether total war in its present form is justifiable, even when it serves a just purpose. Does it not have material and spiritual evil as its consequences which far exceed whatever good that might result? When will our moralists give us a clear answer to this question?

Source: Chapter 25 of The Manhattan Engineer District, *The Atomic Bombings of Hiroshima and Nagasaki* (29 June 1946), from The Avalon Project: The Atomic Bombings of Hiroshima and Nagasaki, URL: http://www.yale.edu/lawweb/avalon/abomb/mp25.htm.

AFTERMATH

American officials recorded Siemes's recollections and included them, apparently uncensored, as one chapter of the June 1946 report on the Hiroshima and Nagasaki bombings published by the Manhattan Project. Even though the full implications of radiation poisoning were not yet known, the report's authors clearly had the intellectual honesty to wish to include material illustrating the human consequences of the employment of atomic bombs. For many decades, Truman's decision to employ atomic weapons continued to provoke popular and historical controversy and dissent, which intensified when scientists and the general public became more familiar with the long-term medical and genetic consequences of radiation contamination and poisoning, which afflicted many of the survivors of Hiroshima and Nagasaki and even their children.

ASK YOURSELF

1. Many scientists who worked on the Manhattan Project later confessed to personal uneasy consciences over whether the devastation their invention had brought to Hiroshima and Nagasaki and the potential for further such destruction was morally excusable. Should scientists be held responsible for the uses that political and military officials make of their inventions?

FATHER WILHELM KLEINSORGE (1907–1977)

Siemes's colleague Father Kleinsorge featured prominently in John Hersey's nonfiction account, *Hiroshima* (1946), published in the *New Yorker* magazine one year after the atomic attacks, which caused many Americans to view the atom bomb's victims as individualized human beings for the first time. Already weak from his inadequate wartime diet, Father Kleinsorge initially tended Japanese sufferers, but later became ill from radiation poisoning. His postexplosion experiences gave him a new sense of solidarity and identification with the people he was serving and he became a Japanese citizen, taking the name Father Makoto Takakura. He spent the rest of his life working as a priest in Japan, although his Japanese friends still thought him unshakably German.

2. Only in July 1945, after the first successful atomic test, did British and American leaders inform **Josef Stalin** that they had developed this weapon. What impact was their earlier secrecy on the subject likely to have upon their relations with the Soviet Union? Is it surprising that, once Hiroshima and Nagasaki demonstrated the power of atomic weapons, Stalin immediately launched a crash program to develop a Soviet atomic bomb?
3. In the late 1940s, American scientists disagreed among themselves over whether their country should develop the far more powerful hydrogen bomb. Ultimately, both the United States and Soviet Union did so. When states are involved in a race to develop ever more technologically advanced weapons, is it ever possible for them to call a halt?
4. The bombings of Hiroshima and Nagasaki were the only times nuclear weapons have ever been used in war. Many people argue that the devastation wrought on those cities was so great that the memory deterred all nations from using such weapons again. Do you agree?
5. Some historians have alleged that the Allies were willing to use atomic bombs against Japan, an Asian nation, but would not have done so against the Germans, because they were Europeans. Given how heavily British and American bombers pounded German cities from 1943 to 1945, how plausible is this view?

TOPICS TO CONSIDER

1. In 1995 a Smithsonian Museum exhibit featuring portions of the fuselage of the *Enola Gay,* the B-29 bomber that delivered the first atomic bomb, provoked enormous controversy and discussion when World War II veterans and others charged that the accompanying recorded commentary was overly critical of President Truman's decision to use atomic devices against Japan. Is it ever possible for museums to insulate themselves from such politically and emotionally charged debates? Should museum staff even attempt to do so?
2. In recent years, India and Pakistan have both developed nuclear weapons, and North Korea and Iran have established scientific ventures with the apparent goal of doing likewise. What, if anything, do present-day nations gain by equipping themselves with nuclear bombs? Given that the United States, Russia, China, France, and Britain have had nuclear weapons for many years and never used them in conflict situations, why does the prospect of additional nations getting their own independent nuclear bombs seem so alarming?

Further Information

Alperovitz, Gar. *Atomic Diplomacy: Hiroshima and Potsdam: The Use of the Atomic Bomb and the American Confrontation with Soviet Power.* 2nd expanded ed. Boulder, CO: Pluto Press, 1994.

Alperovitz, Gar, with Sanho Tree. *The Decision to Use the Atomic Bomb and the Architecture of an American Myth.* New York: Alfred A. Knopf, 1995.

Bundy, McGeorge. *Danger and Survival: Choices about the Bomb in the First Fifty Years.* New York: Random House, 1988.

Harwit, Martin. *An Exhibit Denied: Lobbying the History of Enola Gay.* New York: Copernicus, 1996.

Herken, Gregg. *The Winning Weapon: The Atomic Bomb in the Cold War, 1945–1950.* Princeton: Princeton University Press, 1988.
Hersey, John. *Hiroshima.* New York: Alfred A. Knopf, 1946.
Hogan, Michael J., ed. *Hiroshima in History and Memory.* New York: Cambridge University Press, 1996.
Lifton, Robert Jay. *Death in Life: Survivors of Hiroshima.* New York: Random House, 1967.
Ogura, Toyofumi. *Letters from the End of the World: A Firsthand Account of the Bombing of Hiroshima.* Trans. Kisaburo Murakami and Shigeru Fujii. London: Kodansha, 2001.
Rhodes, Richard. *The Making of the Atomic Bomb.* New York: Simon & Schuster, 1986.
Sherwin, Martin J. *A World Destroyed: Hiroshima and Its Legacies.* 3rd ed. Stanford: Stanford University Press, 2000.
Takaki, Ronald. *Hiroshima: Why America Dropped the Atomic Bomb.* Boston: Little Brown, 1995.
Walker, J. Samuel. *Prompt and Utter Destruction: Truman and the Use of Atomic Bombs against Japan.* Chapel Hill: University of North Carolina Press, 1997.

Web Sites

Hiroshima: From the Depths of Destruction to the Heights of Peace. Paul Ketko: Educational Portfolio. http://pketko.com/Hiroshima/index.htm.
Hiroshima & Nagasaki Remembered. http://www.hiroshima-remembered.com.
Trinity Atomic Web site: Nuclear Weapons: History, Technology, and Consequences in Historical Documents, Photos, and Videos. http://www.abomb1.org.

Films and Television

The Atom Strikes (1945). U.S. Army Signal Corps. http://video.google.com/videoplay?docid=2284993057251583384#.
Hiroshima (1996), starring Wesley Addy, Jeffrey DeMunn, and David Gow.
Hiroshima, Mon Amour (1960), starring Emmanuelle Riva and Eiji Okada.
White Light/Black Rain: The Destruction of Hiroshima and Nagasaki (2007). HBO Home Video.

18. Toshikazu Kase, Account of the Japanese Surrender Ceremony, September 2, 1945

INTRODUCTION

One of the war's great symbolic moments was the formal surrender of Japan. Even though he had commanded his subjects to cease fighting and accept defeat, the Shōwa Emperor **Hirohito** was absent from the surrender ceremony. Eleven Japanese delegates attended the ceremony of surrender to the Allied powers, on board the battleship USS *Missouri* in Tokyo Bay. Toshikazu Kase (1903–2004), one of three Foreign Ministry representatives, gave a vivid account of Japan's moment of utmost humiliation.

KEEP IN MIND AS YOU READ

1. Kase, one of the less prominent figures in the Japanese delegation, was a moderate in Japanese political terms. As a mid-level Foreign Office bureaucrat, for at least a year before these events he had tried to facilitate efforts to negotiate peace with the Allied powers.
2. Despite Kase's claims in his final paragraphs, superior American military force had undoubtedly been the key factor in the Allied defeat of Japan.
3. Although the Emperor had announced the Japanese surrender on August 15, 1945, some Japanese military figures still deeply resented his decision. Fears that extremists might still attack and try to kill the surrender delegation were not entirely unfounded, especially given the number of moderate Japanese politicians assassinated by their opponents in the first decades of the 20th century.
4. The two top Japanese representatives at this ceremony felt very differently about their participation. While Shigemitsu welcomed the coming of peace and saw the war's end, however difficult, as a chance for a new beginning, Umezu believed Japan should have fought on to the bitter end. Only the Emperor's direct command impelled him to attend the surrender ceremony.
5. The official surrender was a carefully choreographed event. Its orchestrators correctly anticipated that the media would quickly disseminate newsreel and print accounts of the proceedings around the world. It was an opportunity for the United States, in particular, to display its unparalleled military might and strength.

Toshikazu Kase, Account of the Japanese Surrender Ceremony, 2 September 1945

We left Tokyo at about five o'clock in the morning. There were nine of us, three each from the Foreign Office, and the War and Navy Departments, besides the two delegates, **Shigemitsu**, the Foreign Minister representing the government, and General **Umedzu**, the Chief of Staff of the Army representing the Supreme Command. With the two delegates leading the procession, our cars sped at full speed on the battered and bumpy road to **Yokohama**. Along the highway, we could see nothing but miles and miles of debris and destruction where there had once flourished towns containing a great number of **munitions** factories. The ghastly sight of death and desolation was enough to freeze my heart. These hollow ruins, however, were perhaps a fit prelude to the poignant drama in which we were about to take part for were we not sorrowing men come to seek a tomb for a fallen Empire? They were also a grim reminder that a nation was snatched from an impending annihilation. For were not the scenes of havoc the atomic bomb wrought a sufficient warning? The waste of war and the ignominy of surrender were put on my mental loom and produced a strange fabric of grief and sorrow. There were few men on the road and none probably recognized us. Our journey was kept in utmost secrecy in order to avoid publicity lest extremists might attempt to impede us by violence. . . .

This party arrived in Yokohama in less than an hour's time. It was on this day that the spearhead of the Eighth Army landed at the same port. Sentries with gleaming bayonets were heavily guarding the streets through which we rode slowly to the port area. All the cars had removed the flags on the **bonnet** and officers had left their swords behind. We had thus furled the banner and ungirt the sword. Diplomats without flag and soldiers without sword—sullen and silent we continued the journey till we reached the quay.

There were four destroyers with white placards hung on the mast marked A to D. We boarded the one marked B, which was the *Lansdown*, a ship which saw much meritorious service in the battle of the Pacific. As the destroyer pushed out of the harbor, we saw in the offing lines on lines of gray warships, both heavy and light, anchored in majestic array. This was the mighty pageant of the Allied navies that so lately belched forth their crashing battle, now holding in their swift thunder and floating like calm sea birds on the subjugated waters. A spirit of gay festivity pervaded the atmosphere.

After about an hour's cruise the destroyer stopped in full view of the **battleship *Missouri,*** which lay anchored some eighteen miles off the shore. The huge 45,000 tonner towered high above the rest of the proud squadron. High on the mast there fluttered in the wind the Stars and Stripes. It was this flag that had lighted the marching step of America's destiny on to shining victory. Today this flag of glory was raised in triumph to mark the Big Day. As we approached the battleship in a motor launch, our eyes were caught by rows of sailors massed on her broadside lining the rails, a starry multitude, in their glittering uniforms of immaculate white.

Shigemitsu: Mamoru Shigemitsu (1887–1957), Japanese Foreign Minister, 1943–1945, 1954–1956
Umedzu: Yoshijirō Umezu (1882–1949), Chief of staff of the Japanese Army, 1944–1945
Yokohama: In 1945, Yokohama was Japan's fourth or fifth largest city and most significant port. In 1944 and 1945 more than 30 Allied bombing raids reduced much of the city to rubble
munitions: armaments
bonnet: hood
USS *Missouri:* *Iowa*-class battleship, also known as Mighty Mo or Big Mo, the last battleship the United States ever built, flagship of the U.S. Pacific fleet at the end of World War II

Soon the launch came alongside the battleship, and we climbed its gangway, Shigemitsu leading the way, heavily limping on his cane. For he walks on a wooden leg, having had his leg blown off by a bomb outrage in Shanghai some fifteen years ago. It was as if he negotiated each step with a groan and we, the rest of us, echoed it with a sigh. As we, eleven in all, climbed onto the veranda deck on the starboard side, we gathered into three short rows facing the representatives of the Allied powers across a table covered with green cloth, on which were placed the white documents of surrender. The veranda deck was animated by a motley of sparkling colors, red, gold, brown, and olive, as decorations and ribbons decked the uniforms of different cut and color worn by the Allied representatives. There were also row upon row of American admirals and generals in somber khaki; but what added to the festive gayety of the occasion was the sight of the war correspondents who, monkey-like, hung on to every cliff-like point of vantage in most precarious postures. Evidently scaffolding had been specially constructed for the convenience of the cameramen, who were working frantically on their exciting job. Then there was a gallery of spectators who seemed numberless, overcrowding every bit of available space on the great ship, on the mast, on the chimneys, on the gun turrets—on everything, and everywhere.

They were all thronged, packed to suffocation, representatives, journalists, spectators, an assembly of **brass, braid, and brand**. As we appeared on the scene we were, I felt, being subjected to the torture of the **pillory**. There were a million eyes beating us in the million shafts of a rattling storm of arrows barbed with fire. I felt their keenness sink into my body with a sharp physical pain. Never have I realized that the glance of glaring eyes could hurt so much.

We waited for a few minutes standing in the public gaze like penitent boys awaiting the dreaded schoolmaster. I tried to preserve with the utmost **sangfroid** the dignity of defeat, but it was difficult and every minute seemed to contain ages. I looked up and saw painted on the wall nearby several miniature Rising Suns, our flag, evidently in numbers corresponding to the planes and submarines shot down or sunk by the crew of the battleship. As I tried to count these markings, tears rose in my throat and quickly gathered to my eyes, flooding them. I could hardly bear the sight now. Heroes of unwritten stories, they were young boys who defied death gaily and gallantly, manning the daily thinning ranks of the suicide corps. They were just like cherry blossoms, emblems of our national character, all of a sudden blooming into riotous beauty and just as quickly going away. What do they see today, their spirit, the glorious thing, looking down on the scene of surrender.

MacArthur walks quietly from the interior of the ship and steps to the microphones. . . .

In a few minutes' time [MacArthur's] speech was over and the Supreme Commander invited the Japanese delegates to sign the instrument of surrender. Shigemitsu signed first followed by Umedzu. It was eight minutes past nine when MacArthur put his signature to the documents. Other representatives of the Allied Powers followed suit in the order of the United States, China, the United Kingdom, the Soviet Union, Australia, Canada, France, the Netherlands and New Zealand.

When all the representatives had finished signing, MacArthur announced slowly: "Let us pray that peace be now restored to the world and that God will preserve it always. These proceedings are closed."

brass, braid, and brand: decorative materials and badges on formal military and diplomatic uniforms, indicating an individual's rank and honors

pillory: medieval punishment device, in which a criminal was held upright, his neck and wrists secured, unable to hide or protect himself from anything thrown at him

sangfroid: coolness and composure (literally French for cold blood)

MacArthur: Douglas MacArthur, American general who was Allied Supreme Commander of the Southwest Pacific Area, 1943–1945, Supreme Commander of the Allied Powers in Japan, 1945–1950

At that moment, the skies parted and the sun shone brightly through the layers of clouds. There was a steady drone above and now it became a deafening roar and an **armada** of airplanes paraded into sight, sweeping over the warships. Four hundred **B-29's** and 1,500 **carrier planes** joined in the aerial pageant in a final salute. It was over. . . .

When the Supreme Commander finished, I wrote in my report the impression his words had made on me. He is a man of peace. Never has the truth of the line "peace has her victories no less renowned than war" been more eloquently demonstrated. He is a man of light. Radiantly, the gathering rays of his magnanimous soul embrace the earth, his footsteps paving the world with light. Is it not a piece of rare good fortune, I asked myself, that a man of such caliber and character should have been designated as the Supreme Commander who will shape the destiny of Japan? In the dark hour of our despair and distress, a bright light is ushered in, in the very person of General MacArthur.

While the destroyer sped home, I wrote down hurriedly the impressions of the surrender which Shigemitsu took to the Throne immediately after our return to the Capital, as the Emperor was anxiously waiting for his report. At the end of this report, in which I dwelt at length upon the superb address of the Supreme Commander, I raised a question whether it would have been possible for us, had we been victorious, to embrace the vanquished with a similar magnanimity. Clearly it would have been different. Returning from the audience, Shigemitsu told me that the Emperor nodded with a sigh in agreement. Indeed, a distance inexpressible by numbers separates us—America from Japan. After all, we were not beaten on the battlefield by dint of superior arms. We were defeated in the spiritual contest by a nobler idea. The real issue was moral—beyond all the powers of algebra to compute.

The day will come when recorded time, age on age, will seem but a point in retrospect. However, happen what may in the future, this Big Day on the *Missouri* will stand out as one of the brightest dates in history, with General MacArthur as a shining **obelisk** in the desert of human endeavor that marks a timeless march onward toward an enduring peace.

armada: armed fleet
B-29: B-29 Superfortress four-engined bombers, responsible for numerous highly destructive bombing raids on Japanese cities in late 1944 and 1945, as well as the mining of shipping routes and harbor approaches
carrier airplanes: aircraft based on naval aircraft carrier ships, rather than on land
obelisk: monumental tapering pillar of stone, usually erected to commemorate some great event

Source: Toshikazu Kase, *Eclipse of the Rising Sun,* David Nelson Rowe, ed. (London: Jonathan Cape, 1951). Reprinted by permission of Yale University Press.

AFTERMATH

For the following five years, Japan remained under Allied occupation. American military and civilian officials effectively supervised Japan's administration, and economic and political reconstruction, deliberately transforming it into a nonmilitarized but economically strong bastion of western Cold War strategy. American leaders turned to pro-Western Japanese politicians and bureaucrats willing to work with them, of whom the most prominent was Yoshida Shigeru (1878–1967), Japan's prime minister from May 1946 to May 1947, and again from 1948 to 1954. Like Premier Yoshida, Kase became a strong supporter of Japan's alliance with the United States. He helped to negotiate Japan's full membership of the new postwar United Nations (UN) organization, to which he was appointed Japan's first ambassador in 1955. He died in 2004 at the age of 101. Shigemitsu, convicted of war crimes and sentenced to seven years in prison, was paroled in 1950, and from 1954 to 1956

DOUGLAS MACARTHUR (1880–1964)

MacArthur, among the most forceful 20th-century U.S. military figures, commanded U.S. forces in the Pacific from 1941 to 1945. From a career military family, he served as U.S. army chief of staff during the early 1930s. From 1935 to 1941 MacArthur was military adviser to the newly independent Philippine Commonwealth Government, his mission to develop a Philippine army capable of withstanding the Japanese. In July 1941, as the Pacific crisis intensified, the U.S. War Department recalled MacArthur to active duty, appointing him commander of United States army forces in the Far East. In December 1941, immediately after Pearl Harbor, Japanese troops attacked and soon overran the Philippines, killing or capturing many American soldiers. MacArthur escaped to Australia. Although the American navy was primarily responsible for victory in the Pacific campaign, MacArthur's forces played an important supporting role. President Harry S. Truman appointed MacArthur supreme commander of Allied occupation forces in Japan, where from 1945 to 1950 he presided over extensive political, economic, and military reforms. His support for the retention of Emperor **Hirohito** as the figurehead of the Japanese state was crucial to the Japanese monarchy's survival. MacArthur also anchored Japan firmly in the Western, anti-Soviet camp of the Cold War in Asia, preparing the ground for the long-term treaty of security and alliance the United States and Japan signed in September 1951.

served once again as Japan's foreign minister. On December 18, 1956, he was Japan's chief representative in the UN General Assembly when his country became its 80th member. He died six weeks later of heart problems. The International Military Tribunal for the Far East also tried Umezu for war crimes. In 1948, he was found guilty of waging a war of aggression. Sentenced to life imprisonment in November 1948, while in jail he converted to Christianity, dying of cancer in January 1949.

ASK YOURSELF

1. In his own memoirs, General Douglas MacArthur later quoted at length from Kase's account of the surrender ceremony, which he said was his favorite of all the descriptions of that event. Why did MacArthur find Kase's narrative so appealing? How sincere was Kase's extravagant praise of MacArthur?
2. As a young man, during the 1920s Kase studied for several years at Amherst College, Massachusetts, and Harvard University. In the 1930s, when he began his diplomatic career, he was posted to Japan's embassies in London and Berlin, Germany? How did these experiences affect his feelings towards the United States and other Western countries?
3. Was Kase's decision to publish his memoirs in English in 1951 motivated in part by his desire to facilitate Japan's re-acceptance into the international community? To what extent did his book represent the Japanese government's official position at that time?

TOPICS TO CONSIDER

1. Top and mid-level political figures in states defeated by outside powers often face a choice between working with their conquerors or refusing to cooperate with them. This is particularly the case when individuals have disagreed, either openly or tacitly, with the policies of earlier regimes in their own country. If

such individuals decide to collaborate with their nation's new masters, should they be considered patriots whose foremost interest is their country's survival and prosperity, or opportunists whose foremost interest is their own survival and prosperity? Or can both views be compatible with each other?

2. After 1945, Japanese leaders gravitated into the orbit of the United States and other Western powers in the Cold War. Japan was demilitarized, with tens of thousands of American troops, together with U.S. strategic bombers and nuclear weapons, located on bases in Okinawa and elsewhere in Japan. Japan's own military spending, forces, and activities were greatly restricted. Simultaneously, from the 1950s onward Japan enjoyed very high economic growth rates, its exports to the rest of the world expanded dramatically, and it became a leading economic power in Asia and beyond. Some commentators even suggested that post-1945 Japan had snatched victory from the jaws of defeat and, while protected against external enemies by the U.S. security umbrella, had succeeded in establishing the Greater East Asia Co-Prosperity Sphere that had been one of the objectives of Japanese policymakers of the 1930s and early 1940s. How valid is this viewpoint?

Further Information

Dower, John. *Embracing Defeat: Japan in the Wake of World War II.* New York: Norton, 1999.

Dower, J.W. *Empire and Aftermath: Yoshida Shigeru and the Japanese Experience, 1878–1954.* Cambridge, MA: Council on East Asian Studies, Harvard University, 1979.

Finn, Richard B. *Winners in Peace: MacArthur, Yoshida, and Postwar Japan.* Berkeley: University of California Press, 1992.

Schaller, Michael. *The American Occupation of Japan: The Origins of the Cold War in Asia.* New York: Oxford University Press, 1985.

Schoenberger, Howard B. *Aftermath of War: Americans and the Remaking of Japan, 1945–1952.* Kent State, OH: Kent State University Press, 1989.

Web Site

American Occupation of Japan: Voices of the Key Participants. Claremont Colleges Digital Library. http://ccdl.libraries.claremont.edu/cdm4/browse.php?CISOROOT=/aoc.

Film and Television

Japan under American Occupation (2002). The History Channel.

WARTIME VICTIMS AND SURVIVORS

19. A Pacifist Point of View: Rev. Arle Brooks, Statement upon His Conviction for Draft Evasion, January 1941

INTRODUCTION

Oklahoma-born Arle Brooks (1909–1953), an ordained Christian minister in the Disciples of Christ Church, studied at Texas Christian University and Chicago Theological Seminary, after which he did social work in Chicago and with the Texas prison system. In 1940 he began work for the summer work camp program of the American Friends Service Committee. From 1940 onward, Brooks, admired by many for his religious fervor, took up the pacifist cause. Although he could have claimed exemption from Selective Service on the grounds that he was a religious minister, he chose instead to break the law by refusing to register for the draft at all, on the grounds that this was unconstitutional. Charged with draft evasion and tried and convicted in January 1941, Brooks was sentenced to a year and a day in prison for refusing to register. Before his sentencing, Brooks made a public statement.

KEEP IN MIND AS YOU READ

1. By 1940, the Society of Friends (Quakers), which employed Brooks, had a very long established and well-recognized pacifist tradition, dating back to the 17th century, when they founded the then colony of Pennsylvania.
2. Brooks deliberately courted arrest, in order to make a political point, and give him an opportunity to win maximum publicity for his views. Upon his conviction, he took advantage of the fact that before sentencing every convicted man has the right to speak on his own behalf to make a stirring public avowal, widely reported in the press, of his personal beliefs.
3. The **Selective Training and Service Act**, passed by the United States Congress in September 1940, when the United States was still supposedly neutral, under which all young American men between 21 and 35 years of age were required to register with their local draft boards, and liable to be called up for a year of military training, was politically highly controversial. Its opponents argued that it was bringing the United States closer to outright war.
4. Brooks realized that, if the government arrested and convicted a respectable religious minister for draft evasion, this would have far greater public impact than the trial and sentencing of an ordinary young man for similar reasons.

AMERICAN TREATMENT OF PACIFISTS IN WORLD WAR II

Given that the Allied governments claimed to be fighting for liberal principles, excessively harsh repression of pacifists might well have backfired on them. Moreover, committed pacifists represented a very small portion of the population, around one in every 200 in the United States, so posed no great threat to the effective prosecution of the war. Thanks to vigorous lobbying by the Historic Peace Churches, the Mennonites, American Friends (Quakers), and the Church of the Brethren, the Selective Service Act passed in September 1940 contained provisions for exemption from military service on religious grounds, though not on those of conscience alone. Conscientious objectors could choose between noncombatant service in the military, prison, or accepting work under the Civilian Public Service (CPS) scheme established in February 1941, under whose aegis all three Historic Peace Churches and the Roman Catholic Church established and administered work camps. Just over 6,000 conscientious objectors were imprisoned, and a further 15,700 draft evaders. Between 25,000 and 50,000 opted for noncombatant military service, either formally or informally, and the 12,000 Seventh-Day Adventists among them won numerous military decorations for bravery. In all, CPS set up 67 camps and 130 detached service units, which provided work for 12,000 conscientious objectors from over 200 religious denominations and some nonsectarians. Most worked on conservation projects or farming, though about 2,000 went to mental hospitals and training schools, and 500 served as experimental human guinea pigs in medical or scientific research.

Rev. Arle Brooks, Statement upon His Conviction for Draft Evasion, January 1941

My conscience forbade me to register under the Selective Service Training Act of 1940.

The present wars are the natural product of our economic system and our way of living. Preparation for war is easier than going through the painful process of reconstructing our social and economic system and improving our own lives.

Wars destroy human lives. Individuals have the right to give their lives for a cause. They have no right to take the life of another. Wars are destructive, futile and immoral. Wars have failed to solve the basic problems of the world. Participation in war to settle international or national differences does not do justice to man's intelligence.

The people of America are filled with fear of an invasion. Are we so morally weak that the power of one man could control 130,000,000 free people? Free people cannot be enslaved unless they allow it. Are we too lethargic to find a better method of settling international affairs? The people of India have almost won their freedom from Great Britain without firing a shot. They are willing to give their lives but refuse to take the lives of the British soldiers.

Democracy does not mean a blind following of the will of the majority. In a democracy the minority has a right and a duty to follow its ideals. Sometimes the ideals of the minority have eventually been adopted by the majority. [Mohandas] **Gandhi** said, "We are sunk so low that we fancy that it is our duty and our religion to do what the law lays down. If man will only realize that it is unmanly to obey laws that are unjust no man's tyranny will enslave him. . . . It is

Gandhi: Mohandas Gandhi (1869–1948), prominent leader of the movement for the political independence of India from British rule, a noted exponent of nonviolent tactics and civil disobedience

a superstition and an ungodly thing to believe that an act of a majority binds a minority." I believe in and have worked for the brotherhood of man, which is the highest form of democracy and which recognizes no national boundaries. I have worked with children of the slums of Chicago, with **transients**, **relief people**, prisoners in Texas, and with **sharecroppers** in Mississippi.

Conscription is a denial of the democracy for which I have worked. Under conscription the individual is required blindly to obey his superior officer even when the superior officer is wrong. **Hitler** could not wage his war if the people of Germany had not granted him the power to conscript them. The United States is adopting a system of conscription which may produce tyranny instead of freedom.

I cannot agree with those who believe that registration is a mere **census.** Registration is the first and necessary step in conscription. My conscience will not permit me to take this first step.

As a minister I could have received complete exemption. I felt it my moral duty to do all within my power to protest against conscription which will eventually weaken and destroy democracy. I am not evading the draft. I am opposing it. I am defending democracy.

transients: people with no settled residence in the United States, who might or might not be immigrants from elsewhere
relief people: individuals who were receiving government welfare benefits
sharecroppers: tenant farmers, frequently living in extreme poverty, who gave their landlords a share of the crop they produced as a form of rent for the land they farmed
census: an official survey and listing of the population

Source: *Christian Century* 58 (5 February 1941), 181.

AFTERMATH

Upon his release, Brooks still refused to carry a draft card, for which he was once more arrested and imprisoned for a further two years. Once freed, Brooks worked for the Prison Service Committee of the American Friends Service Committee, serving throughout 1946 as its secretary. This body originally provided practical and spiritual assistance to imprisoned wartime conscientious objectors, endeavors that sparked off broader initiatives to improve the conditions of all prisoners and nationwide prison visitation programs. In 1947, Brooks and his wife were among the founders of an utopian community at Celo Valley in North Carolina, where he died of a brain tumor in 1953.

ASK YOURSELF

1. In more totalitarian countries, such as Germany, Italy, or Japan, press censorship would have prevented the reporting of Brooks's speech. Conscription, he charged, was a step toward "tyranny instead of freedom," and its imposition would eventually weaken American democracy. Could one argue that Brooks was paradoxically using the freedoms of American democracy to attack his country for not being sufficiently democratic?
2. Like many political radicals of the 1930s, Brooks blamed wars upon economic injustices, condemning them, moreover, as "destructive, futile and immoral." How convincing was his analysis of the underlying causes of World War II? Are there circumstances in which war is the only means of righting injustices?
3. Why did the United States government not simply refuse to respond to Brooks's challenge, and fail to prosecute him for draft evasion?

TOPICS TO CONSIDER

1. If all potential soldiers took the same stance as Brooks did, there would be no wars. Yet in all countries, the majority of individuals drafted for military service sign up, however reluctantly, and accept their enlistment in the armed forces. In most wars, a substantial number of young men volunteer to join the military, even if they are not compelled to do so, and may even face substantial public and social pressure to take this course of action. How likely is it that pacifism will ever become the majority viewpoint, in the United States or any other country?
2. Although staunch pacifists who traditionally refused to fight, members of the Society of Friends, often known as Quakers, for which Brooks was working in 1940, won genuine renown and respect for their extensive wartime provision of medical facilities in hazardous conditions on and behind the battlefields, and for their work with refugees, for which the American and British Friends received the 1947 Nobel Peace Prize. From the mid-1930s onward, they were particularly active in assisting Jewish refugees from German persecution, and often criticized American diplomats and other officials for being reluctant to admit more such refugees to the United States. When pacifists in nongovernmental organizations work with state authorities that are waging war, are they implicitly collaborating with the power structures responsible for wars?
3. Brooks's position was by no means the only one for pacifists. In Western nations overall, World War II generated far less in the way of pacifist dissent than World War I (1914–1918) 25 years earlier. In Britain, the events of March 1939, when **Adolf Hitler** effectively annexed what remained of Czechoslovakia, shattered the existing peace movement. To many on the left, the need to oppose Nazism seemed so compelling as to justify war and conscription. During the **phony war** of September 1939 to April 1940, some peace activists still supported a negotiated settlement, but once British Premier **Winston Churchill** decided to reject this option, most fell silent; often they even came to believe that prevailing circumstances made war, however distasteful, the lesser evil. Some former pacifists metamorphosed into staunch supporters of the war. Many turned their attention primarily to humanitarian efforts to alleviate the impact of war by helping refugees, campaigning for food shipments to the peoples of occupied Europe, and attempting to moderate such military tactics as the saturation bombing of cities with large civilian populations. Could such undertakings be considered more useful than the three years Brooks spent in prison?

Further Information

Appelbaum, Patricia. *Kingdom to Commune: Protestant Pacifist Culture between World War I and the Vietnam Era.* Chapel Hill: University of North Carolina Press, 2009.

Brooks, Arle. *We the Offenders.* Philadelphia: American Friends Service Committee, 1947.

Brooks, Arle, and Robert J. Leach. *Help Wanted: The Experience of Some Quaker Conscientious Objectors.* Philadelphia: American Friends Service Committee, 1940, reprint ed. New York: Garland Publishers, 1972.

Brooks, Arthelia. *The Backside of Yesterday: My Life and Work.* Burnsville, NC: Celo Valley Books, 1994.

Chatfield, Charles with Robert Kleidman. *The American Peace Movement: Ideals and Activism.* New York: Twayne, 1992.
Frazer, Heather T., and John O'Sullivan. *We Have Just Begun Not to Fight: An Oral History of Conscientious Objectors in Public Service during World War II.* New York: Twayne, 1996.
Gara, Larry, and Lenna Mae Gara, eds. *A Few Small Candles: War Resisters of World War II Tell Their Stories.* Kent, OH: Kent State University Press, 1999.
Goodall, Felicity. *A Question of Conscience: Conscientious Objection in the Two World Wars.* Stroud, UK: Sutton Publishing, 1997.
Hicks, George L. *Experimental Americans: Celo and Utopian Community in the Twentieth Century.* Urbana: University of Illinois Press, 2001.
Mollin, Marian. *Radical Pacifism in Modern America: Egalitarianism and Protest.* Philadelphia: University of Pennsylvania Press, 2006.

Web Site

Swarthmore College Peace Collection. http://www.swarthmore.edu/ Library/peace/.

Films and Television

Conscience and the Constitution (2000). Corporation for Public Broadcasting. http://www.pbs.org/itvs/thegoodwar/resources.html.
The Farmer at War (1943). Columbia Pictures and the U.S. Office of War Information.
The Good War and Those Who Refused to Fight It (2000). Corporation for Public Broadcasting. http://www.pbs.org/itvs/thegoodwar/resources.html.
The Pacifist Who Went to War (2002), directed by David Neufeld. National Film Board of Canada. http://onf-nfb.gc.ca/eng/collection/film/?id=51136.

20. Conditions in the Warsaw Ghetto: The Diary of Stanislaw Rozycki, November–December 1941

INTRODUCTION

As a prelude to embarking on the outright extermination of Jews in Germany and occupied Europe, in 1940 German authorities established ghettos, segregated areas for Jews alone, in most East European cities and towns. Jews from areas further west were deported to these. The largest such ghetto was that in Warsaw, the Polish capital, under German occupation since September 1939, where more than 450,000 Jews were at one point confined. The official food allocation for ghetto Jews was 300 calories a day; housing was overcrowded and often unheated in winter, and sanitation was basic. One Polish Jew normally resident in Warsaw, Stanislaw Rozycki, made his way back from Lwow to the Warsaw ghetto. In his diary, Rozycki described the brutal conditions prevailing there.

KEEP IN MIND AS YOU READ

1. Rozycki was one of a Jewish resistance group within the ghetto, the *Oynes Shabes* (Sabbath Joy), led by historian Dr. Emanuel Ringelblum (1900–1944), who decided to keep a historical record of what was happening there. It included several dozen economists, historians, poets, sociologists, rabbis, and social workers.
2. The survivors of this group buried thousands of the documents they had collected in August 1942, when mass deportations of surviving Jews to Treblinka extermination camp had been in progress for several weeks, and it was clear that their chances of living much longer were slim.
3. Around 100,000 Jews in the Warsaw ghetto died of starvation and disease before deportations began in July 1942.
4. At the time he was writing, Rozycki knew that his long-term chances of surviving the war were poor.

Emanuel Ringelblum (1900–1944) was a Polish Jewish historian, specializing in the history of Polish Jewry from the Middle Ages to the 18th century. A social worker and political activist, he gave assistance to Polish Jews expelled from Germany in 1938 and 1939. With his family, he was among those Jews whom German officials resettled in and confined to the Warsaw Ghetto—the city's Jewish quarter—from 1939 onward, where they were crowded together in extremely harsh conditions. While living there, Ringelblum was the originator and leader of the Oyneg Shabbos or Oneg Shabbat (Joy of the Sabbath) venture, an initiative to gather together and preserve all possible documentation on the Warsaw ghetto, to serve as lasting testimony to the lives and experiences of that community, even if most of its residents died during the war. Setting an example, he himself kept an extensive diary, handwritten in ink on cheap paper. This diary was among many thousands of pages of documents of every kind, including underground newspapers, accounts of life in the ghetto, diaries, letters, ration coupons, chocolate and candy wrappers, concert and lecture announcements, and other written materials, that Ringelblum and his colleagues collected between September 1939 and January 1943. Initially, they intended these to serve as raw data for a book. As evidence of widespread German killings of Polish Jews reached the ghetto's inhabitants in 1942, they focused particularly upon collecting materials documenting the persecution and extermination of European Jews, some of which were smuggled out to the Western allies.

With their prospects of surviving the war ever poorer, and well-founded fears mounting that German officials intended to empty and destroy the ghetto, either killing its inhabitants or consigning them to concentration camps, at intervals in late 1942 and January and April 1943, the Oyneg Shabbos group buried three caches of documents, protected in metal cans, in different locations within the ghetto. Ringelblum and his family escaped from the ghetto later in 1943, finding temporary refuge elsewhere, shortly before the Warsaw ghetto uprising in which its remaining inhabitants fought bitterly against German forces, inflicting heavy casualties before their own ultimate destruction. In March 1944, however, an informer betrayed the Ringelblums, and German occupying forces executed them, together with the family that had sheltered them. Ringelblum's diary was among the 25,000 pages of documents retrieved when a survivor of the Oyneg Shabbos group unearthed two of the three hoards of documents—the third is still missing—from the ruins of Warsaw, one in 1946 and the second in 1950. With the rest of the archive, it was subsequently preserved in the Zydowski Instytut Historyczny/Jewish Historical Institute, Warszawa, Poland.

Source: First page of entry of March 18, 1941 (File no. ARG I 446, former Ring. I/504). Zydowski Instytut Historyczny/Jewish Historical Institute, Warszawa, Poland. Used by permission.

The Diary of Stanislaw Rozycki, November–December 1941

I entered. I crossed the boundary not just of a residential quarter but of a zone of reality, because what I saw and experienced cannot be understood by our reason, thoughts, or imagination. . . the very act of crossing reminded me of some **rite of passage**, a ceremonial initiation, a crossing into the realm of **Hades**.

. . . . The majority are nightmare figures, ghosts of former human beings, miserable destitutes, pathetic remains of former humanity. One is most affected by the characteristic changes which one sees in their faces: as a result of misery, poor nourishment, the lack of vitamins, fresh air and exercise, the numerous cares, worries, anticipated misfortunes, suffering and sickness, their faces have taken on a skeletal appearance. The prominent bones around their eye sockets, the yellow facial colour, the slack pendulous skin, the alarming emaciation and sickliness. And, in addition, this miserable, frightened, restless, apathetic and resigned expression like that of a hunted animal. I pass my closest friends without recognizing them and guessing their fate. Many of them recognize me, come up to me and ask curiously how things are 'over there' behind the walls—there where there is enough bread, fresh air, freedom to move around, and above all freedom. . . .

On the streets children are crying in vain, children who are dying of hunger. They howl, beg, sing, moan, shiver with cold, without underwear, without clothing, without shoes, in rags, sacks, flannel which are bound in strips round the emaciated skeletons, children swollen with hunger, disfigured, half conscious, already completely grown-up at the age of five, gloomy and weary of life. They are like old people and are only conscious of one thing: 'I'm cold', 'I'm hungry'. They have become aware of the most important things in life that quickly. Through their innocent sacrifice and their frightening helplessness the thousands upon thousands of these little beggars level the main accusation against the proud civilization of today. Ten per cent of the new generation have already perished: every day and every night hundreds of these children die and there is no hope that anybody will put a stop to it.

There are not only children. Young and old people, men and women, **bourgeois** and **proletarians**, intelligentsia and business people are all being declassed and degraded. . . . They are being gobbled up by the streets on to which they are brutally and ruthlessly thrown. They beg for one month, for two months, for three months—but they all go downhill and die on the street or in hospitals from cold, or hunger, or sickness, or depression. Former human beings whom no one needs fall by the wayside: former citizens, former 'useful members of human society'.

I no longer look at people; when I hear groaning and sobbing I go over to the other side of the road; when I see something wrapped in rags shivering with cold, stretched out on the ground, I turn away and do not want to look. . . . I can't. It's become too much for me. And yet only an hour has passed. . . .

For various reasons standards of hygiene are terribly poor. Above all, the fearful population density in the streets with which nowhere in Europe can be remotely compared. The fatal over-population is particularly apparent in the streets: people literally rub against each other, it is impossible to pass unhindered through the streets. And then the lack of light, gas,

rite of passage: a formal ceremony or ritual, to mark a major change in one's life or circumstances
Hades: in Greek mythology the underworld or hell, home of the dead
bourgeois: middle class
proletarians: working class

and heating materials. Water consumption is also much reduced; people wash themselves much less and do not have baths or hot water. There are no green spaces, gardens, parks; no clumps of trees and no lawns to be seen. For a year no one has seen a village, a wood, a field, a river or a mountain: no one has breathed slightly better air for even a few days this year. Bedding and clothing are changed very rarely because of the lack of soap. To speak of food hygiene would be a provocation and would be regarded as mockery. People eat what is available and when it is available. Other principles of nutrition are unknown here. Having said all this, one can easily draw one's own conclusions as to the consequences: stomach typhus and typhus, dysentery, tuberculosis, pneumonia, influenza, metabolic disturbances, the most common digestive illnesses, lack of vitamins and all other illnesses associated with the lack of bread, fresh air, clothing, and heating materials. Typhus is systematically and continually destroying the population. There are victims in every family. On average up to a thousand people are dying each month. In the early morning the corpses of beggars, children, old people, young people and women are lying in every street—the victims of the hunger and the cold. The hospitals are so terribly overcrowded that there are 2–3 patients lying in every bed. Those who do not find a place in a bed lie on the floor in rooms and corridors. The shortage of the necessary medicines in sufficient quantities makes it impossible to treat the sick. Moreover, there is a shortage of food for the sick. There is only soup and tea. . . .

While this cruel struggle for a little bit of bread, for a few metres of living space, for the maintenance of health, energy and life is going on, people are incapable of devoting much energy and strength to intellectual matters. In any case, there are German restrictions and bans. Nothing can be printed, taught or learnt. People are not allowed to organize themselves or exchange cultural possessions. We are cut off from the world and from books. We are not allowed to print anything, neither books nor newspapers; schools, academic institutions etc. are not permitted to open. There are no cinemas, radio, no contacts with world culture. Nothing reaches us, no products of the human spirit reach us. We have to smuggle in not only foodstuffs and manufactured goods, but also cultural products. For that reason everything which we achieve in this respect is worthy of recognition irrespective of how much there is or what it consists of. . . .

Source: J. Noakes and G. Pridham, eds., *Nazism 1919–1945: Volume 3: Foreign Policy, War and Racial Extermination: A Documentary Reader* (Exeter: University of Exeter Press, 1988), 460–462. Used by permission of the University of Exeter Press.

AFTERMATH

In the first episode of popular resistance to German rule, in January 1943 the remaining inhabitants of the ghetto decided to stage a revolt and resist the deportations. Despite their debilitated condition, they fought ferociously, and the Germans did not suppress the rebellion until April 1943. Most of the members of the Oyneg Shabbes group, including Emanuel Ringelblum, the moving spirit behind its activities, were killed during the war. In August 1942, they had buried the documents they had collected in different three locations, in three milk cans and ten metal boxes. One cache was unearthed in 1946 and a second in 1940, leaving only one milk canister—reportedly buried beneath the current site of the Chinese embassy in Warsaw—still unaccounted for. The surviving 25,000 pages of documents became a major historical source on the Jewish community in Poland during World War II. It is unclear whether or not Rozycki survived the war; his name is not listed in the Yad Vashem list of **Holocaust** deaths.

ASK YOURSELF

1. The final sentence of this diary excerpt gives Rozycki's reason for writing it. Why did he and others in the Oyneg Shabbes group feel that recording their experiences and those of their community was so significant an undertaking that, despite all their other problems, they devoted an enormous amount of energy to writing about their situation and collecting other relevant documentary materials? Are people who lack documentary records of some kind people without history?
2. Rozycki's picture of the state of the Jews in the Warsaw ghetto in late 1941 is extremely depressing. Yet almost 18 months later, those who remained still found the resilience, courage, and energy to mount an uprising against German rule. Does this suggest that he exaggerated the sufferings of the Jewish population? Or had the physically and emotionally weaker residents already succumbed to hunger and illness by early 1943?
3. Only one of the people who helped to hide the Oyneg Shabbes documents survived. If he had not done so, they would probably have remained lost after the war. In what ways would their absence have affected historians' ability to reconstruct that period?
4. Within the Warsaw ghetto, wealthy Jews with access to funds or valuables they could trade for black-market food, fuel, or other goods, were far better equipped to survive, at least temporarily, than those with nothing. Rozycki's diary does not recognize or at least does not emphasize this, even though his own family did have resources it could liquidate or barter. Nor does he mention that some forms of cultural life, including recreation centers, schools, libraries, and a symphony orchestra, continued to function. Why did he omit these aspects of ghetto life?

TOPICS TO CONSIDER

1. One of the more controversial aspects of the Oyneg Shabbes archive was its documentation of discreditable behavior by both Jews and non-Jews. Jews and Poles alike sometimes collaborated with the German authorities, in particular by betraying Jews who were trying to conceal their Jewish identity. Within the ghetto and in concentration camps, particular Jewish inmates served as *kripos* (criminal police) or *kapos* (camp police), thereby winning extra rations and other privileges, and enhancing their chances of survival. When the war was over, historians sometimes came under community pressure to ignore such matters, since dredging up memories of them might call into doubt the genuine sufferings of others and disturb the equilibrium of often fragile social harmony with fruitless recriminations. Should such behavior ever be passed over in silence, even in the interests of what is seen as the greater social good? Is historical memory sometimes an act of collective forgetting, or at least of remembering only selected facts?
2. The Nazi regime were responsible for the deaths of many other civilians besides Jews, including German political opponents of all kinds, many noncombatants in occupied countries, prisoners of war, slave laborers from across Europe, gypsies, the mentally handicapped, and others considered socially or physically degenerate and therefore unfit to live. The term "Holocaust," however, normally refers to the

killing of 6 million European Jews by the Nazis and their collaborators. Should the fact that **Adolf Hitler's** regime tried to exterminate the entire European Jewish community, in an act of what is now termed genocide, make a difference to our perceptions of those deaths?

Further Information

Berg, Mary. *The Diary of Mary Berg: Growing Up in the Warsaw Ghetto*. London: Oneworld Publications, 2007.

Engelking, Barbara, and Jacek Leociak. *The Warsaw Ghetto: A Guide to the Perished City*. Trans. Emma Harris. New Haven, CT: Yale University Press, 2009.

Fritz, Stephen G. *Ostkrieg: Hitler's War of Extermination in the East*. Lexington: University Press of Kentucky, 2011.

Grynberg, Michal, ed. *Words to Outlive Us: Voices from the Warsaw Ghetto*. Trans. Philip Boehm. New York: Metropolitan Books, 2002.

Gutman, Israel. *Resistance: The Warsaw Ghetto Uprising*. Boston, MA: Houghton Mifflin, 1994.

Kassow, Samuel D. *Who Will Write Our History? Emanuel Ringelblum, the Warsaw Ghetto, and the Oyneg Shabes Archive*. Bloomington: Indiana University Press, 2007.

Kermish, Joseph, ed. *To Live with Honor and Die with Honor: Selected Documents from the Warsaw Underground Ghetto Archives "O.S."* Jerusalem: Yad Vashem, 1986.

Ringelblum, Emanuel. *Notes from the Warsaw Ghetto*. New York: McGraw Hill, 1958.

Snyder, Timothy. *Bloodlands: Europe Between Hitler and Stalin*. New York: Basic Books, 2010.

Web Sites

"Let the World Read and Know": Witness to the Holocaust—The Oneg Shabbat Archives. http://www1.yadvashem.org/yv/en/exhibitions/ringelbum/intro.asp.

Poetry in Hell: Yiddish Poetry in the Ringelblum Archives. http://poetryinhell.org.

Films and Television

A Day in the Warsaw Ghetto: A Birthday Trip in Hell (1991). Kuper Productions Limited.

Kanal (2003), starring Teresa Izewska, Tadeusz Janczar, and Wienczyslaw Glinski.

The Pianist (2002), starring Adrien Brody and Thomas Kretschmann.

Uprising (2001), starring Leelee Sobieski, Hank Azaria, David Schwimmer, Jon Voight, and Donald Sutherland.

The Wall (1982), starring Tom Conti and Lisa Eichhorn.

The Warsaw Ghetto (c. 1940–1943) (2009). Quality Information Publishers.

21. The Final Solution: Minutes of the Wannsee Protocol, January 20, 1942

INTRODUCTION

From the time the Nazis took power in Germany in 1933, all Jews who fell under their authority were subjected to ever-increasing persecution, designed to make their lives unbearable and if possible to drive them out of Germany. Nazi ideology, as expressed in Führer **Adolf Hitler's** testament of faith *Mein Kampf* (1924), held that Jews—defined not simply as those of the Jewish faith, but also nonpracticing individuals of Jewish ancestry—were *Untermenschen* (subhumans) who were genetically ineradicably inferior to those of **Aryan** (white Caucasian or Teutonic) blood. Indeed, according to this perspective all races—Slavs, Latins, Asians, Arabs, and Africans— were graded according to a hierarchy, with Aryans in the top rank, and Jews at the bottom, together with gypsies.

On July 31, 1941 *Obergruppenführer* **Reinhard Heydrich**, head of the *Reichssichterheitshauptamt* (RSHA), the major German security and police authority, obtained authority from Reischsmarshall **Hermann Goering** to devise and implement an overall "final solution" to the Jewish problem. Heydrich summoned a group of German ministers, civil servants, and security officials to a conference eventually held at scenic Wannsee House, near Berlin, in January 1942. Detailed minutes were kept of this meeting, written by SS Lt. Col. **Adolf Eichmann**, head of the RSHA Jewish section. Able-bodied male and female Jews were to be evacuated east to labor camps, to be worked to death. Since, according to crude Darwinian logic, anyone who survived would be the fittest of their race, and hence the nucleus of a future Jewish renascence, they would "have to be treated accordingly," ambiguous language that undoubtedly meant killed. Jews over 65 would be sent to a special old-age camp. The administrator of the General Government, namely, German-occupied Poland, volunteered those Jews under his control as the first Jewish population scheduled for evacuation under this scheme.

In all, these discussions envisaged disposing of over 11 million Jews throughout Europe. Effectively, the meeting sanctioned genocide on a massive scale, where possible to be implemented by methods adapted from industrial processes designed to handle large quantities of raw materials or animals. Overall the Nazis were responsible for the deaths of around 6 million Jews, mass murders subsequently termed the **Holocaust**.

KEEP IN MIND AS YOU READ

1. This document was kept extremely secret, and did not become public until after the war had ended.
2. The Wannsee Protocol envisaged the ultimate elimination not just of Jews then resident in Germany and territories occupied by Germany, but also in countries allied with Germany, neutral, or not yet conquered.
3. By the beginning of 1942, most German Jews had been driven out of Germany proper and those central European areas, especially Czechoslovakia and Austria, under German rule since the late 1930s. Those who could not emigrate or escape as refugees were first confined to Jewish ghetto areas of their own cities, and then shipped eastward, usually under dreadful conditions in cramped and overcrowded railroad cars at the mercy of the weather and without sanitation, food, or water, and forced into camps or ghettos in other cities close to the main railway lines, such as Lodz and Warsaw.
4. German conquests, especially in the east, greatly enhanced what the Nazi regime saw as its Jewish problem. About three million Jews lived in Poland, two-thirds in the area under German occupation and one-third in the portion first occupied by Soviet troops, and then taken over by German forces in June 1941. The Soviet Union likewise had a substantial Jewish population, many residing in the Ukraine and other western areas first invaded by Germany.

Minutes of the Wannsee Protocol, 20 January 1942

Top Secret

Minutes of Meeting

This meeting of top German officials with responsibility for Jews under their control was held on 20 January 1942 in Berlin, at Grossen Wannsee No. 56/58. Those present included **Gauleiter** Dr. Meyer and **Reichsamtleiter** Dr. Leibbrandt of the Ministry for the Occupied Eastern territories; Dr. Stuckart, Secretary of State of the Ministry for the Interior; Secretary of State Neumann, Plenipotentiary for the Four Year Plan; Dr. Freisler, Secretary of State of the Ministry of Justice; Dr. Bühler, Secretary of State of the Office of the General Government [of Poland]; Dr. Luther, Under Secretary of State of the Foreign Office; SS-**Oberführer** Klopfer of the Party Chancellery; **Ministerialdirektor** Kritzinger of the Reich Chancellery; SS-**Gruppenführer** Hofmann of the Race and Settlement Main Office; SS-Gruppenführer Müller and SS-**Obersturmbannführer** Eichmann of the Reich Main Security Office; SS-Oberführer Dr. Schöngarth of the Security Police, Security Department, Commander of the Security Police, Security Department (SD) of the General Government [of Poland]; SS-**Sturmbannführer** Dr. Lange of the Security Police, Security Department, Commander of the Security Police and the Security Department for the General-District of Latvia, in his capacity as deputy to the Commander of the Security Police and the Security Department for the Reich Commissariat **"Eastland."**

Gauleiter: regional Nazi Party leader
Reichsamtleiter: departmental director
Oberführer: colonel
Ministerialdirektor: permanent secretary
Gruppenführer: major general
Obersturmbannführer: lieutenant colonel
Sturmbannführer: major
"Eastland": occupied Eastern territories, including the Baltic states and much of Byelorussia

II

Obergruppenführer: General

At the beginning of the discussion Chief of the Security Police and of the SD, SS-**Obergruppenführer** Heydrich, reported that the Reich Marshal [Hermann Goering] had appointed him delegate for the preparations for the final solution of the Jewish question in Europe and pointed out that this discussion had been called for the purpose of clarifying fundamental questions. The wish of the Reich Marshal to have a draft sent to him concerning organizational, factual and material interests in relation to the final solution of the Jewish question in Europe makes necessary an initial common action of all central offices immediately concerned with these questions in order to bring their general activities into line. The Reichsführer-SS [Heinrich Himmler] and the Chief of the German Police (Chief of the Security Police and the SD) [Reinhard Heydrich] was entrusted with the official central handling of the final solution of the Jewish question without regard to geographic borders. The Chief of the Security Police and the SD then gave a short report of the struggle which has been carried on thus far against this enemy, the essential points being the following:

a) the expulsion of the Jews from every sphere of life of the German people,
b) the expulsion of the Jews from the living space of the German people.

In carrying out these efforts, an increased and planned acceleration of the emigration of the Jews from Reich territory was started, as the only possible present solution.

By order of the Reich Marshal, a Reich Central Office for Jewish Emigration was set up in January 1939 and the Chief of the Security Police and SD was entrusted with the management. Its most important tasks were

a) to make all necessary arrangements for the preparation for an increased emigration of the Jews,
b) to direct the flow of emigration,
c) to speed the procedure of emigration in each individual case.

The aim of all this was to cleanse German living space of Jews in a legal manner.

All the offices realized the drawbacks of such enforced accelerated emigration. For the time being they had, however, tolerated it on account of the lack of other possible solutions of the problem.

The work concerned with emigration was, later on, not only a German problem, but also a problem with which the authorities of the countries to which the flow of emigrants was being directed would have to deal. Financial difficulties, such as the demand by various foreign governments for increasing sums of money to be presented at the time of the landing, the lack of shipping space, increasing restriction of entry permits, or the cancelling of such, increased extraordinarily the difficulties of emigration. In spite of these difficulties, 537,000 Jews were sent out of the country between the takeover of power and the deadline of 31 October 1941. Of these

approximately 360,000 were in Germany proper on 30 January 1933
approximately 147,000 were in Austria (Ostmark) on 15 March 1939
approximately 30,000 were in the Protectorate of Bohemia and Moravia [formerly Czechoslovakia] on 15 March 1939.

The Jews themselves, or their Jewish political organizations, financed the emigration. In order to avoid impoverished Jews' remaining behind, the principle was followed that wealthy Jews have to finance the emigration of poor Jews; this was arranged by imposing a suitable tax, i.e., an emigration tax, which was used for financial arrangements in connection with the emigration of poor Jews and was imposed according to income.

Apart from the necessary **Reichsmark** exchange, foreign currency had to be presented at the time of landing. In order to save foreign exchange held by Germany, the foreign Jewish financial organizations were—with the help of Jewish organizations in Germany—made responsible for arranging an adequate amount of foreign currency. Up to 30 October 1941, these foreign Jews donated a total of around 9,500,000 dollars.

Reichsmark: German currency

In the meantime the Reichsführer-SS and Chief of the German Police had prohibited emigration of Jews due to the dangers of an emigration in wartime and due to the possibilities of the East.

III

Another possible solution of the problem has now taken the place of emigration, i.e. the evacuation of the Jews to the East, provided that the Führer gives the appropriate approval in advance.

These actions are, however, only to be considered provisional, but practical experience is already being collected which is of the greatest importance in relation to the future final solution of the Jewish question.

Approximately 11 million Jews will be involved in the final solution of the European Jewish question, distributed as follows among the individual countries: [The document proceeds to list the number of Jews living not only in states such as France, Hungary, and Rumania already currently under German occupation or control, but also in countries at war with Germany including Britain and Russia, allied with it, such as Italy, sympathetic but neutral, such as Spain and Portugal, and simply neutral, including Ireland, Sweden, and Switzerland.]. . . .

Under proper guidance, in the course of the final solution the Jews are to be allocated for appropriate labor in the East. Able-bodied Jews, separated according to sex, will be taken in large work columns to these areas for work on roads, in the course of which action doubtless a large portion will be eliminated by natural causes.

The possible final remnant will, since it will undoubtedly consist of the most resistant portion, have to be treated accordingly, because it is the product of natural selection and would, if released, act as a the seed of a new Jewish revival (see the experience of history).

In the course of the practical execution of the final solution, Europe will be combed through from west to east. Germany proper, including the Protectorate of Bohemia and Moravia, will have to be handled first due to the housing problem and additional social and political necessities.

The evacuated Jews will first be sent, group by group, to so-called transit ghettos, from which they will be transported to the East.

SS-Obergruppenführer Heydrich went on to say that an important prerequisite for the evacuation as such is the exact definition of the persons involved.

It is not intended to evacuate Jews over 65 years old, but to send them to an old-age ghetto—Theresienstadt is being considered for this purpose.

In addition to these age groups—of the approximately 280,000 Jews in Germany proper and Austria on 31 October 1941, approximately 30% are over 65 years old—severely wounded veterans and Jews with war decorations (Iron Cross I) will be accepted in the old-age ghettos. With this expedient solution, in one fell swoop many interventions will be prevented.

The beginning of the individual larger evacuation actions will largely depend on military developments. Regarding the handling of the final solution in those European countries occupied and influenced by us, it was proposed that the appropriate expert of the Foreign Office discuss the matter with the responsible official of the Security Police and SD.

In Slovakia and Croatia the matter is no longer so difficult, since the most substantial problems in this respect have already been brought near a solution. In Rumania the government has in the meantime also appointed a commissioner for Jewish affairs. In order to settle the question in Hungary, it will soon be necessary to force an adviser for Jewish questions onto the Hungarian government.

With regard to taking up preparations for dealing with the problem in Italy, SS-Obergruppenführer Heydrich considers it opportune to contact the chief of police with a view to these problems.

In occupied and unoccupied France, the registration of Jews for evacuation will in all probability proceed without great difficulty.

Under Secretary of State Luther calls attention in this matter to the fact that in some countries, such as the Scandinavian states, difficulties will arise if this problem is dealt with thoroughly and that it will therefore be advisable to defer actions in these countries. Besides, in view of the small numbers of Jews affected, this deferral will not cause any substantial limitation.

The Foreign Office sees no great difficulties for southeast and western Europe.

SS-Gruppenführer Hofmann plans to send an expert to Hungary from the Race and Settlement Main Office for general orientation at the time when the Chief of the Security Police and SD takes up the matter there. It was decided to assign this expert from the Race and Settlement Main Office, who will not work actively, as an assistant to the police attaché.

IV

[Intermarriages between Jews and non-Jews could give rise to problems in precisely who qualified as a Jew, and here it was proposed to follow the guidelines given in the earlier **Nuremberg Laws** of the 1930s, though in many cases exceptions and exemptions for meritorious conduct or the reverse were at least theoretically possible, as were compulsory sterilization and the forced dissolution of mixed marriages.]

With regard to the issue of the effect of the evacuation of Jews on the economy, State Secretary Neumann stated that Jews who are working in industries vital to the war effort, provided that no replacements are available, cannot be evacuated.

Nuremberg Laws: German legislation passed in 1935, depriving Jews of German citizenship, forbidding intermarriage between Jews and non-Jews, and forbidding Jewish participation in civic life

SS-Obergruppenführer Heydrich indicated that these Jews would not be evacuated according to the rules he had approved for carrying out the evacuations then underway.

State Secretary Dr. Bühler stated that the General Government would welcome it if the final solution of this problem could be begun in the General Government, since on the one hand transportation does not play such a large role here nor would problems of labor supply hamper this action. Jews must be removed from the territory of the General Government as quickly as possible, since it is especially here that the Jew as an epidemic carrier represents an extreme danger and on the other hand he is causing permanent chaos in the economic structure of the country through continued black market dealings. Moreover, of the approximately 2-1/2 million Jews concerned, the majority is unfit for work.

State Secretary Dr. Bühler stated further that the solution to the Jewish question in the General Government is the responsibility of the Chief of the Security Police and the SD and that his efforts would be supported by the officials of the General Government. He had only one request, to solve the Jewish question in this area as quickly as possible.

In conclusion the different types of possible solutions were discussed, during which discussion both Gauleiter Dr. Meyer and State Secretary Dr. Bühler took the position that certain preparatory activities for the final solution should be carried out immediately in the territories in question, in which process alarming the populace must be avoided.

The meeting was closed with the request of the Chief of the Security Police and the SD to the participants that they afford him appropriate support during the carrying out of the tasks involved in the solution.

Source: Minutes of the Wannsee Protocol, 20 January 1942. Available at House of the Wannsee Conference Memorial and Educational Site. http://www.ghwk.de/engl/protengl.htm.

AFTERMATH

Implementation of the Wannsee Protocol began virtually immediately. Indeed, in December 1941, one month before this meeting took place, an extermination camp modeled on those established for Germany's earlier 1939–1941 euthanasia program for adults and children defined as physically or mentally unfit to live, had been set up at Chelmo, near Lodz in Poland. More quickly followed. In the first half of 1942, three more began operations, at Belzec, Sobibor, and Treblenka, to where over the next two years much of Poland's Jewish population was deported. Later that year, three huge labor camps and extermination centers, established in Polish territory, supplemented them: Majdanek, Auschwitz I (first established as a concentration camp in May 1940), and Auschwitz II or Auschwitz-Birkenau. Existing concentration camps, such as that first established at Dachau, Bavaria, in 1933, were now equipped with additional extermination facilities, gas chambers—for some reason those at Dachau were never used, though numerous deaths nonetheless occurred there—and also mass crematoria for the disposal of bodies. Others, such as Buchenwald, served as staging camps for the death camps themselves.

Between 1941 and 1945, about 6 million European Jews, between 100,000 and 200,000 gypsies, perhaps 100,000 Poles, and thousands of Soviet prisoners of war, communists, homosexuals, Jehovah's Witnesses, criminals, and others considered socially undesirable were murdered. New arrivals were separated into those unfit or unable to work, who were killed immediately, usually in large gas chambers; and those considered sufficiently able-bodied to do useful labor. Not all were gassed: some were worked to death, often finally succumbing to starvation and illness, and some fell victim to the casual brutality of camp guards and work-party supervisors.

ASK YOURSELF

1. Killing and disposing of several million people is not a simple undertaking. How many individuals were in some way involved in German efforts to destroy Europe's German population?

2. Initially, Nazi tactics focused on forcing German Jews to emigrate, usually in return for substantial payments. What factors were responsible for the switch to measures designed to eliminate all European Jews?
3. The Wannsee Conference was a businesslike gathering, summoned to decide on how best to implement a "final solution" that would eventually eliminate all European Jews, even those in neutral or enemy countries who were presumably beyond the Nazi reach at that time. Perhaps the most chilling aspect was the degree to which all present took it for granted that the extermination of all European Jews was an entirely acceptable goal, which none saw fit to question. What tangible and concrete advantages, if any, was Nazi Germany likely to gain by killing Europe's entire Jewish population?
4. The Wannsee Protocol was somewhat evasive in its references to Jewish deaths, using the slightly squeamish euphemism that, of those Jews assigned to forced labor, "doubtless a large portion will be eliminated by natural causes," a tactful intimation that many would essentially be worked to death in conditions so abysmal as to guarantee a high mortality rate. In an even more mealy mouthed circumlocution, any survivors would "have to be treated accordingly," a remarkably oblique intimation that they would be executed. Does this language suggest that those German officials attending this meeting had a vestigial bad conscience, or merely that they were cautious when creating a documentary record of their decision?

TOPICS TO CONSIDER

1. Some revisionist historians on the far right, most notably David Irving, have sought to use the Wannsee memorandum as evidence that in reality the Nazis did not intend to murder Jews en masse, but simply to use them as forced laborers, and argue this meeting bore no relation to the contemporaneous establishment of extermination camps, many though not all of whose victims were Jews. Given remarks on the expected mortality rates among such laborers and the need to eliminate the survivors, together with comments by the administrator of the General Government (formerly Poland) that most of the estimated 2.5 million Jews in his area whom he wished to take priority under this scheme were in any case unfit for work, this interpretation seems remarkably strained. Why have some historians strenuously tried to deny the reality of Nazi efforts to eliminate all Jews in Europe?
2. Irving has also suggested that German Führer Adolf Hitler remained unaware of the establishment and operations of labor and extermination camps and the factory-style mass murders that took place in them. Given the Nazi regime's authoritarian character, with fierce competition and backstabbing the rule among its highest echelons, meaning that every top leader was liable eagerly to inform Hitler of any instance in which a rival disregarded the Führer's authority, it is inconceivable that enterprises on this scale, involving numerous high officials, could for several years have been implemented without his knowledge. Even if the final solution had been implemented behind Hitler's back, would this make any difference to historians' understanding of it?
3. Austria has passed legislation making it a serious crime to deny the occurrence of the Holocaust by claiming that Hitler's Germany did not deliberately murder

several million Jews. Many historians believe that such laws are mistaken, and the only effective way to refute such allegations is through rational argument, not by restricting freedom of speech. Which approach do you consider preferable?

Further Information

Bartov, Omer. *Germany's War and the Holocaust: Disputed Histories.* Ithaca, NY: Cornell University Press, 2003.

Breitman, Richard. *The Architect of Genocide: Himmler and the Final Solution.* New York: Alfred A. Knopf, 1991.

Cohn-Sherbok, Dan. *Understanding the Holocaust: An Introduction.* New York: Cassell, 2002.

Dawidowicz, Lucy S. *The Holocaust and the Historians.* Cambridge, MA: Harvard University Press, 1981.

Engel, David. *The Holocaust: The Third Reich and the Jews.* New York: Longman, 2000.

Friedlander, Henry. *The Origins of Nazi Genocide: From Euthanasia to the Final Solution.* Chapel Hill: University of North Carolina Press, 1995.

Gerwarth, Robert. *Hitler's Hangman: The Life of Heydrich.* New Haven, CT: Yale University Press, 2011.

Goldhagen, Daniel Jonah. *Hitler's Willing Executioners: Ordinary Germans and the Holocaust.* New York: Alfred A. Knopf, 1996.

Jewish Black Book Committee. *The Black Book: The Nazi Crime against the Jewish People.* Reprint ed. New York: Nexus Press, 1981.

Longerich, Peter. *Heinrich Himmler: A Life.* New York: Oxford University Press, 2012.

Longerich, Peter. *The Unwritten Order: Hitler's Role in the Final Solution.* Stroud: Tempus, 2001.

McCale, Donald M. *Hitler's Shadow War: The Holocaust and World War II.* New York: Cooper Square Press, 2002.

Roseman, Mark. *The Wannsee Conference and the Final Solution: A Reconsideration.* New York: Metropolitan Books, 2002.

Web Sites

"The 'Final Solution.'" The Holocaust: A Learning Site for Students: United States Holocaust Memorial Museum. http://www.ushmm.org/outreach/en/article.php?ModuleId=10007704.

Genocide Under the Nazis. BBC: World Wars in-depth. http://www.bbc.co.uk/history/worldwars/genocide/.

House of the Wannsee Conference: Memorial and Educational Site. http://www.ghwk.de/engl/kopfengl.htm.

Yad Vashem: The Holocaust. http://www1.yadvashem.org/yv/en/holocaust/index.asp.

Films

The Boy in the Striped Pyjamas (2008), starring Sheila Hancock and David Thewlis.

The Devil's Arithmetic (1999), starring Kirsten Dunst, Brittany Murphy, and Paul Freeman.

Out of the Ashes (2002), starring Christine Lahti, Beau Bridges, and Richard Crenna.

Sophie's Choice (1982), starring Meryl Streep and Kevin Kline.

22. Conspiracies of Silence: Oral History of Martin Koller on German Massacres of Jews

INTRODUCTION

Until early 1942, the Nazi regime relied on ad hoc measures, primarily mass killings and other brutal atrocities, to reduce the numbers of Jews in the east. One of the most dramatic of these was the two-day massacre of 33,000 Ukrainian Jews at Babi Yar ravine near Kiev over September 28–29, 1941, but throughout the area under German occupation thousands of smaller-scale episodes occurred. Polish and Russian partisans who offered resistance to German occupation were treated equally harshly. By the end of 1941, between 500,000 and 1,000,000 Jews had died. German leaders nonetheless felt that such uncoordinated measures had hardly dented the problem, and a more systematic strategic approach was essential. Shooting, the most common method of execution, was moreover somewhat inefficient, and subjected those who wielded the guns to some stress.

Martin Koller, born in 1923, was the son of a Protestant pastor who had fought in World War I at Verdun. His father revered combat soldiers but disliked Hitler and the Nazis. In 1939, Koller, who wanted to learn to fly, applied to join the **Luftwaffe**, the German air force. He became a skilled pilot, flying tactical reconnaissance missions on the Eastern front, where he learned by chance of one massacre of the Jews.

KEEP IN MIND AS YOU READ

1. At the time this episode occurred, Koller was only 19 or 20 years of age and extremely inexperienced. He was a lieutenant, the lowest rank in the officer corps, and took pride in belonging to the German military.
2. Koller recorded these memories of World War II in the mid-1980s, more than 40 years after these events took place. This incident had clearly lodged itself deeply in his mind.
3. Some post–World War II critics charged that all Germans claimed to have had no idea of how the Nazi regime treated the Jews. This was not true of Koller, who had no doubt, moreover, that he had stumbled on an "injustice" he found "so monstrous that I couldn't grasp it."

4. If Koller's report had reached higher authorities, he might well have been arrested himself. His superior officer was trying to ensure his safety.
5. Koller later recalled how small units within the German military had a very strong sense of camaraderie, "almost like a family," which helped them endure and sometimes survive very adverse circumstances.

Oral History of Martin Koller

After three weeks' leave, I took a train back to the front. Something happened to me en route that I still think about to this day: my encounter with injustice. At one point, a strange officer came into our compartment. He was amiable and polite, and introduced himself in broken German with a Baltic accent as a lieutenant from Latvia. We talked about all kinds of things, everyday subjects, war and private life. And then he said he'd taken part in shooting Jews somewhere in the Baltic. There had been more than 3,000 of them. They had had to dig their own mass grave "as big as a soccer field." He told me all this with a certain pride.

Wehrmacht: German military

I was completely at a loss and asked stupid questions like "Is that really true? How was it done? Who led this operation?" And I got a precise answer to each. It was true; anybody could check it; they did it with 12 men armed with machine pistols and one machine gun. The ammunition had been officially provided by the **Wehrmacht**, and a German SS lieutenant, whose name he didn't remember, had been in command. I became confused and started to sweat. This just didn't fit into the whole picture—of me, of my country, of the world, of the war. It was so monstrous that I couldn't grasp it.

"Can I see your identification?" I asked, and "Do you mind if I note it down?" He didn't mind, and was just as proud of what he had done as I was of the planes I'd shot down. And while I scribbled his strange name down on a cigarette package, my thoughts somersaulted: either what he's told me is true, in which case *I* can't wear a German uniform any longer, or he's lying, in which case *he* can't wear a German uniform any longer. What can, what should I do? My military instinct told me, "Report it!"

I returned to the squadron and was right back in action. I flew and fought as best I could. I didn't think about the Latvian's story. Then my orderly came to collect my laundry. That's when I found the shirt I'd worn on the train. I emptied the pockets, and there was that piece of paper with the address. I finally had to do something. The same night, I wrote a report to the squadron leader.

The commander remained seated behind his desk when I came, still in my flight suit, to report. He pointed to my paper: "What do you want me to do with this?" I shrugged and ventured, "Forward it, of course, Captain."

I had done my duty; now I could forget it. Then I received a message that told me I was to report to Colonel Bauer at Simferopol in the Crimea two days later.

The colonel had my report in hand. With all the stamps and entries on it, it had become an official document.

"I wanted to speak with you," said the colonel, "before I act on this report. Do you understand that?" "No, Colonel," I said stupidly.

He leaned back, took a deep breath, and said, "My dear young friend. . . ." My dear young friend? No superior had ever said that to me before. I felt good.

"What do you think I should do with this?" I sat stiffly on the sofa and didn't know what to do with the question. What does a colonel do with reports? I swallowed and said, "I don't know, Colonel. Maybe forward it?"

The colonel slid closer and put an arm around my shoulder. I smelled his good aftershave and was frozen. "Son," said the colonel with a frown. Son? He was talking like my father, but I liked it. Then he offered me cigarettes. We smoked. The colonel said, "If I pass on this report, you'll be jumping out of the frying pan and into the fire."

Then he nudged me and said, "You know what, son?" I shook my head and looked at him. "If we get out of this alive, we'll go home and clean up that mess. Thousands, believe me, thousands will be with us!"

And the colonel picked up my report, held it over the wastebasket and asked, "So, do you want to jump into the fire, or do you want to be there with the rest of us, for the big clean-up? Can I quash your report?" "Yes, sir, *Herr Oberst,*" I said, convinced.

"Thank you, Lieutenant," the colonel said, and dropped my report about the Latvian lieutenant and the execution of the Jews into the wastebasket.

Source: From the book *Voices from the Third Reich: An Oral History* by Johannes Steinhoff, Peter Pechel, and Dennis Showalter, eds., 344–346.

AFTERMATH

In 1943 Koller's airplane crashed in the Crimea, somewhere between the Russian and German lines, hit by an antitank shell as he tried to strafe a Russian artillery emplacement. Seriously wounded in one leg, he was dragged to safety by German soldiers, who fought off a Russian patrol to rescue Koller and his radio operator. The accident ended his flying career, as his leg was amputated at the hip in hospital. After the war, he became a West German civil servant, living at Troisdorf in the Rhineland. He does not mention whether his paternal colonel also survived the war.

ASK YOURSELF

1. Realistically, was there any way in which Koller, or even his superior officers in the German military, could have prevented further massacres of Jews and other so-called undesirables in territory under German occupation? Or indeed have sabotaged the operations of the death camps and concentration camps?
2. Many ordinary soldiers who took part in German atrocities claimed that they were only following the orders of their superiors, and would have been punished had they disobeyed these. How far can or should individuals be expected to go in terms of jeopardizing not just their own lives and safety but also those of their families or others close to them, in order to oppose or prevent actions that they believe to be unjustifiably cruel or morally wrong? Are those who try to remain ignorant of wrongdoing as guilty as those who commit crimes?
3. In every country, some individuals took considerable risks to help at least some Jews escape the **Holocaust**. Well-known examples include the German businessmen Oskar Schindler, who was responsible for the survival of several hundred Jews working at Auschwitz; the Japanese diplomat Chiune Sugihara, who issued visas that allowed up to 10,000 Jews to leave Latvia; and the Swedish diplomat Raoul Wallenberg, who saved the lives of thousands of Hungarian Jews in 1944. Substantial numbers of ordinary people also jeopardized their own safety when they

RAOUL WALLENBERG (1912–1947?)

Wallenberg, who came from a wealthy Swedish banking family, was part-owner and international director of the Central European Trading Company, a Stockholm-based business that traded extensively with Hungary, and travelled frequently to that country. Hungary was allied with Germany and, though facing defeat, and in the spring of 1944 began mass deportations of Hungarian Jews to concentration camps, at the rate of 12,000 daily. In 1944 Wallenberg became first secretary of the Swedish legation in Budapest, a position he used to issue thousands of Swedish protective passports to Hungarian Jews facing deportation camps. Although not legal, these documents won acceptance from German and Hungarian officials, some of whom were bribed. Wallenberg also rented 32 buildings in Budapest, declared them Swedish territory under diplomatic immunity, and housed around 10,000 Jews in them. Swiss diplomats, British intelligence operatives, and many others, 350 in all, assisted these efforts. When Soviet Red Army forces approached Budapest in January 1945, they detained Wallenberg as a suspected spy, possibly hoping to exchange him for Soviet defectors in Sweden, and he disappeared into Russian custody, his subsequent fate unknown. Soviet officials reported his death in March 1945, but later stated Wallenberg died in prison in Moscow in July 1947. As late as 1987 there were reported sightings of him in Soviet jails. Russian government enquiries in 1991 and 2000 claimed he was shot in July 1947 for unspecified crimes, but others dispute this. Wallenberg's ultimate fate still remains mysterious.

helped Jews to hide or escape. In most cases, those who did so had little to gain and a good deal to lose. What motivated such "good Gentiles," as they were later known?

4. After Germany's defeat, Nazi officials who had ordered the deaths or mistreatment of Jews and others in their power, together with those who had carried out their directives, stood trial for crimes against humanity. Some received death sentences and others lengthy prison terms. The newly created Jewish state of Israel also put enormous effort into tracking down Nazis responsible for atrocities of various kinds who had escaped from Germany at the end of World War II. The most spectacular such operation was the capture in 1960 of Adolf Eichmann, one of the leading architects of the **Final Solution**, whom Israeli intelligence agents tracked down to Argentina and kidnapped. He was tried, convicted, and executed by hanging in 1962. By 2010, even those who were teenagers at the end of World War II, old enough to have taken part in atrocities, were reaching their 80s. Does there come a point at which efforts to identify and punish such criminals should be abandoned? Or should they not be given up until the last perpetrator has died? Can any such trials ever truly compensate for the deaths and sufferings of the victims? If not, what is their purpose?

TOPICS TO CONSIDER

1. In the first decade of the 21st century, Americans who failed to take any effective action to prevent the government of President George W. Bush committing gross human rights abuses against American citizens and even more against non-Americans when prosecuting the war against terror have been compared to those "good Germans" who did little or nothing to stop Hitler's persecution of the Jews. Is this analogy well-founded?

2. In 1948 the United Nations passed a Convention on the Prevention and Punishment of the Crime of Genocide, defined as systematic efforts to destroy all or part of an ethnic, religious, racial, or national group. Since that time, mass murders of entire population groups that fit this description have occurred in many countries and conflicts, notably Biafra in Nigeria, the Congo, Cambodia, Rwanda, Chechnya, the former Yugoslavia, and Darfur in Sudan. Despite growing interest in the subject on the part of international and nongovernmental organizations, effective measures to prevent genocide and successful trials and convictions of those accused of perpetrating genocide have been rather few. Most nations are reluctant to intervene with military force to end such abuses in other states. In today's international system, are there any practicable means of preventing genocide? How does one define the difference between genocide and other methods of warfare?

Further Information

Bierman, John. *Righteous Gentile: The Story of Raoul Wallenberg, Missing Hero of the Holocaust.* New York: Viking, 1981.

Crowe, David M. *Oskar Schindler: The Untold Account of his Life, Wartime Activities, and the True Story Behind the List.* New York: Basic Books, 2007.

Fensch, Thomas, ed. *Oskar Schindler and His List: The Man, the Book, the Film, the Holocaust, and its Survivors.* Forest Dale, VT: Paul S. Eriksson, 1995.

Gilbert, Martin. *The Righteous: The Unsung Heroes of the Holocaust.* New York: Henry Holt, 2003.

Kershaw, Alex. *The Envoy: The Epic Rescue of the Last Jews of Europe in the Desperate Closing Months of World War II.* New York: Da Capo Press, 2010.

Levine, Hillel. *In Search of Sugihara: The Elusive Diplomat Who Risked His Life to Rescue 10,000 Jews from the Holocaust.* New York: Free Press, 1996.

Satloff, Robert. *Among the Righteous: Lost Stories from the Holocaust's Long Reach into Arab Lands.* New York: PublicAffairs Press, 2006.

Wallenberg, Raoul. *Letters and Dispatches1924–1944.* New York: Arcade Publishers, 1995.

Web Sites

Davidson, David. "Looking for the Good Germans." *American Heritage Magazine,* June/July 22, no. 4 (1982): http://www.americanheritage.com/articles/magazine/ah/1982/4/1982_4_90.shtml.

The Holocaust: Crimes, Heroes and Villains. http://auschwitz.dk.

Prevent Genocide International. http://www.preventgenocide.org/prevent/.

Righteous Gentiles: Holocaust Education and Archive Research Team. http://www.holocaustresearchproject.org.

Films and Television

Good Evening, Mr. Wallenberg (2002), starring Stellan Skarsgård and Katharina Thalbach.

Miracle at Midnight (1998), starring Sam Waterston, Mia Farrow, and Justin Whalin.

The Only Way (1970), starring Jane Seymour and Ebbe Rode.

The Power of Conscience: The Danish Resistance and the Rescue of the Jews (1994). Direct Cinema Education.

Schindler's List (1993), starring Liam Neeson, Ralph Fiennes, and Ben Kingsley.

23. The Internment of Japanese Americans: Recollections of Mary Tsukamoto

INTRODUCTION

Mary Tsukamoto (1915–1998), then Mary Tsuruko Dakuzaku, was born in San Francisco, the second of five children of parents who had emigrated from Okinawa. In 1925, the family moved to Florin, California, where they operated a market garden, growing strawberries for the nearby cities. Their children had to attend segregated schools, where Dakuzaku's teachers themselves paid part of the cost of her subsequent education at the College of the Pacific, Stockton, inspiring her to become a teacher herself. In 1936, Dakuzaku married Alfred Tsukamoto, the son of another Florin market gardener; the couple had a daughter the following year. By the time of Pearl Harbor, Mary Tsukamoto, then 27, was a leader in the Japanese American Citizens League, which soon assumed the responsibility of serving as an intermediary between the government and Japanese Americans, some of whom spoke no English.

KEEP IN MIND AS YOU READ

1. On February 19, 1942 President **Franklin D. Roosevelt** issued Executive Order 9066, authorizing the United States military to ban any American citizen from a zone 60 miles wide along the American West Coast, extending from Washington state, through Oregon and California, and inland into Arizona.
2. The continental United States had a population of 47,000 Issei, foreign-born Japanese who had emigrated there before 1924 and were therefore ineligible for citizenship under existing immigration rules and approximately 80,000 Nisei, American citizens of Japanese ancestry, most of whom had been born in the country.
3. During 1942, 110,000 Japanese Americans were forced to leave their homes and relocated to hastily constructed camps within and outside the affected states. Unless they joined the American military, most remained there until January 1945.
4. The U.S. government deported and interned Japanese Americans living on the West Coast en masse, children included, making no effort to identify those who might represent a genuine security threat and separate these from loyal American citizens.

Recollections of Mary Tsukamoto

I do remember Pearl Harbor Day. I was about twenty-seven, and we were in church. It was a December Sunday, so we were getting ready for our Christmas program. We were rehearsing and having Sunday School class, and I always played the piano for the adult **Issei** service. Of course, because there were so many Japanese, all of it was in Japanese; the minister was a Japanese, and he preached in Japanese. But after the service started, my husband ran in. He had been home that day and heard on the radio. We just couldn't believe it, but he told us that Japan attacked Pearl Harbor. I remember how stunned we were. And suddenly the whole world turned dark. We started to speak in whispers, and because of our experience [with earlier anti-Japanese sentiment] in Florin, we immediately sensed something terrible was going to happen. We just prayed that it wouldn't, but we sensed that things would be very difficult. The minister and all of the leaders discussed matters, and we knew that we needed to be prepared for the worst.

Then, of course, within a day or two, we heard that the **FBI** had taken Mr. Tanigawa and Mr. Tsuji. I suppose the FBI had them on their list, and it wasn't long before many of them were taken. We had no idea what they were going through. We should have been more aware. One Issei, Mr. Iwasa, committed suicide. So all of these reports and the anguish and the sorrow made the whole world very dark. Then rumors had it that we were supposed to turn in our cameras and our guns, and they were called in. Every day there was something else about other people being taken by the FBI. Then gradually we just couldn't believe the newspapers and what people were saying. And then there was talk about sending us away, and we just couldn't believe that they would do such a thing. It would be a situation where the whole community would be uprooted. But soon enough we were reading reports of other communities being evacuated from San Pedro and from Puget Sound. After a while we became aware that maybe things weren't going to just stop but would continue to get worse and worse.

Issei: Japanese Americans born in Japan
FBI: Federal Bureau of Investigation, in charge of internal American security
Hakujin: white

We read about President Roosevelt's Executive Order 9066. I remember the Japanese American Citizens League (JACL) people had a convention in San Francisco in March. We realized that we needed to be able to rise to the occasion to help in whatever way we could in our community. We came home trying to figure out just how we could do that. We had many meetings at night and the FBI was always lurking around. We were told we couldn't stay out after eight o'clock in the evening.

Meanwhile, **Hakujin** [white] neighbors were watching us and reporting to the FBI that we were having secret meetings. We were not supposed to meet after eight o'clock, but often we couldn't cut off our JACL meeting at eight o'clock, and so we would have tea or coffee and keep talking. We would be reported and the police would come. There were so many people making life miserable for us. Then we heard that we had been restricted to traveling five miles from our homes; it was nine miles to Sacramento, and at that time everything was in Sacramento, like doctors, banks, and grocery stores. So it just was a terrible, fearful experience. Every time we went anywhere more than five miles away, we were supposed to go to the Wartime Civilian Control Administration (WCCA) office in Sacramento, nine miles away, to get a permit. It was ridiculous.

A lot of little things just nagged at us and harassed us, and we were frightened, but even in that atmosphere I remember we frantically wanted to do what was American. We were Americans and loyal citizens, and we wanted to do what Americans should be doing. So we were wrapping Red Cross bandages and trying to do what we could to help our country. By May 1942, more than a hundred of our boys were already drafted. We worried about them, and they were worried about what was going to happen to their families. We knew what we wanted to do. We started to buy **war bonds**, and we took first aid classes with the rest of the Hakujin people in the community. We went out at night to go to these classes, but we worried about being out after eight o'clock. It was a frightening time. Every little rule and regulation was imposed only on the Japanese people. There were Italian and German people in the community, but it was just us that had travel restrictions and a curfew. . . .

I had anxieties for Grandpa and Grandma. They were old and had farmed all their lives, and after more than fifty years here, the thought of uprooting these people and taking them away from their farm and the things they loved was terrible. Grandpa growing tea and vegetables, and Grandma growing her flowers. It was a cruel thing to do to them in their twilight years. But we had to get them ready to leave, anxious for their health and their safety. And my daughter, who was five, had to be ready to go to school. Al [Tsukamoto] had had a hemorrhage that winter, so we all had our personal grief as well.

The **Farm Security Administration** told us that we should work until the very last moment. Yet we had to worry about selling our car and our refrigerator and about what we should do with our chickens and our pets. . . . I wrote to the President of the United States and the principal of the high school and the newspaper editors thanking them for whatever they did for us. I don't know if I was crazy to do this, but I felt that history was happening, and I felt that it was important to say good-bye in a proper way, speaking for the people who were leaving and trying to tell our friends that we were loyal Americans and that we were sorry that this was happening. We needed to say something, and that's what I did.

We left early in the morning on May 29, 1942. Two days earlier we sold our car for eight hundred dollars, which was just about giving it away. We also had to sell our refrigerator. But some wonderful friends came to ask if they could take care of some things we couldn't store. . . .

It happened so suddenly to our community. You know, we grew up together, we went through the hardships of the **Depression**, and then finally things were picking up. . . . These were our people, and we loved them. We wept with them at their funerals and laughed with them and rejoiced at their weddings. And suddenly we found out that the community was going to be split up. The railroad track was one dividing line, and Florin Road the other dividing line. We were going to Fresno; the ones on the other side went to Manzanar; and the ones on the west side went to Tule. The ones on the west and north went to Pinedale and Poston. We never dreamed we would be separated—relatives and close friends, a community. The village people, we were just like brothers and sisters. We endured so much together and never dreamed we would be separated. Suddenly we found out we wouldn't be going to the same place. That was a traumatic disappointment and a great sadness for us. We were just tied up in knots, trying to cope with all of this happening. I can't understand why they had to do this. I don't know why they had to split us up.

. . . .

I don't know, we had been a very happy family. When we left, we swept our house and left it clean, because that's the way Japanese feel like leaving a place. I can just imagine everyone's emotions of grief and anger when they had to leave, when the military police

war bonds: securities issued by the United States government to pay for the war effort, bought by Americans in massive numbers during World War II, who were encouraged to buy these as a patriotic duty

Farm Security Administration: government agency dealing with agriculture

Depression: the Great Depression of the 1930s, the longest and most severe economic downturn in American history

came and told them, "Get ready right now. You've got two hours to get ready to catch this train."

. . . . Nobody could take pets, and this was a sad thing for our daughter. There were tears everywhere; Grandma couldn't leave her flowers, and Grandpa looked at his grape vineyard. We urged him to get into the car and leave. I remember that sad morning when we realized suddenly that we wouldn't be free. It was such a clear, beautiful day, and I remember as we were driving, our tears. We saw the snow-clad Sierra Nevada mountains that we had loved to see so often, and I thought about God and about the prayer that we often prayed.

I remember one scene very clearly: on the train, we were told not to look out the window, but people were peeking out. After a long time on the train somebody said, "Oh, there's some Japanese standing over there." So we all took a peek, and we saw this dust, and rows and rows of **barracks**, and all these tan, brown Japanese people with their hair all bleached. They were all standing in a huddle looking at us, looking at this train going by. Then somebody on the train said, "Gee, that must be Japanese people in a camp." We didn't realize who they were before, but I saw how terrible it looked: the dust, no trees—just barracks and a bunch of people standing against the fence, looking out. Some children were hanging onto the fence like animals, and that was my first sight of the assembly center. I was so sad and discouraged looking at that, knowing that, before long, we would be inside too.

barracks: military-style mass accommodation

Source: From Mary Tsukamoto, "Jerome," in John Tateishi, *And Justice for All: An Oral History of the Japanese American Detention Camps* (Seattle: University of Washington Press, 1984), 3–13. Used by permission.

AFTERMATH

From the spring of 1942 until January 1945, Tsukamoto and her family were interned at a camp in Jerome, Arkansas. After the war, the Tsukamotos returned to Sacramento, and Mary spent 26 years as a teacher. Her dynamism was such that eventually a district elementary school was renamed in her honor. She also became a prominent activist in the campaign to win compensation for the Japanese American internees. In 1988 the surviving internees finally won a formal apology from the U.S. government, together with individual compensation of $20,000 apiece. Tsukamoto aggressively amassed artifacts and materials relating to Japanese American immigrants in California, a collection eventually donated to California State University, Sacramento, together with a major oral history collection on the Japanese American experience.

ASK YOURSELF

1. Japanese Americans in California had always been the targets of much racist resentment and suspicion. Local business competitors on the West Coast also coveted their property and economic assets. In the atmosphere of national hysteria immediately following Pearl Harbor, was superheated patriotism a plausible disguise for covert racism and economic exploitation?
2. In Hawaii 37.8 percent of the population were of Japanese descent and reasonably well-organized politically. Had all been interned, the islands' economy would have collapsed. The United States was also at war with Germany and Italy, but only a

few thousand among the many millions of American citizens of ethnic German and Italian ancestry were arrested and incarcerated on the grounds that they represented a security threat. German Americans and Italian Americans enjoyed substantial political clout. Did the fact that the West Coast Japanese American community was relatively small and noninfluential politically make it an easy, perhaps even symbolic, target for government harassment? Was the government taking the easy path in yielding to political pressure to disregard the civil rights of Japanese Americans? If so, what does this reveal about the administration of President Franklin D. Roosevelt?

3. At their own request, in 1943 about 8,000 of the Japanese American internees, including one in every four young Nisei liable to serve in the American military, were repatriated to Japan. Nonetheless, 33,000 Nisei joined the U.S. armed forces, where most served in all-Nisei regiments, which became renowned for their courage in battle, and 6,000 of them worked in military intelligence. What accounted for the diametrically opposite decisions different young Japanese American men chose to make?
4. Mary Tsukamoto recorded her recollections when she was prominent in the campaign to obtain compensation for surviving Japanese American internees. How might this have affected both what she included in her reminiscences and also what she might have chosen not to record?

TOPICS TO CONSIDER

1. In late 1944 the U.S. Supreme Court paved the way for the release of the internees when it decided that the existing Executive Order had given the government only the authority to remove Japanese Americans from the West Coast, but not to imprison the evacuees, leaving undecided the question whether additional legislation to do so would be constitutionally invalid. Why did the Supreme Court take more than two years to issue this decision?
2. Since September 11, 2001, many Americans have shown intense fear and suspicion of Muslim Americans and immigrants of Middle Eastern or South Asian descent, regarding all as potential terrorists. On many occasions, the U.S. government has also ridden roughshod over the civil rights of individuals and groups American officials believe may threaten the country's security. Are there any discernible parallels between the current position of Muslim Americans and that of Japanese Americans during World War II? Can one ever justify destroying or ignoring democratic values in the interests of defending democracy?

Further Information

Daniels, Roger. *Concentration Camps, North America: Japanese in the United States and Canada during World War II.* Updated ed. Malabar, FL: Krieger Publications, 1993.

The Florin Japanese American Citizens League Oral History Project, California State University, Sacramento, California.

Harth, Erica, ed. *Last Witnesses: Reflections on the Wartime Internment of Japanese Americans.* New York: Palgrave, 2001.

Hayashi, Brian Masaru. *Democratizing the Enemy: The Japanese American Internment.* Princeton, NJ: Princeton University Press, 2004.

Irons, Peter. *Justice at War.* Berkeley: University of California Press, 1993.
Kashima, Tetsuden. *Judgment without Trial: Japanese American Imprisonment during World War II.* Seattle: University of Washington Press, 2003.
The Mary Tsukamoto Japanese American Collection, California State University, Sacramento, California.
Murray, Alice Yang, ed. *What Did the Internment of Japanese Americans Mean?* New York: St. Martin's Press, 2000.
Okihiro, Gary Y. *Whispered Silences: Japanese Americans and World War II.* Seattle: University of Washington Press, 1996.
Robinson, Greg. *By Order of the President: FDR and the Internment of Japanese Americans.* Cambridge, MA: Harvard University Press, 2001.
Shimabukuro, Robert Sadamu. *Born in Seattle: The Campaign for Japanese American Redress.* Seattle: University of Washington Press, 2001.
Weglyn, Mishi Nichiura. *Years of Infamy: The Untold Story of America's Concentration Camps.* Updated ed. Seattle: University of Washington Press, 1996.

Web Sites

Exploring the Japanese American Internment. http://www.asianamericanmedia.org/jainternment/.
The Japanese American Archival Collection. http://library.csus.edu/collections/jaac/overview.html.
Japanese American National Museum. http://www.janm.org/.

Films

American Pastime (2007), starring Aaron Yoo, Olesya Rulin, and Carlton Bluford.
Come See the Paradise (1991), starring Dennis Quaid, Tamlyn Tomita, and Sab Shimono.
Unfinished Business (1984), starring Amy Hill, Gordon Hirabayashi, Fred Korematsu, and Min Yasui.

24. Roy M. "Max" Offerle Recalls Working on the Burma–Thailand "Death" Railway

INTRODUCTION

After Pearl Harbor, Japanese troops swept through much of Southeast Asia and by mid-1942 had taken prisoner around 140,000 European and North American and 180,000 Chinese, Filipino, Indian, and other Asian troops. Roy M. "Max" Offerle, born in Texas in 1921, was among 668 American soldiers of the Second Battalion captured on the Indonesian island of Java in March 1942. Recovering from amoebic dysentery, he was set to work on the Burma–Thailand Railway and sent to 18 Kilo[meter] Camp, where his elder brother Oscar, who later died of a tropical ulcer, also worked.

KEEP IN MIND AS YOU READ

1. Japan had signed—but not ratified—the 1929 Geneva Convention governing conditions for prisoners of war (POWs), and in 1942 pledged to observe it in its spirit. This convention forbade forcing POWs to undertake grueling forced labor.
2. Most POWs in Japanese hands were generally assigned to labor camps, working on industrial, construction, mining, and agricultural enterprises. Conditions were usually poor, with inadequate food, clothing, and medical facilities, primitive sanitation, and overcrowded accommodation.
3. About 50,000 Australian, British, Dutch, and American POWs and around 250,000 local Asian slave laborers worked on the railway linking Rangoon and Bangkok, the capitals of Burma and Thailand. About one-third of Western prisoners and almost half the Asians laborers died working on the "death railway," often from horrific tropical ulcers, cholera, dysentery, malaria, or other diseases.

Roy M. "Max" Offerle Recalls Working on the Burma–Thailand "Death" Railway

Basically, 18 Kilo was like one of the many camps we were to be in the future. You're talking about, like, maybe three, four, five thousand men in these camps, a lot of men. They had long huts made out of bamboo frames tied together with atap, which are leaves wrapped over thin pieces of bamboo about three feet long. They'd leave the walls open, and they had atap leaf roofs that were then overhanging. . . . The men worked hard because they knew they were off as soon as they moved a meter of dirt. After we got accustomed to pick-and-shovel work and carrying dirt, we would finish at three or four o'clock in the afternoon.

Well, then the Japs just gave us a larger quota. So we went to a meter-and-a-tenth, a meter-and-a-quarter, a meter-and-a-half per man per day. Later on up country, they went to two meters of dirt. When they went to one-and-a-half meters of dirt, you'd get in about dark. Two meters of dirt would get you in at about ten or eleven o'clock at night. They eventually went to this, and by then, too, we got food that didn't have all of your vitamins. You weren't keeping your strength up. The men's physical strength gradually wore down and our quotas gradually went up, which set us up for disease and sickness and a lot of the things that were to follow.

At this time, our group, which was one of the largest groups of Americans working on the railroad, hadn't yet experienced real hardship. We were getting a little sickness, some malaria, maybe a few people hurt. From 18 Kilo we went to 80 Kilo Camp. Now, we had larger quotas to meet. We were up in a lot more jungle. Conditions were not so good. We were farther away, so supplies were harder to get up there. We got away from canteens and extra food that you could buy.

From 80 Kilo, which was a smaller camp, we went to 100 Kilo, which was a larger camp. Incidentally, we were at 85 Kilo Camp for a while—80, 85, 100. But 100 Kilo Camp seemed to be a larger camp. I believe it was in 100 Kilo Camp where we got the full brunt of the rainy season. When you talk about rainy season in Burma, you're talking about three or four months where it comes out like you're pouring it from a bucket, day in and day out. It's possibly three or four hundred inches of rain in a season. Actually, creeks and rivers form, and you can almost watch vegetation grow. The rainy or monsoon season turned everything to soup or mud. They couldn't get supplies up there easily. Then the speedup on work came. We went from one meter, to a meter-and-a-half, to two meters of dirt per day. Well, the men's health broke down. We started getting lots of malaria, beriberi, dysentery, and tropical ulcers, because it seemed that the germ that causes tropical ulcers was more prevalent in the rainy season. We started getting a multitude of diseases.

The more people that got sick, the less the Japs had for working parties, so more sick people had to work. They'd set a quota of men everyday that had to go out, and they'd fill it. . . . This **kumi** of fifty men that I was in was originally all sergeants, and it was down after the rainy season started to thirteen or fourteen men. That didn't mean they were all dead; some of them were, but most of them were just sick. They were sick enough that if they had been in the United States, they'd have been in an isolation ward with a nurse twenty-four hours a day. Yet here they were in a bamboo hut in the rainy season eating a little rice and water stew; no medication and no one to take care of them, except our own medics and doctor who had no medicine.

kumi: group

This developed into a situation where we started losing men fast. . . .

Source: Robert S. La Forte and Ronald E. Marcello, eds., *Building the Death Railway: The Ordeal of American POWs in Burma, 1942–1945* (Wilmington, DE: Scholarly Resources, 1993), 171–173. Used by permission of Scholarly Resources.

AFTERMATH

Of the 668 Americans working on the Burma Railway, including Max's elder brother Oscar, 130 died there. Working conditions were worst from February to October 1943, when

Japanese officials launched a campaign to expedite completion of the railway, and those supervising its construction demanded still more work from men whose health and strength were rapidly declining. Many Allied soldiers who had been Japanese prisoners felt lifelong hatred for their captors.

ASK YOURSELF

1. The Japanese military ethos decreed that soldiers should fight to the death, so there was no real concept of POWs, who were despised as dishonorable cowards. Was this one reason why Japanese guards treated Western POWs so brutally?
2. High-ranking Japanese military officers often treated subordinates with great brutality, punishing them severely for offenses against military regulations, and superiors enforced stringent discipline upon inferiors. Lower-ranking soldiers in turn showed enormous callousness to those below them. What part did this chain reaction play in Japanese abuses of Western prisoners, especially harsh punishments for minor offenses?
3. Asian laborers on the "death railway" had substantially higher mortality rates than Western POWs. Was this evidence that Japanese guards in reality treated Westerners better than they did Asians?

TOPICS TO CONSIDER

1. The final year of the Pacific War, a period when revelations of Japanese abuses of American POWs were already appearing in print, was one of great savagery on both sides. American B-29 airplanes firebombed Japanese cities; American troops took Japanese ears, skulls, and hands as trophies in hand-to-hand fighting and massacred any Japanese who tried to surrender; and until the war's last day Japan executed American POWs in retaliation for the destruction of Japanese urban centers. Why had both sides in the Pacific War come to feel such atavistic hatred for each other?
2. How genuine was the post-1945 rapprochement between the United States and Japan? To what extent was it merely an alliance of convenience on either side?

Further Information

Crager, Kelly E. *Hell Under the Rising Sun: Texan POWs and the Building of the Burma–Thailand Death Railway.* College Station: Texas A & M University Press, 2008.

Daws, Gavin. *Prisoners of the Japanese: POWs of World War II in the Pacific.* New York: William Morrow, 1994.

Dower, John W. *War without Mercy: Race and Power in the Pacific War.* New York: Pantheon Books, 1986.

Havers, R.P.W. *Reassessing the Japanese Prisoner of War Experience: The Changi POW Camp, Singapore, 1942–45.* New York: RoutledgeCurzon, 2003.

Lomax, Eric. *The Railway Man: A POW's Searing Account of War, Brutality and Forgiveness.* New York: Norton, 1995.

McCormack, Gavan, and Hank Nelson, eds. *The Burma–Thailand Railway: Memory and History.* St. Leonard's, NSW, Australia: Allen and Unwin, 1993.

Rees, Laurence. *Horror in the East: The Japanese at War 1931–1945.* London: BBC Books, 2001.

Thompson, Kyle. *A Thousand Cups of Rice: Surviving the Death Railway.* Austin, TX: Eakin Press, 1994.

Towle, Philip, *Japanese Prisoners of War.* London: Hambledon Continuum, 2003.

Web Site

Japanese-POW Home Page. West Point. http://www.west-point.org/family/japanese-pow/.

Prisoners of War of the Japanese 1942–1945. http://www.pows-of-japan.net/

Films and Television

The Bridge on the River Kwai (1957), starring William Holden, Alec Guinness, and Jack Hawkins.

Horror in the East: Japan and the Atrocities of World War II (2000). BBC series. Directed by Laurence Rees.

A Town Like Alice (1956), starring Virginia McKenna, Peter Finch, and Kenji Takaki.

A Town Like Alice (1981). BBC. Starring Helen Morse, Bryan Brown, and Gordon Jackson.

25. Japan's Occupation of the Philippines: Claro M. Recto to Lt. Gen. Takaji Wachi, June 15, 1944

INTRODUCTION

Claro M. Recto (1890–1960), a nationalist Filipino lawyer and poet and longtime advocate of greater Philippine independence from the United States, served as both minority and majority floor leader in the Philippine Senate, switching parties in the mid-1930s in protest against the economic and military terms on which the United States was prepared to grant Philippine independence. In 1934, Recto presided over the convention that drafted the new Philippine Constitution. He was appointed to the Philippine Supreme Court in 1935. In January 1942, Recto was one of 32 leading Filipino politicians who accepted an invitation from occupying Japanese forces to join a government under their aegis headed by President José P. Laurel. From 1942 to 1943, Recto was commissioner for education, health, and public welfare; he then became minister of state for foreign affairs. In June 1944, Recto sent Takaji Wachi, director general of the Japanese Military Administration in the Philippines, a lengthy letter protesting against Japanese mistreatment and abuse of the population. He warned that, unless Japan granted the Philippines genuine independence, Filipinos would be unwilling to resist the anticipated American invasion of the islands.

KEEP IN MIND AS YOU READ

1. As Japanese forces moved into much of Southeast Asia in 1941 and 1942, they urged the leaders and peoples of the Philippines, the Dutch East Indies (present-day Indonesia), Malaya, Burma, and India to transfer their allegiance from their former imperialist overlords to Japanese-sponsored governments of national liberation and join a Japanese-led "Greater East Asia Co-Prosperity Sphere."
2. In October 1943, Japan formally recognized the independence of the Philippine government, but Japanese military forces remained in the Philippines and continued to exercise ultimate authority.
3. A significant indigenous Philippine anti-Japanese resistance movement existed in the Philippines. Between 1942 and 1944, the American military and intelligence operatives delivered equipment and supplies to Philippine guerrillas.
4. By mid-1944, it was clear that it was only a matter of time before the Allies would succeed in defeating Japan.

Claro M. Recto to Lt. Gen. Takaji Wachi, 15 June 1944

. . . one of the most important and pressing problems which confront the Filipino leaders today is how to convince the people of the reality of the Philippine independence in order that they may all support the government of the Republic and cooperate with the Japanese forces by living in peace, and engaging in useful and productive activities.

. . . . To this end, we have appealed to our people, trying to convince them that the independence of our country is real, that Japan's intentions in sponsoring and recognizing it were sincere, and that therefore they should have faith in their Government, assisting it in the work that it is doing, and cooperating to the fullest extent with the Japanese authorities in the Philippines for the accomplishment of the noble purposes envisaged in the said Pact of Alliance [between the Philippines and Japan].

If the Filipino leaders have not thus far been as successful in their efforts as might be desired, their failure is due to a number of causes, many of them traceable to certain practices which should have been discontinued after our independence was declared. Foremost among these is the kind of treatment to which, from the very beginning of the occupation of the Philippines, a great number of our people have been subjected. . . .

The practice, for instance, of slapping Filipinos in the face, of tying them to posts, of making them kneel in public, in the heat of the sun, and then beating them up—this upon the slightest fault, mistake or provocation, or without any other reason than failure to understand each other's language, is certain to create resentment on the part not only of the victim but also of the members of his family, his friends, and the general public. Even more serious is the practice of inflicting cruel, unusual and excessive punishment upon persons arrested on mere suspicion, during their investigation and before their guilt has been established. There have been even cases wherein, because of overcrowding in public places, such as **street-cars**, some Japanese, military or civilians who were inadvertently jostled or pushed, immediately slapped or beat the persons they thought guilty of pushing them.

Thousands of cases have been reported of people being either burned alive, killed at the point of the **bayonet**, beheaded, beaten without mercy, or otherwise subjected to various methods of physical torture, without distinction as to age or sex. Women and children below fifteen years are known to have been among those who were victims of such punishment. On many occasions, these killings and punishments were purposely done in public. . . . The unfortunate thing about all this is that in many cases the victims are really innocent of any crime but are punished merely upon suspicion or false denunciation by informers who harbor some private or personal grudge against them, or if they are guilty at all, do not deserve the excessive penalties inflicted upon them. Many have no fault at all except the fact that they have sons or brothers who are members of the "**guerrilla**" bands, or that they have given food to the latter, under threat of death or physical injuries. If they are released maimed, crippled, or sick they lament, and naturally the feeling is shared by their families and friends and by those who have knowledge of such things.

Many also are the cases wherein people have been arrested, taken for questioning, and then disappeared completely. No information is ever given to their relatives as to their whereabouts and the nature of the charges against them. . . .

street-cars: trams
bayonet: knife, dagger, or sword fixed on the end of a gun or rifle
guerrilla: unofficial civilian resistance fighter

The proclamation of the independence of the Philippines and the establishment of the Government of the Republic have not minimized these occurrences. They used to be done before but they have continued and continue to be done now. Most of the towns in the provinces are still actually governed by the commanders of the local Japanese garrisons, who are in the majority of cases with only the rank of Sergeant, and who treat the municipal mayors as their subordinates even to the extent of beating them publicly, and who continue to arrest and punish people without advising either the local civil authorities or the national government. The only sign of independence is the display of the Filipino flag. Even Japanese civilians consider themselves above Philippine laws, and Filipinos working in Japanese companies are sometimes punished summarily by their employers instead of being turned over to the appropriate Philippine authorities.

Another matter that needs to be mentioned is the practice of exacting collective responsibility for individual acts. If a "guerrilla" happens, for instance, to ride in a ***carretella*** with other peace-loving and law-abiding citizens who are completely unaware of the former's identity, and that "guerrilla" is arrested, all those who, by pure accident, are riding with him are also arrested, and punished in the same way. . . . Oftentimes there is no distinction between innocent and guilty, between old and young, or between strong and weak, to such an extent that there have been instances where women and children below fifteen have died as a result of the **concentration**, excessive punishments and outright executions. In fact, the innocent are usually the only ones who suffer, because the culprits manage to get out or otherwise escape punishment. . . .

carretella: cart
concentration: concentration camps

The incidents and practices which I have described are the cause of constant requests for assistance received by the Philippine Government from the people concerned, and in making representations in their behalf to the Japanese authorities, the Ministry of Foreign Affairs finds itself in the strange role of an embassy trying, none too successfully, to protect its nationals in the foreign country to which it is accredited.

It is for the foregoing reasons that many Filipinos seem to have but little faith in their government today. They doubt the reality of their country's independence. They consider it hardly anything more than display of the Filipino flag, since independence has not minimized the rigors of military rule, particularly in the provinces. . . . It becomes, therefore, an increasingly difficult task for the Filipino leaders to convince their people of the noble intentions of Japan in waging the present war and of the sincerity of the pronouncements of Japanese leaders that Japan came to the Philippines not as conqueror but as liberator. . . .

The existence of "guerrilla" elements or of outright banditry, particularly in the provinces, is not principally due to any fundamental political motive. It is doubtful whether those who are engaged in such activities are pro-American by conviction. . . . The main reason why many of them have turned "guerrillas" and bandits is not the desire that America should win the war, but simply because of the cruel treatment that they or their relatives, friends and countrymen had received at the hands of the Japanese and their fear that if they go out of hiding and live normal lives, they will be punished or put to death. . . .

. . . Is it not natural for a great portion of our people to believe that this Government is only a puppet, having no independent authority of its own, seeing that it is often subject to dictation or now violent interference by the Japanese authorities?

. . .

In view of the impending developments in the war situation, it is especially important to bring about more harmonious relations between Filipinos and Japanese and to arouse Filipino loyalty to the Republic. . . .

Asia for the Asians: well-known Japanese propaganda slogan

[T]he Filipino must be given a real stake in the war. He must be given something concrete to fight for—his land, his honor, his freedom and independence—something that will invest with living substance such high principles as **Asia for the Asians** or such large ideals as the establishment of the Co-Prosperity Sphere.

Source: Gregorio F. Zaide, ed., *Documentary Sources of Philippine History*, Volume 12 (Metro Manila, Philippines: National Book Store, Inc., Publishers, 1990), 57–74.

AFTERMATH

With the help of Philippine guerrillas, Allied forces regained control of most of the Philippines in April 1945, after a hard-fought campaign that lasted six months. In this campaign, 336,000 Japanese died and 12,000 were captured, in return for 14,000 American deaths and 48,000 wounded, a total of 64,000 American casualties. Up to 1 million Filipino civilians also lost their lives. When the war ended, Recto was accused of collaboration with Japan, arrested, and charged with treason. Rather than taking advantage of the subsequent amnesty proclamation by President Manuel Roxas, Recto insisted on fighting his case in the courts, pleading not guilty and winning acquittal after proving that he had maintained connections with the underground Philippine resistance movement. Elected to the Senate in 1949 and 1955, he ran unsuccessfully against Ramon Magsaysay for the presidency in 1957. Recto vehemently opposed allowing the United States to maintain military bases in the Philippines, causing the U.S. Central Intelligence Agency (CIA) to conduct black propaganda intended to undermine his presidential bid. When Recto died suddenly of a heart attack in 1960, rumor—probably ill-founded—suggested that the CIA had murdered him.

ASK YOURSELF

1. Decades after World War II, bitter memories of the behavior of Japanese occupiers lingered persistently among both elites and ordinary people throughout China and Southeast Asia. Why, despite using rhetoric that they sought to liberate Asia from Western colonial domination and establish a mutually beneficial Greater East Asia Co-Prosperity Sphere, did Japanese officials then treat subject peoples so harshly?
2. Like many leaders who had collaborated with occupying forces, Recto justified his behavior on the grounds that he did so in order to protect his own people and mitigate the harshness of Japanese rule. He could not have done so had he, like some Philippine politicians, gone into exile. Faced with such a choice, what would you do?
3. Throughout Asia, independence leaders often argued that there was no real difference between Western colonial rulers and the Japanese. How valid was this viewpoint?

TOPICS TO CONSIDER

1. In Asia, the issue of wartime collaboration with Japan was extremely sensitive after 1945, opening issues of imperialism and legitimacy most were reluctant to

scrutinize too closely. Returning colonial overlords rarely contemplated serious reprisals against those who had collaborated with the Japanese, and many who had joined Japanese-sponsored governments later enjoyed successful political careers. In Burma Lord Mountbatten, British commander-in-chief for Southeast Asia, specifically ordered that only Burmese responsible for actual atrocities during the Japanese occupation should be punished. In the Philippines, Allied commander-in-chief General Douglas MacArthur and President Sergio Osmeña issued similar instructions. Why did China, France, and various other European nations wreak far greater retribution and vengeance on their own nationals who had collaborated in Japanese or German rule?

2. Relatively few people in occupied countries had the option of fleeing into exile. For many, the first priority was the safety and survival of themselves and their families. What compromises, bargains, and arrangements with occupying forces did this involve them in, either tacitly or openly?

Further Information

Agoncillo, Teodoro A. *Burden of Proof: The Vargas-Laurel Collaboration Case.* Mandaluyong: University of the Philippines Press, 1984.

Duus, Peter, Ramon H. Myers, and Mark R. Peattie, eds. *The Japanese Wartime Empire, 1931–1945.* Princeton: Princeton University Press, 1996.

Li, Narangoa, and Robert Cribb, eds. *Imperial Japan and National Identities in Asia, 1895–1945.* New York: Routledge, 2003.

Mayo, Marlene J., and J. Thomas Rimer with H. Eleanor Kirkham. *War, Occupation, and Creativity: Japan and East Asia, 1920–1960.* Honolulu: University of Hawaii Press, 2001.

Recto, Claro M. *Three Years of Enemy Occupation: The Issue of Collaboration in the Philippines.* Manila: People's Publishers, 1946.

Smith, Robert Thompson. *Empires on the Pacific: World War II and the Struggle for the Mastery of Asia.* New York: Basic Books, 2001.

Tarling, Nicholas. *Imperialism in Southeast Asia: "A Fleeting, Passing Phase."* New York: Routledge, 2001.

Tarling, Nicholas. *A Sudden Rampage: The Japanese Occupation of Southeast Asia, 1941–1945.* Honolulu: University of Hawaii Press, 2001.

Thorne, Christopher. *The Issue of War: States, Societies, and the Coming of the Far Eastern Conflict of 1941–1945.* New York: Oxford University Press, 1985.

Web Site

Philippine History. http://www.philippine-history.org.

Films

Aishite Imasu 1941/Mahal Kita/I Love You (2004), starring Judy Ann Santos, Raymart Santiago, and Dennis Trillo.

The Call of the River (Panaghoy sa Suba) (2004), starring Cesar Montano, Juliana Palermo, and Jackie Woo.

Fires on the Plain (1959), starring Eiji Funakoshi, Osamu Takizawa, and Mickey Curtis.

Oro, Plata, Mata (*Gold, Silver, Death*) (1982), starring Cherie Gil, Sandy Andolong, and Liza Lorena.

Tatlong Taong Walang Diyos (1976), starring Nora Aunor, Christopher De Leon, and Bembol Roco.

26. Japanese Biological Experiments: Testimony of Anonymous Hygiene Specialist of Unit 731

INTRODUCTION

From the early 1930s until 1945, Japanese doctors habitually conducted a wide range of medical and biological experiments on prisoners of every nationality, to test the effectiveness of biological, chemical, and other weapons and human reactions to extreme stress of all kinds. Physicians performed unnecessary operations of every type on human subjects, often without anesthetics, exposed them to biological infection, chemical weapons, and extremes of heat, cold, starvation, thirst, and deprivation, and tested bayonets, guns, grenades, and other weapons on live prisoners. In 1932, the Japanese army established Unit 731 Liaison Office, an army medical unit, to undertake such enterprises. The headquarters for these medical researches was a sprawling complex of more than 150 buildings covering six square kilometers in Pingfang, Manchuria, the northeastern provinces that Japan seized from China in 1931 and made into the puppet Japanese satellite of Manchukuo, headed by former Chinese emperor **Pu Yi**. In 1994, an elderly onetime hygiene specialist from Japan who spent more than four years working at Pingfang and a Unit 731 sub-branch at Hailar, Manchuria, recounted some of his experiences.

KEEP IN MIND AS YOU READ

1. Until the 1980s, the existence of this program remained largely secret, deliberately concealed by the Western allies after World War II ended.
2. In the 1980s and 1990s, journalists, historians, and writers began to investigate the operations of Unit 731 and reveal some of their findings in print. Japanese officials destroyed many documents relating to it as they faced defeat in 1945, but many individuals associated with it were still alive and some agreed to be interviewed, though often anonymously.
3. Prisoners involved were known as *maruta,* a term that literally means blocks of wood. Between 3,000 and 10,000 prisoners, the majority Chinese and Koreans, some from Southeast Asia, and a few Australians, North Americans, and British, are believed to have died during Japanese experiments on human subjects. No such prisoners survived to recount their own stories.
4. The hygiene specialist whose testimony is given here was working in an ancillary role, assisting with human experiments rather than conducting them himself.

5. The Japanese are believed to have used germ warfare against Chinese targets in World War II, spreading bubonic plague, typhus, and other deadly diseases and causing between 200,000 and 580,000 Chinese deaths.

Testimony of Anonymous Japanese Hygiene Specialist of Unit 731, 1994

Five people were selected from each prefecture to become hygiene specialists, and I was one of **Iwate**'s five. In January 1941, we arrived in **Dalian**. We spent three months training in a unit there, and in March I was transferred to Pingfang and entered Unit 731. I was eighteen years old.

At the former unit we were always hit around by the senior soldiers, and it was rough. But at Unit 731, there was harmony. There were only medical officers and civilian doctors. There was no seniority among soldiers, no noncommissioned officers. The facilities and the food were good, and we didn't get hit.

From April to July we had general education. There were about two hundred of us in the same residence hall. Later, we worked at dissecting dogs. After I opened up a dog, the instructor explained the organs.

Part of our work was growing bacteria in glass dishes. They warned us not to touch the bacteria with our hands. We were told, "Don't remove the cover until you get the order to do so." We were ordered to apply the bacteria culture medium to the glass dish as a preparation stage and leave it overnight. In twenty-four hours, the bacteria would generate. The medium was sweet, like jelly, and we would eat it. The officer would scream at us, "If you eat that, you'll die."

Iwate: Japan's second largest prefecture, located on Honshu Island
Dalian: major city in Manchuria
Ishii: General Shirō Ishii (1892–1959), chief medical officer of the Japanese army, head of Unit 731

. . .

Ishii, the unit leader, was an exalted man—he was higher than the emperor. I thought that he was a great man because of the water filtration system he had invented. I almost cried from appreciation.

Sometimes I drove truckloads of Chinese for tests. Around May 1941—we were still wearing winter uniforms—we were told to load some Chinese prisoners into a truck. There was just a rush mat on the floor of the truck. We had guns, but I don't think they were loaded. The newest members of our group had less than half a year of service.

The officers told us where to take the Chinese. We pulled the canopy over the back of the truck and started out. There were between twenty and thirty of them. We drove for about three or four hours and we were told to stop and unload the Chinese. We were in an open plain; there was nothing around. The interpreter told the Chinese "Go!" and they were happy to be running around. They were all men, all built better than we were, some in good clothing with shoes, others in sandals. Some were coal carriers, still black with coal dust the way they had been when they were picked up. Others were dirty with the soil of whatever work they had been doing.

The truck went back empty. A couple of civilian employees and four or five soldiers stayed. A few days later, I carried another load of about the same number of people out there to the same place. The ones we had brought before were still there, lying huddled together on the ground in groups of five or six, blue with cold, begging, "Help . . . help." So we carried them by hand back to the truck. When we got back to the unit, we were ordered back to the **barracks**. That was the only time I ever carried anyone in such bad shape, but I made three or four trips out to the plain carrying prisoners. They were strong and healthy when we hauled them out there, but later they were shaking, screaming: "My stomach hurts!"; "I'm finished!"; I'm dying!"

barracks: military accommodation block

The third time I brought a load of Chinese out to the plain, there were two or three trucks that were returning empty stopped by the side of the road. I pulled my truck over, and there was an old man sitting there on a mat rush holding a skylark. I started up the truck again and heard some gunshots. I stopped and looked back, and the old man was lying dead. Later, I asked a researcher about it. He told me, "Don't ever say a word about that. He was a spy."

There was an airfield near the unit headquarters. There were lots of planes, and when they took off in the morning it was noisy. Planes from other units used to land there often. I was once told that a plane that had just left had gone for a plague germ attack on the Chinese army. But a civilian researcher told us, "The bacteria that you fellows cultivated were spread in Nanjing, or somewhere in China." Once, someone said that the bacteria that we made had been cultivated well, and four or five Chinese had died. We cheered ourselves. "We're medal earners," we said. We were really proud.

There was a big smokestack in the unit. On some days it poured smoke, sometimes there was none. It was far from our barracks. Once, we asked what was burning. The answer was "prisoners."

Source: Hal Gold, *Unit 731: Testimony* (Tokyo: Yenbooks, 1996), 178–181. Used by permission of Tuttle Publishing.

AFTERMATH

As Russian troops invaded Manchuria in August 1945 and Japan faced defeat, Ishii disbanded Unit 731, telling all its personnel to keep its existence and activities strictly secret. U.S. General **Douglas MacArthur**, the Allied Supreme Commander who headed the Allied occupation regime in Japan from 1945 to 1950, granted Unit 731's physicians and scientists immunity from prosecution for war crimes on condition that they handed over their experimental data on biological and chemical warfare to the U.S. government. Many of those involved later held high positions within Japan's medical and scientific establishment. Until the 1980s, this bargain remained highly confidential. In 1949, Soviet authorities tried 12 high-ranking Japanese military officials and scientists they had captured in Manchuria for war crimes, including germ warfare and abuses against human subjects. The perpetrators received prison sentences of between two and 25 years in labor camps. The Russians also established a biological weapons facility in the city of Sverdlovsk, where they made use of data contained in documents captured from Unit 731.

From the early 1980s, Japanese and Western writers and journalists began to expose the operations of Unit 731 and Allied complicity in concealing these, and Japanese citizens groups took up the issue. In the mid-1990s, a Unit 731 Exhibition toured 61 Japanese cities over a period of 18 months. The organizers solicited oral histories, including the one above, from former Unit 731 employees. Chillingly, at the end its author, who claimed that he had only heard rumors of atrocities but not committed any himself, stated: "[P]ersonally, I feel no shame. I thought that I was really doing a good thing."

ASK YOURSELF

1. Around 3,000 people probably worked in Unit 731 during its operations. Why did they remain silent about its activities for so long?
2. Unit 731 was an elite facility, whose operatives enjoyed far higher pay and better working conditions than other Japanese soldiers or officials. What part did these practical benefits play in encouraging Unit 731 employees, including highly trained physicians and scientists, to take part in sometimes horrific experiments?
3. The victorious Allies prosecuted German medical men responsible for human experimentation at Dachau and elsewhere. By choosing to protect Japanese accused of similar crimes, most of whose victims were Asian rather than European, were the American occupation authorities implicitly sending a racist message that Asian lives were less important than Western ones?
4. Was it morally justified for Western and Russian scientists to make use of data from experiments on humans and animals conducted at Unit 731?

TOPICS TO CONSIDER

1. Historical museums in such Chinese cities as Nanjing (site of the 1937 Nanjing Massacre) and Changchun and Shenyang (Mukden) in Manchuria contain very extensive exhibits highlighting Japanese wartime medical experimentation on Chinese people, as well as other Japanese atrocities. What useful purposes do such exhibits fulfill?
2. Chinese government officials have recently attacked Japanese school history textbooks for downplaying Japanese atrocities against the Chinese during World War II. Nationalist Japanese, by contrast, either deny that such atrocities ever occurred or claim that Chinese authors have greatly exaggerated how extensive and systematic such behavior was. Japanese historians who have written controversial books condemning their government's past involvement in such episodes as the Nanjing massacre, the military abuse of comfort women, and Japanese crimes against Chinese prisoners and civilians in World War II often attract heavy criticism from many of their own countrymen. World War II ended more than 65 years ago. Why do these topics remain so politically loaded in both Japan and China? Will they ever cease to be so sensitive?

Further Information

Barenblatt, Daniel. *A Plague upon Humanity: The Hidden History of Japan's Biological Warfare Program*. New York: Harper & Row, 2004.

Endicott, Stephen, and Edward Hagerman. *The United States and Biological Warfare: Secrets from the Early Cold War and Korea*. Bloomington: Indiana University Press, 1999.

Harris, Sheldon H. *Factories of Death: Japanese Biological Warfare, 1932–45 and the American Cover-Up*. New York: Routledge, 2002.

Tanaka, Yuki. *Hidden Horrors: Japanese War Crimes in World War II.* Boulder, CO: Westview, 1997.
Williams, Peter, and David Wallace. *Unit 731: Japan's Secret Biological Warfare in World War II.* New York: Free Press, 1989.

Web Sites

Japanese War Crimes: Resources for Researchers. U.S. National Archives. http://www.archives.gov/iwg/japanese-war-crimes/.
A Plague upon Humanity: The Continuing Story. http://web.archive.org/web/20091026234608/http://geocities.com/dib10280/.
Unit 731: Auschwitz of the East. AII Prisoners of War—Missing in Action. http://web.archive.org/web/20071017024424/www.aiipowmia.com/731/731caveat.html.
Unit 731: Japanese Experimentation Camp (1937–1945). http://www.unit-731.com/.

Films and Television

Men Behind the Sun (1988), starring Hsu Gou, Wang Gang, Andrew Wu Dai Yao, and Wang Run Shen.
Philosophy of a Knife (2008), directed by Andrey Iskanov.
Unit 731: Nightmare in Manchuria (1998). History Channel.

27. Comfort Women: Account of Ms. K, an Anonymous Korean Woman

INTRODUCTION

Sexual exploitation and abuse of vulnerable women has always been common in war, but until recently governments and historians alike tended to ignore it. This is the story of one of around 200,000—estimates range from a low of 20,000 up to 410,000—attractive young Korean, Chinese, Southeast Asian, Indonesian, and Dutch women forced to work in military brothels throughout Asia serving Japanese troops as wartime prostitutes or "comfort women." Around 75 percent of them are thought to have died in the course of the war, of venereal disease, other illnesses, starvation, or mistreatment.

KEEP IN MIND AS YOU READ

1. If recorded earlier than the 1990s, this oral history would probably not have been so frank. Many comfort women felt permanently shamed and remained silent.
2. Even though prepared to tell her story, this Korean woman, identified only as Ms. K, still wished to remain anonymous.
3. From 1905 to 1945, Korea was under Japanese occupation, run by Japanese officials, many of whom settled in the country.
4. From 1932, the Japanese military recruited women for its brothels overseas, initially advertising for Japanese prostitutes ready to work voluntarily in these establishments, but turning to kidnapping and coercion of women from occupied areas of Asia when the supply of willing applicants proved inadequate.
5. Japanese soldiers often paid up to half their monthly wage for one visit to a prostitute, but the comfort women never received this money, which went to the army.

Comfort Women: Account of Ms. K, an Anonymous Korean Woman

I was born in Ulsan, a small town in the southern part of Korea, in 1928. I was the oldest among several children in my family.

My Japanese name was Kikuko Kanazima. . . . I was about 15 years old when a tragic fate took hold of me. A town clerk and policeman visited my home and told me that I had to appear at the county office by a certain date. I was told that young girls had to join "*Jungshin-dae,*" the women's labor corps, to fight for the Emperor so that the war would soon be won. They also told me that I would work at a military factory and that I would be paid wages.

My mother resisted this order. However, at the end of September, a policeman came again and took me to the county office by force. When I arrived, there were about 30 girls of my age there. The police put us on a truck that took us to a military cargo train. On the train I could see 30 or 40 Korean men who were drafted as laborers. We were put into a **box-car** which had no windows, with lighting only from a dim candle. Two soldiers guarded us.

After about one week's ride, we arrived at Uonkil Station in Manchuria. They separated us into different groups and put us into military trucks. After riding quite a while through the night, I and a few other girls were discharged at a military camp. Some young girls, including those of Chinese origin, were already at the camp. Each girl received two blankets, one towel, and a military-type uniform. Then guards took us to a wooden warehouse surrounded by barbed wire. They put one girl into each of the small cubicles. Our supervisors were Japanese soldiers or men wearing militia uniform. They told us to obey them.

For the first three days, only officers visited me. After that I was forced to have sex with 20 to 40 soldiers a day. I worked from eight in the morning till ten at night, but there were many nights I had to sleep overnight with an officer. A military doctor inspected us on a regular basis, but we all ended up having **venereal diseases**. Some girls died from these and other illnesses. Some girls became hysterical and crazy. In exchange for sex, soldiers apparently paid some kind of military money, but our supervisors took the money, saying that they would save it for us. In any case, I never received a penny from them.

During this horrifying enslavement, I was moved to three different military camps. The last unit was called "Koyabashi 8000" stationed near Jijiharu. Whenever we were moved, we were guarded by military policemen and kept under constant watch. I tried to escape several times, but I was caught each time by the soldiers and severely beaten by the supervisors. On one occasion, I jumped off a truck and tried to run away in the dark. But they caught me and my supervisor beat me savagely all over my body and then cut off my three left fingers with a knife.

boxcar: rectangular railway wagon
venereal diseases: sexually transmitted diseases of various kinds
hysterectomy: surgical removal of the uterus (womb)

Life in the camp became devastating toward the end of the war. We were starving. Those who were sick had no medical treatment. Then, one day, the camp became completely silent. I went outside. There were no soldiers in the camp. Finally, a Chinese told me that the war was over.

It took me about two months to walk back to Korea. I had to beg food from the Chinese on the way. I was glad to have survived, but very ashamed and angry about my past life. I decided not to go back to my home because of the shame and potential harm to my family.

I settled down in Pusan and worked as a waitress in restaurants and as a house maid. Eventually, I contacted an aunt who arranged a meeting with my mother. My mother asked me to come back to her, but I decided to live by myself. As time passed, I became sick and had to undergo a **hysterectomy**.

In 1979, my younger sister who was living in New York City invited me to live with her. So I came to America. At present, I live alone with financial assistance from my sister, the U.S. government, and the South Korean government. I wait for death.

Source: Sangmie Choi Schellstede, ed., *Comfort Women Speak: Testimony by Sex Slaves of the Japanese Military* (New York: Holmes and Meier, 2000), 102–105. Used by permission of Holmes & Meier Publishers, Inc.

AFTERMATH

Although Ms. K, then aged 17, begged her way back to her own country when the war ended and made contact with her mother and other female relatives again, she was too ashamed of what had befallen her ever to rejoin her family. She later suffered from gynecological problems, which were probably the result of her two years as a prostitute. She was, however, luckier than many such women, in that her family did not repudiate her and helped her financially. Her recollections were among those collected several decades later by advocates for the Korean women who sought to win them compensation from the Japanese government.

ASK YOURSELF

1. Many Japanese military and civilian officials stood trial for war crimes after 1945, with some accused of having forced non-Japanese women into sexual slavery. Allied prosecutors usually charged those military officers involved with having committed personal breaches of the Japanese army's code of conduct, not of acting in their official capacity. Why did prosecutors of the late 1940s decide not to hold the Japanese military bureaucracy officially responsible for sexually exploiting women of other nationalities?
2. Numerous surviving comfort women remained permanently traumatized by their experiences and often suffered long-term health problems, with most unable to bear children. Many also faced social ostracism from their families and communities, and even suggestions that any decent woman would have killed herself rather than endure repeated rapes. Why do so many societies treat vulnerable sexually abused women as having been somehow complicit in their own sufferings and as having shamed and disgraced not just themselves but their broader social community and even their country?

ANG LEE'S *LUST, CAUTION* (2007)

In 2007 the Taiwanese director Ang Lee proved that World War II sexual politics remain controversial, when he brought out the film *Lust, Caution.* Based on a short story by the well-known Chinese author Eileen Chang, it follows a young Chinese woman, a student revolutionary in the anti-Japanese resistance who is instructed to seduce and then deliver for assassination a top official in the Shanghai-based puppet collaborationist government of China headed by Wang Ching-wei, who worked with Japanese occupation forces from 1939 to 1944. The young woman, played by actress Tang Wei, falls in love with her target and warns him of the plot against him, whereupon she and all her coconspirators are arrested and shot. The film provoked heated discussion within China over the accuracy of its portrayal of the young woman, with some critics furiously arguing that no Chinese female revolutionary would ever have betrayed the anti-Japanese resistance and placed her personal feelings above the patriotic cause. The Chinese government banned the airing of advertisements featuring Tang Wei, and the actress moved to Hong Kong to pursue her career. This controversy over a fictional dramatization revealed just how politically loaded and sensitive issues of wartime female behavior and collaboration still remain in today's China.

3. In all occupied countries, many individuals and organizations collaborated with occupying forces. Did women who, willingly or not, had some form of sexual relationship with the occupiers serve as scapegoats for broader collective guilt?
4. For decades, many Japanese historians and government officials sought to deny that these events ever took place. Why?

TOPICS TO CONSIDER

1. In the 1980s and 1990s, women's groups and historians began to investigate the extent of the Japanese government's culpability in the exploitation of World War II comfort women. The Japanese government first denied all responsibility, until historians in the early 1990s discovered substantial incriminating documentary evidence of top-level official military involvement, some former comfort women launched legal proceedings seeking financial compensation, and the United Nations took up the issue. In 1993 the Japanese government therefore issued a qualified apology to these women, without accepting legal responsibility for their travails. In 1995, Japan also established an Asia Women's Fund, financed by private donations, to provide compensation to surviving comfort women, and the Japanese prime minister apologized to them. Many, however, believed the government had still failed to accept responsibility for its past actions; some rejected these payments, continuing to campaign for an official apology and compensation. Why, more than 50 years later, have top Japanese politicians been so reluctant to admit that their predecessors officially sanctioned these activities?
2. The growing strength of female activism at all levels, global, international, and national, is one reason underlying greater openness on sexual exploitation of women since the 1980s. Women's groups have also taken up the issue of sexual violence against women in other recent conflicts, in Serbia, Bosnia, Kosovo, Rwanda, Darfur, and elsewhere, making the topic less taboo in international organizations and forums. Has this changed climate of opinion made it easier for earlier female victims of sexual abuse to speak up with some expectation of winning a respectful hearing?

Further Information

Henson, Maria Rosa. *Comfort Woman: A Filipina's Story of Prostitution and Slavery under the Japanese Military.* Lanham, MD: Rowman and Littlefield, 1999.

Hicks, George. *The Comfort Women: Japan's Brutal Regime of Enforced Prostitution in the Second World War.* New York: Norton, 1997.

Howard, Keith, ed. *True Stories of the Korean Comfort Women: Testimonies.* Trans. Young Joo Lee. New York: Cassell, 1995.

Schellstede, Sangmie Choi, ed. *Comfort Women Speak: Testimony by Sex Slaves of the Japanese Military.* New York: Holmes and Meier, 2000.

Schmidt, David Andrew. *Ianfu, The Comfort Women of the Japanese Imperial Army of the Pacific War: Broken Silence.* Lewiston, NY: Edwin Mellen Press, 2000.

Soh, C. Sarah. *The Comfort Women: Social Violence and Postcolonial Memory in Korea and Japan.* Chicago: University of Chicago Press, 2009.

Stetz, Margaret, and Bonnie B.C. Oh, eds. *Legacies of the Comfort Women of World War II.* Armonk, NY: M. E. Sharpe, 2001.
Tanaka, Yuki. *Japan's Comfort Women: Sexual Slavery and Prostitution during World War II and the U.S. Occupation.* New York: Routledge, 2002.
Yoshiaki, Yoshimi. *Comfort Women: Sexual Slavery in the Japanese Military during World War II.* Trans. Suzanne O'Brien. New York: Columbia University Press, 2000.

Web Sites

Amnesty International Australia: Justice for Comfort Women. http://www.amnesty.org.au/comfort.
comfort-women.org: Washington Coalition for Comfort Women Issues. http://www.comfort-women.org.
Digital Museum: The Comfort Women Issue and the Asian Women's Fund. http://www.awf.or.jp.

Films

Behind Forgotten Eyes (2006), directed by Anthony Gilmore.
My Heart Is Not Yet Broken (2007), directed by Ahn Hae-ryong.
Silence Broken: Korean Comfort Women (2008), directed by Dai Sil Kim-Gibson. Center for Asian American Media.

28. GERMAN WOMEN IN WARTIME: REMINISCENCES OF JULIANE HARTMANN

INTRODUCTION

With millions of German men absent in the armed forces and a massive manpower shortage, German women increasingly took over a wide variety of tasks, working long hours on farms and in factories. Women bore the brunt of ever-intensifying food shortages. Many German women in areas taken and occupied by Russian forces were also subjected to repeated rape, as well as the looting of all their possessions. The Soviet siege and eventual capture in early May 1945 of Germany's capital Berlin, symbolic heart of **ADOLF HITLER'S** empire and the earlier Prussian state, effectively marked the end of Nazi rule. Juliane Hartmann, the sheltered daughter of an upper-middle-class family who owned a large house in a Berlin suburb, later recalled her experiences in the final year of the war.

KEEP IN MIND AS YOU READ

1. Between November 1943 and March 1945, Berlin was subjected to 314 Allied air raids. The German authorities encouraged all nonessential civilians, especially families with young children, to leave Berlin and go elsewhere. By 1944, 1.2 million people, two-thirds of them women and young children, constituting a quarter of the city's population, had been evacuated.
2. In January 1945, the remaining population of Berlin numbered around 2.9 million, of whom only 100,000 were young men between 18 and 30, and another 100,000 forced laborers. The city's population was therefore disproportionately female.
3. Red Army forces took Berlin in a battle lasting from April 20 to May 2, 1945, one of the war's bloodiest engagements, in which 100,000 German troops and 1,200 tanks fought against 1.5 million Soviet soldiers equipped with 20,000 tanks and heavy artillery pieces. On April 30, 1945, Hitler committed suicide in the city. Berlin was left in ruins and rubble.

GERMAN WOMEN IN WARTIME

Nazi ideology precluded Germany making the most effective wartime use of women. It sought to restrict women to the supposedly appropriate spheres of children, kitchen, and church, and mass mobilization of women, even though some of **Adolf Hitler's** subordinates urged this, would have challenged the prevailing mindset. Legislation passed in 1940 required German women to register for work, but in practice its scope was restricted, applying only to women who had already held jobs and to the working class, which proved a fruitful source of social tensions and resentments. Over time, efforts to recruit women intensified, with a new registration decree passed in early 1943, whose enforcement became far more draconian from mid-1944 onward. From 1939 onward, all young single German girls were expected to work for 6 to 12 months as nurses, or agricultural or industrial workers, and 1.5 million German women entered the workforce during the war. Like the Allies, the German forces also had women's auxiliary units, which provided support services and freed men for combat duty, and their numbers eventually grew to over 500,000. About 100,000 German women served in anti-aircraft units, and some who later became notorious worked as guards in concentration camps. A few much feted German women even served as test pilots.

Reminiscences of Juliane Hartmann

It was the autumn of 1944. My father was at war, and, in the meantime, my stepmother had moved with my younger brothers and sisters to a farm in Bavaria. I was 19 and decided to stay in Berlin. Berlin was, after all, my home. Not much later I was drafted into the labor service and had to work 64 hours a week in an ammunition factory. Thank God I didn't end up in the main hall, but instead was sent to work with two wounded soldiers in a small room. It was said that we were doing **solder** work on some secret weapon, but all I recall soldering were pots and pans. I got up at five o'clock every morning and rode my bike to the factory to begin work at six. I worked 10 hours a day, 64 hours a week for "our Führer."

About that time, we began to really feel the food shortage at home. There was nothing left to hoard, and we had used up what we had in reserve. We relied totally on the official rations. Our noon meal consisted of cabbage and potatoes, while in the evening we generally ate potatoes and carrots. Besides my aunt and me, there were up to 35 refugees living in our house. I remember having to divide a tiny piece of butter up into "Monday to Friday"; the daily portions were never even enough to spread on one piece of bread.

I remember distinctly, it was April 14, 1945, when there was a major attack on **Potsdam**. From that day on, we had neither running water nor electricity. The telephones weren't working either. The first wave of Russians arrived shortly after that. The first thing we did was to hang a **white sheet** out the window. What followed was worse than anything we had ever imagined. Today, I am able to say that "I was the first victim on the street." The never-ending stealing and looting became a daily occurrence over the following weeks and months.

The man who lived next door had been bombed out of his house in Berlin. One night he was visited by an entire horde of **Mongolians** who pointed their guns at him and asked, "Where woman?" Since he lived alone, the only thing he could say was that there were none in his house. And so they went to the next house, which was ours. They forced their way through the front door. I can't tell you now exactly how many of them there were. They

solder: joining two pieces of metal together with a heated alloy
Potsdam: capital city of Brandenburg state, 15 miles southwest of Berlin
white sheet: signal of surrender
Mongolians: Asiatic Russian soldiers

went through the entire house—which was very large—with flashlights, from the basement to the attic. Some of the people living in the house were able to hide. As for myself, I fell into the hands of one of the Mongolians.

That was actually the second time. The first time occurred when I mentioned I was the first victim on the street. It was the middle of the day. One Russian went into the garage and the other headed for the house. Not having the slightest idea of what would happen, I followed the man into the house. First, he locked all of the doors behind him and put the keys in his pocket. I began to feel a bit funny when we got to one of the bedrooms. I wanted to go out on the balcony, but he pointed his gun at me and said, ***"Frau komm!"*** We had already heard about a few of the horrible things going on, so I knew one thing for certain and that was "Don't try to defend yourself." An upper-middle-class child, I had never been told about the facts of life. . . .

Frau komm!: Come here, lady!

I was 19, not that young by today's standards. We were just so happy that the war was over, that we were still alive, and that no more bombs would fall. Of course, we contemplated what the future would have in store for us, but primarily we thought we were lucky to be alive at all. I was examined, and fortunately I hadn't been infected with venereal disease. At least I knew I was all right, though I admit that I did have nightmares for quite a while after that. But looking back at what happened to me, it's as though *I* wasn't really being violated. Instead I was standing next to myself, alongside my body, a detached observer. That feeling has kept the experience from dominating the rest of my life.

Source: From the book *Voices from the Third Reich: An Oral History* by Johannes Steinhoff, Peter Pechel, and Dennis Showalter, eds. (Washington, DC: Regnery Gateway, 1989), 453–455.

AFTERMATH

Juliane Hartmann went on to have a fulfilling personal and professional life, joining the German Foreign Service and working as a diplomat in the United States. She eventually settled in Bonn, capital of the West German Federal Republic.

ASK YOURSELF

1. Juliane Hartmann was only one of around 2 million German and Hungarian women raped by invading Soviet soldiers as they battled their way across Eastern and Central Europe in 1944 and 1945 and during the German occupation. Many had experiences far worse than hers, being gang-raped repeatedly, often leaving them permanently traumatized psychologically, and up to 240,000 died, either of brutal mistreatment or because they chose to commit suicide. Russian, Polish, Ukrainian, and Belorussian women taken to Germany as slave laborers received the same treatment from Red Army forces, as did Jewish and Communist women, some freed from concentration camps, who initially welcomed the invading Red Army. Russian troops also looted without restraint. Why did Soviet political and military leaders permit this behavior, which undercut their ability to win the loyalties of East European populations in states that later became Russian satellites?

2. Under Communist rule, German women in the East German Democratic Republic were subsequently pressured to sign statements that Red Army troops had not raped them. Women were forced to remain silent because the official government line was that the Soviets were heroic liberators. How often have governments sacrificed the interests of women to what are seen as more important political objectives? What do such narrative fictions reveal about the sociopolitical status of women?
3. Although precise figures are difficult to obtain, German troops were likewise responsible for the rape, sometimes followed by murder, of several hundreds of thousands, perhaps even millions, of Jewish, Polish, and Russian women, mostly on the Eastern front and in concentration camps between 1939 and 1945. Some historians suggest that the Red Army's treatment of German women represented retaliation for such atrocities. Even if this was true, was such behavior justified? Does war tend to become an ever escalating spiral of brutality?

TOPICS TO CONSIDER

1. In his book on the fall of Berlin in 1945, published in 2002, the British historian Antony Beevor graphically described the mass rapes of German and other women by Red Army soldiers. The Russian ambassador to Britain and leading Russian historians denounced this volume as neo-Nazi propaganda, questioning Beevor's sources while characterizing Soviet reprisals against German civilians for Russian sufferings during the previous years of war as well-justified revenge. Beevor pointed out that his book relied heavily upon evidence from Russian archives to document its allegations and other prominent Western historians defended the accuracy of his sources. Why, more than half a century after the events Beevor's book portrayed, did Russian officials and historians protest so vehemently against it?
2. The recent film *A Woman in Berlin,* based upon an authentic diary from this period, depicts not just Russian sexual violence against German women, but also how during the occupation many such women turned to prostitution in order to survive and support themselves and their families, or struck up opportunistic relationships with occupying military personnel whereby they bartered sexual favors for food and other commodities, and protection against other predatory men. Such arrangements are common in every conquered state or city, reflecting asymmetries of power without necessarily being nonconsensual. Why did the Red Army so exceed these norms in terms of abusing and terrorizing women?
3. During their occupation of Germany, many Russian officers acquired German "occupation wives," steady girlfriends, or mistresses with whom they had long-term affairs, and some even deserted from the Red Army to remain in Europe with these women. Wives, fiancés, and girlfriends in Russia bitterly condemned these relationships. Is it ever feasible for military authorities to prevent fraternization between lonely soldiers far from home and local women?

Further Information

Anonymous [Hillers, Marta]. *A Woman in Berlin: Eight Weeks in the Conquered City: A Diary.* New York: Metropolitan Books, 2005, originally published 1954.

Beevor, Antony. *The Fall of Berlin 1945.* New York: Viking, 2002.

Cosner, Shaaron, and Victoria Cosner. *Women under the Third Reich: A Biographical Dictionary*. Westport, CT: Greenwood Press, 1998.
Krockow, Christian von. *Hour of the Women*. Trans. Krishna Winston. New York: HarperCollins, 1991.
MacDonogh, Giles. *After the Reich: The Brutal History of the Allied Occupation*. New York: Basic Books, 2007.
Naimark, Norman M. *The Russians in Germany: A History of the Soviet Zone of Occupation, 1945–1949*. Cambridge, MA: Harvard University Press, 1995.
Owings, Alison. *Frauen: German Women Recall the Third Reich*. New Brunswick, NJ: Rutgers University Press, 1993.
Rupp, Leila J. *Mobilizing Women for War: German and American Propaganda, 1939–1945*. Princeton: Princeton University Press, 1978.
Saywell, Shelley. *Women in War*. Markham, ON: Viking, 1986.

Web Site

History in Images: Mass Rape of German Women. http://historyimages.blogspot.hk/2011/10/mass-rape-of-german-women-when-germany.html.

Film

A Woman in Berlin (2008), starring Nina Hoss, Evgeny Sidikhin, and Irm Hermann.

THE WAR'S SOCIAL AND ECONOMIC IMPACT

29. The Aryan Obsession: Heinrich Himmler, Order to the Members of the German SS and Police, October 28, 1939

INTRODUCTION

National Socialist racial theory urged all **Aryan** men to father as many children as possible to carry on the German or Teutonic race. Racially suitable German women were encouraged to have large families, with access to birth control increasingly difficult under Nazi rule, while those considered unsuitable on racial or other grounds found themselves the targets for forced abortion and sterilization. Single women who became pregnant were encouraged to continue their pregnancy to full term, and they and their children were accommodated in *Lebensborn* (Fount of Life) homes, run by the **SS**. At the beginning of the war, **Heinrich Himmler**, head of the German SS and Police, went further and directed all members of those two organizations to father as many children as possible, whether legitimate or not. He was concerned that otherwise they might die in battle with no offspring to perpetuate their genetic heritage.

KEEP IN MIND AS YOU READ

1. In the 1930s, bearing an illegitimate child out of wedlock normally carried a major social stigma, especially for the woman involved. Legally, an unmarried mother had no rights over her own child, and often faced dismissal from her job.
2. For a widow or single woman, bringing up a child or children without the support of a husband could be extremely difficult, both financially—since the woman would often need to work to support her child—and in terms of having the time to care for the child.
3. Nazi ideology sought to restrict the role of women in public life, and to confine them to the spheres of *kinder, kirche, und küche* (children, church, and kitchen). Overly elegant or sophisticated clothes and the use of cosmetics were also frowned upon; a wholesome homespun simplicity—rarely embraced by women prominent in the Nazi movement—was the stated ideal.
4. Since the late 19th century, throughout the Western world, many political leaders had been dismayed by declining birthrates, especially among educated middle class families, and had sought to persuade well-to-do women to produce more rather than fewer children. In Europe, such concerns were accentuated by the deaths of millions of young men during World War I.

5. Despite official encouragement to Germans to have large families, during the 1930s birthrates rose slightly, to between 18 and 20 births per 1,000 population, but never reached the 21–25 level of 1920–1923, let alone the rates of between 26 and 35 prevalent from 1900 until World War I began in 1914. Parents of large families received official recognition and honor from the Nazi state, but practical financial or other help from the authorities to support and bring up their numerous children was limited.

Heinrich Himmler, Order to the Members of the German SS and Police, 28 October 1939

To all men of the **SS** and Police

The old proverb that only he can die in peace who has sons and children must again hold good in this war, particularly for the SS. He can die in peace who knows that his clan and everything that his ancestors and he himself have wanted and striven for will be continued in his children. The greatest gift for the widow of a man killed in battle is always the child of the man she has loved.

Beyond the limits of **bourgeois** laws and conventions, which are perhaps necessary in other circumstances, it can be a noble task for German women and girls of good blood to become even outside marriage, not light-heartedly but out of a deep moral seriousness, mothers of the children of soldiers going to war of whom fate alone knows whether they will return or die for Germany. . . .

During the last war, many a soldier decided from a sense of responsibility to have no more children during the war so that his wife would not be left in need and distress after his death. You SS men need not have these anxieties; they are removed by the following regulations:

SS: *Schutzstaffeln* or Protection Police. The much feared German security force, responsible for internal and subsequently external security
bourgeois: middle class
Reichsführer SS: the head or director of the SS, at this time Himmler himself
good blood: racially pure, according to Nazi classifications

1. Special delegates, chosen by me personally, will take over in the name of the **Reichsführer SS**, the guardianship of all legitimate and illegitimate children of **good blood** whose fathers were killed in the war. We will support these mothers and take over the education and material care of these children until they come of age, so that no mother and widow need suffer want.
2. During the war, the SS will take care of all legitimate and illegitimate children born during the war and of expectant mothers in cases of need. After the war, when the fathers return, the SS will in addition grant generous material help to well-founded applications by individuals.

SS-Men and you mothers of these children which Germany has hoped for show that you are ready, through your faith in the Führer and for the sake of the life of our blood and people, to regenerate life for Germany just as bravely as you know how to fight and die for Germany.

Source: Jeremy Noakes, ed., *Nazism 1919–1945, Volume 4: The Home Front in World War II* (Exeter: University of Exeter Press, 1998), 368–369. Used by permission of the University of Exeter Press.

AFTERMATH

Despite official encouragement, relatively few German soldiers took advantage of Himmler's exhortation to perpetuate the race during the war. Himmler's order attracted criticism from both the Roman Catholic Church and some leaders of the Nazi Women's Group, an elite organization within the **Nazi Party**, for destabilizing the family. The government did begin paying cash grants to single women in full-time employment who produced a child, and women who lost a fiancé in action could apply for a post-mortem marriage that would entitle them to a widow's pension and legitimize any children. Even many Nazis, however, felt that Himmler's vision of a group of SS supermen who should be encouraged to impregnate as many women as possible, and perhaps to contract bigamous marriages, was too extreme.

There was a wave of marriages after August 1939, when the German government relaxed the regulations whereby couples first had to be certified as suitable for marriage. Under these controls, couples who could not satisfy officials that they were racially qualified for wedlock and in good physical and mental health were liable to forced sterilization. With the coming of war, however, fertility declined, from 20.4 live births per 1,000 in 1939 to a mere 14.9 in 1942. As the fortunes of war began to turn against Germany from 1941 onward, with casualties on the Eastern Front against Russia rising steadily and heavy bombing of German cities, very few Germans wanted to bring more children into increasingly insecure and dangerous circumstances.

ASK YOURSELF

1. Since the late 19th century, numerous countries—France, Germany, Singapore, China, India, and Romania, for example—have tried to implement population policies, in some cases to increase the numbers of children born, especially to parents considered in some way desirable, in others, notably China and India, to decrease the number of births. In what circumstances, if any, are government efforts to increase or limit population numbers likely to be successful?
2. No other government took measures comparable to those of Himmler in World War II to encourage young German men and women to produce children, even if there was a risk that the fathers would be killed in action, and the government would have to support these children. Why was Germany alone in trying to implement such a program?
3. If you were a young German man or woman in 1939, would you have found Himmler's order convincing? Why?

TOPICS TO CONSIDER

1. Jutta Rüdiger, head of the Nazi League of German Girls from 1937 to 1945, later denied that Himmler's stance represented official Nazi policy, describing such allegations as enemy propaganda or at most "the work of a few fanatics during the war." In her words, during his speech on the subject, "even Himmler never went so far as to say 'you must give the Führer a child,' or 'every woman should get pregnant.' He didn't dare. All of us were glaring at him, and he probably noticed it." According to Rüdiger, she and other female Nazi officials were anxious that unmarried women who became pregnant by German soldiers

MAGDA GOEBBELS

Magda Goebbels (1901–1945). The wife of **Josef Goebbels** (1897–1945), a Nazi zealot and fervent anti-Semite who was German minister of propaganda from 1933 to 1945, Magda was a favorite of Adolf Hitler, in part because she seemed to personify the ideal of German womanhood that he and the Nazis sought to propagate. Beautiful and blonde (albeit with some chemical assistance), she produced six attractive children, giving each a name beginning with H, to demonstrate her devotion to Hitler. In practice, her marriage to the small, dark, less than Aryan-looking Goebbels, her second husband, was stormy, and both were unfaithful to each other. Magda also departed from the purported Nazi template of the perfect *Hausfrau* (housewife), in that she wore elegant, stylish, and sophisticated clothes and used cosmetics. She often functioned as the de facto first lady of the Nazi regime, frequently serving as a hostess for Hitler. At the end of the war, in May 1945, the Goebbels family joined Hitler in his bunker in Berlin, where—despite pleas from Hitler not to do so—they drugged and killed all their six children, and committed suicide themselves.

should be well looked after in special government-sponsored homes, rather than driven to suicide, as had too often happened. Which perspective, that of Himmler or Rüdiger, was likely to be the more influential within top Nazi circles during World War II?

2. At the same time that SS-men were encouraged to procreate with suitably Aryan women, Nazi Germany sought to control and reduce reproduction by other groups in the population, and eventually to eliminate those groups altogether. Jews (including individuals of partial Jewish descent), Gypsies, and Slavs were initially forbidden to marry Aryans, and later subject to forced sterilization and abortion, before finally becoming targets for mass murder. Homosexuals and leftists, who were generally defined as degenerate, were frequently sterilized and sent to concentration camps, where many died of illness or overwork. The physically or mentally handicapped often became victims of euthanasia, supposed mercy killings. To justify these policies, the Nazis invoked supposedly scientific racial theories, based on perverted Darwinian principles of the survival of the fittest and the need to eliminate the unfit. How, if at all, is it possible to prevent the misuse of science for such purposes?
3. Later during the war, British propagandists untruthfully invented a fictitious club of German women, mostly married to soldiers or with fiancés away in the military, who would sleep with any German officer who was back on leave in Germany. Invitation cards purporting to be from this club were distributed among German troops at the front, with the objective of destroying the morale of those who had left wives or girlfriends behind them. Might the Himmler order have served as one inspiration for the British propaganda specialists who devised this scheme? And why did the British believe that spreading such rumors and disinformation would nonetheless damage German morale?

Further Information

Klabunde, Anja. *Magda Goebbels*. Boston: Little, Brown, 2002,

Koonz, Claudia. *Mothers in the Fatherland: Women, the Family, and Nazi Politics*. New York: St. Martin's Press, 1987.

Longerich, Peter. *Heinrich Himmler: A Life*. New York: Oxford University Press, 2012.
Manrich, Roger, and Heinrich Fraenkel. *Doctor Goebbels: His Life and Death*. New York: Skyhorse Publishing, 2010.
Reuth, Ralph Georg. *Goebbels*. Trans. Krishna Winston. New York: Harcourt, 1993.
Stephenson, Jill. *Women in Nazi Germany*. Harlow, UK: Longman, 2001.
Thacker, Toby. *Joseph Goebbels: Life and Death*. New York: Palgrave Macmillan, 2009.

Web Site

George Duncan's Women of the Third Reich. http://members.iinet.net.au/˜gduncan/women.html.

Film

Eva Braun: Her Home Movies Complete and Uncut (2004 release). Produced by Kent Kiefer. Kiefer Entertainment.

30. The British Home Front: Recollections of Pamela Lazarus, October 10, 2001

INTRODUCTION

This oral history by Pamela Lazarus—then Pamela Rodker—recounts the wartime story of a young Jewish girl living in the East End of London throughout World War II. Three when the war began and nine when it ended, she was at an age when one's memories are perhaps most vivid, as a child begins to focus on the outside world. Like most oral histories, her recollections tend to center on two sets of issues: memorable highlights, such incidents as meetings with American GIs or the return of her father, and the prevailing long-term conditions of life. Many of her memories brought up almost conventional themes common to many recollections: the shortages of food during rationing, the blackout, the fear and horrors of bombing, the dramatic impact of American soldiers upon the British population, the absence of her father in the armed forces, and the street party that celebrated the ending of the war in 1945.

One also, however, gains a sense of the darker side of the war. Pamela Rodker Lazarus belonged to a Yiddish-speaking Jewish family from Russian Poland, with ramifications extending into Berlin, Warsaw, Paris, London, and Prague. Her grandparents were among the many hundreds of thousands of Jews who left Eastern Europe at the turn of the century to escape pogroms and persecution. Her paternal grandfather, an affluent corsetier, was among them, moving to London with his wife and children, including Lazarus' father, who became a barber. Although most of the family quickly learned English, her grandmother always refused to speak anything but Yiddish. Lazarus gives a vivid but unromanticized picture of life in wartime London.

KEEP IN MIND AS YOU READ

1. For around five years of her childhood, Lazarus was subjected to constant disruptions, moving from house to air-raid shelter, and town to country and back, as official British government directives decreed. She had more stability than many children and adults, however, in that her home was not destroyed by German bombing, and both her parents survived the war.
2. Numerous British and European children, who had endured the rigors of years of rationing, were dazzled by the affluent lifestyle of the American GIs, especially

AMERICAN SERVICEMEN IN BRITAIN DURING WORLD WAR II

World War II was the height of the Anglo-American alliance. By late 1941, the United States had a massive and ever-growing military mission in Britain, and from 1942 onward, American servicemen began arriving in substantial numbers, initially often as fliers mounting raids on Germany and Italy, later in huge numbers in preparation for the forthcoming Allied invasion of Europe that eventually took place in June 1944. By 1945, 3 million American servicemen had spent time in Britain, in what their fascinated but sometimes resentful hosts on occasion termed the "American occupation" of their country. Famously described as "oversexed, overpaid, overfed, and over here," they tended to be physically large, the product of the superior United States diet, and brash and loud in a culture that emphasized restraint and understatement. In the midst of rationing, austerity, and shortages of every kind, which had by then lasted for several years, lonely American servicemen desiring female companionship—or simply seeking friendship and substitutes for their distant families—could tap the generous supplies of the military PX stores to offer British girls and women otherwise near unobtainable nylon stockings, perfume, chocolates, fruit, and other coveted luxuries. It was hardly surprising that envious British men often felt unable to compete. Many such relationships were undoubtedly short-lived, but during the war and shortly after it ended, between 40,000 and 45,000 British women married their American boyfriends, most going back to the United States with them as "war brides."

their apparently limitless access to otherwise scarce or unobtainable foodstuffs. Countless children remembered the almost casual bounty of unfamiliar fruit, chocolate, and candy they received from individual American soldiers.

3. Even though the country was supposedly safer than the city during the war, many townbred residents hated being sent to rural areas, and despite the dangers involved made great efforts to return to the comfortable familiarity of their own urban surroundings.
4. In the absence of husbands, many women in all countries showed great resilience and coped extremely well with the challenges of hardships of war. This was not true of all women. The mother of Pamela Lazarus was apparently one of those who found it difficult to adjust to the loneliness and other demands of the war.
5. Numerous returning soldiers in all countries found themselves facing children—and, indeed, often wives—who had grown up during their absence and to whom they were near-strangers.

Recollections of Pamela Lazarus, 10 October 2001

It wasn't much fun being a small kid at that time. It was too scary. London was a smoggy city, filled with gray skies, gray fog, rainy days and one seldom saw a blue sky or sunshine. Or so it seemed. And indoors, it always seemed to be night. Everyone had **black curtains** on the windows so that no light would escape into the street, and more importantly, be seen from the German airplanes flying overhead. Lights could show them a good place to drop a bomb. Besides, electricity was expensive, and not to be used if not necessary.

black curtains: Blackout restrictions were tightly enforced in Britain, in an effort to prevent stray light from houses, cars, or other sources guiding German bombers to their targets

THE DORCHESTER HOTEL
LONDON

December 7th [1940]

Dearest Helen:

Your very welcome cable arrived yesterday. Thank you very much indeed for fixing up for Stobbs and Charles to go to Tucson. It will certainly make William very happy and be wonderful for Charles to be in the sunshine. It is grand that you and Frank are going out there for the vacation, it is awfully good of you and will give the children enormous pleasure. I shall never forget your nobility in going out to Philip last year and bycicling and playing tennis with him, you must have needed a month in bed after it.

I gather from Miss Thomas and also in a letter that I had from Philip that William isn't eating very well. I think the great thing is not to bother about it or fuss him. I wish they would just let him eat what he wants. On his holiday when there is less pressure I expect he will eat much less and lose weight, but I will write to Vivian and ask her not to put this at the door of Stobbs! A few days fast would probably do him good.

I am living in London now on my own and I am glad I made the move. I go down five days a week to Whitechapel and work in a social service bureau where all the people come and ask for advice on <u>any</u> subject. However, it is chiefly about air raids, how to get compensation (they can't get more than a few pounds) how to get their houses mended (two months waiting list) and so on. They sleep at night in the shelters and come back by day to wet and cold houses with the rain coming through broken windows and leaking ceilings and rotting their furniture. For every house demolished by a bomb there are six or eight blasted - which means the windows gone and holes in the roof but the people have to hang on in them. They are very uncomplaining, how they stick it I don't know. Some of them have been bombed out three

-2-

or four times times from different places. At night I come back here and live in great comfort. This hotel is very queer and the strangest mixture of people. There are quite a number of very respectable peers and members of the Government, such as Lord Halifax, who live here, have their meals upstairs mostly and aren't seen much. Then there is a large and motley crowd of toughs such as the Duff Coopers and so on who wander about downstairs. The men look like cads and the women all look hardboiled, as if they had been boiled for years in whiskey and gin. There isn't an inch of space anywhere and not a room to be had. I don't know anyone here personally, and I have my dinner in bed every night because I get so terribly tired. I only go downstairs when I have a day off. The raids have been nothing for the last three or four weeks. One night soon after I came they had what was supposed to be the worst raid of the blitz. One heard the bombs coming down with first a long whistle and then a crash for about four or five hours pretty continuously but we had nothing very near here. The nearest was two or three hundred yards away. I imagine it all sounds worse than it is, in the papers - the last few weeks the mess has been tidied up quite a lot and London really looks quite herself. Bombs are much smaller than one would imagine, and do not damage a large area. Land mines do a lot of damage but they don't seem to have used them much lately. You must be sick of the subject of bombs. I haven't been 'round the shelters yet but am going soon. They vary very much I believe, some very good with first aid posts and classes - and others beyond description.

Very much love and thank you a thousand times for fixing it up about Stobbs and Charles.

/s/ Cecily.

From: Mrs. Arthur Godhart
Whitebarn
Boar's Hils
Oxford

C
O
P
Y

Cecily Goodhart to Helen Altschul, December 7, 1940. This typescript of a letter from an Englishwoman, Cecily Goodhart, to her American sister-in-law, Helen Goodhart Altschul, is the only known surviving copy of that letter. Goodhart probably originally wrote it by hand, in her room at the Dorchester Hotel, London, using free hotel stationery, but putting her own address near Oxford on its containing envelope. It may have been mailed to the recipient in the United States, in which case it would probably have gone by sea on the hazardous North Atlantic route, at risk of destruction by the German submarines that were attacking shipping between Britain and the United States. Alternatively, quite possibly it was hand carried to the U.S. East Coast by one of the many British and American officials or authorized civilians who were traveling between Britain and the United States by air on war-related business of some kind. Cecily Goodhart and her American-born husband, Arthur Lehman Goodhart, were close to many individuals in this network, which spanned the Atlantic.

This letter was essentially personal. First, it discussed at some length the well-being of the Goodharts' three young sons, William, Philip, and Charles. The family was visiting the United States in summer 1939. When war began in Europe, the Goodharts returned to Britain themselves, but left their children, accompanied by a nanny, in the care of their wealthy American grandparents and their aunt and uncle, Helen Altschul—Arthur Goodhart's sister—and her husband, Frank Altschul. It was almost certainly Frank, a wealthy banker, who had his secretary type up multiple copies of Cecily Goodhart's ostensibly private letter to Helen, describing the fairly dangerous conditions in which she was living and working in London as a volunteer, assisting working-class families in the East End who had been bombed out during German raids. Goodhart also wrote an article on this subject for a leading American magazine, to win support for the British cause. Paradoxically, she was living in considerable luxury in the up-market Dorchester Hotel, a temporary home for a decidedly mixed bag of British upper-class individuals, most undertaking some kind of government work, who had official or personal reasons to remain in London during the Blitz. Copies of this letter were circulated around the large extended family of Goodhart's American husband, to let all of them know how she was faring during the highly publicized German attacks on Britain. Undoubtedly, Goodhart knew many anxious family members would read her letter, and sought to reassure all of them that, however difficult conditions in Britain were, she was coping well with them. This copy was found in the Papers of Frank Altschul, which are now held by Columbia University, New York.

Source: Papers of Frank Altschul, Rare Book & Manuscript Library, Columbia University in the City of New York. Used by permission of the Goodhart family.

My Dad was away in the army, somewhere in Europe and my mother was very nervous. She was a young woman in her mid 20's, with a little girl (me) and a new baby, and she wanted someone to look after her, and there wasn't anyone to do it. So she cried a lot, and when the siren would go off to warn of an air-raid, she would scream in fear. I always felt responsible for her, like I should be her mother and take care of her. But I was only three and four and five and six and didn't know how, except by not being a burden.

In the beginning, the bombing was at night. She would tell me to quickly! quickly! put on a sweater or coat and shoes and run downstairs. I would hide under the kitchen table until she had dressed herself and wrapped up the baby. Then we would run through the long, narrow garden to the **air-raid shelter**. It seemed always to be night, and dark, with sirens screaming and wailing.

The shelter was simply some corrugated steel sheets made into a shed against the brick, garden wall, with a sloping roof. It had a dirt floor and two wooden benches inside on which to sit. No heat, no light. Mother brought candles if she remembered, or else we sat in the dark. If a stranger was on the street when the sirens began, they could knock at any house door and be taken in to the shelter, and spend the night in the shelter.

Mother was always complaining about the **rations**. She wasn't a good cook and didn't know how to make exotic things like puddings or any treats, so our food was very simple. Mostly something boiled or fried. There was often nothing—nothing at all—to eat and we got used to being hungry. . . .

air-raid shelter: this was apparently the basic version of an Anderson shelter, of which the British government provided a total of 3.6 million, free or at very low cost, for use in the backyards and gardens of houses lacking a cellar

rations: food, clothing, coal, and other necessities were strictly rationed in wartime Britain, restrictions which remained in force until the early 1950s

. . .

The City Authorities would regularly send people (women with small children) out of the City, into the country for safety. Mother would go with much grumbling and complaining. She was a City person.

The train would be packed to the limit with American soldiers coming and going somewhere. Every seat was taken, every foot of ground had someone crammed into it. As a small child, I could not step over the rucksacks or around the people, so the soldiers would pass me down the corridor, from hand to hand, with my mother trying to keep up. And they gave me chewing gum! I learned to say "Any gum, chum?" for a stick of Wrigley's Spearmint gum.

Those yanks! I thought they were the grandest, most glamorous people in the world.

Easy smiling, handsome, glamorous looking, movie-star sounding, generous and friendly.

Yanks! With oranges and chocolate bars in their backpacks, silk stockings in their hip pocket, chewing gum (Wrigley's Juicy Fruit) in their hands. All to be given away, to us, if only we can get to talk to them. If only your young and pretty aunt will go dancing with one, and then invite him home for tea.

They aren't like us English. To be proper we must be standoffish, serious, and quiet. (Children should be seen and not heard). And we shouldn't want or take more than one of anything.

But the Yanks! Their uniforms are smooth and beautiful; their movements are relaxed, spacious. They take up lots of space, just standing there. They have wonderful accents. Sometimes hard to understand, but wonderful to hear when they draaawl their words. It sounds soft, unthreatening, friendly. They talk easily, loudly to each other—they laugh easily, out loud, even in public places!

They like children! How astonishing—they actually like children! Talk to us, tousle our hair, sit us on their laps, tell us we're cute (what's cute??), give us sticks of gum. And we don't have to save it—we can eat it. Before dinner! And they don't get angry if we ask for more. Or if we hang around them, stay close, touch them. This must be what having a father is like.

Age 5—in love. Head-over-heels madly in love—with Yanks. . . .

When the war was over, there was a party on the street. And some time later the soldiers began coming home.

I begged my mother to allow me to run down the stairs and answer the door when my daddy came home. And she said yes.

It seemed a long time later that the doorbell rang, and I remember very well the excitement of that moment. I ran to the door, opened it, and a giant stood there. A tall, tall man in uniform, with a backpack. A total stranger. I don't remember him at all after that moment for many years. My mother told me that I kept asking her when he was going away again, because I didn't like this stranger telling me what to do.

Source: Website Timewitnesses: Memories of the Last Century. http://timewitnesses.org/english/%7Epamelay.html. Used by permission of Pamela Lazarus.

AFTERMATH

Some British children, especially those in country areas relatively remote from the war, undoubtedly enjoyed a relatively tranquil and happy childhood despite the conflict, albeit one marked by austerity, shortages, and the deaths of too many relatives, friends, and acquaintances not greatly older than themselves. Lazarus, however, when asked if she had been happy during the war, retorted: "If I were to be offered one million dollars to relive my childhood, in a heartbeat I'd say 'No way?'. . . . I remember my childhood with shivers." In the mid-1950s, she emigrated with her family, first to Canada, then to the United States, a move which almost certainly gave her the chance of a more affluent lifestyle, but which like many emigrants she also felt cut her off from her extended family and its traditions. A lively, competent, and outgoing woman, with a great sense of humor, she "married a young man from Brooklyn" in 1968, had two daughters and, once they were in school, began an excellent career in "classically men's jobs" selling "first industrial chemicals and tools, then warehouses, land and office buildings." Although she and her husband divorced in 1975, she "made lots of money and made sure my daughters went to and graduated from college." Her daughters both have excellent careers, she has four grandchildren to whom she is clearly devoted, and she describes her life as "a very typical American immigrant success story." It is hard to disagree.

Yet despite all these achievements Lazarus felt she did not escape unscathed from the war. She believed that her wartime experiences and the insecurity caused by "years of living in fear" left her "a young adult with absolutely no sense of self, or of safety, anywhere, at any time." The aftereffects of the war years were, she thought, responsible for a nervous stomach disorder she suffered at the age of 10, and contributed to the breakup of her marriage, difficulties in interpersonal relationships, and her chronic health problems.

ASK YOURSELF

1. Fifty-five years after the war had ended, Pamela Lazarus came across the Timewitnesses Web site for survivors of World War II, set up in January 1994,

its mission to ensure "that the lessons of the past will be learned by a new generation." She quickly volunteered an oral history and also agreed to become one of those participants who were prepared to correspond with children and others seeking to learn more about the war. What are the motivations that lead individuals to record their memories of important experiences in their lives, often many years after the events in question?

2. American expectations of what children should do and how they should behave tended to be far less rigorous and formal and more tolerant than those of Europeans. Overall, the manners and social conduct of Americans were also much more relaxed than those of the British. What advantages and disadvantages did these characteristics give American servicemen when dealing with the British?
3. In what became almost a stereotype, popular memories of the **Blitz** and wartime London have tended to emphasize camaraderie and the positive aspects of the time. Why are many people driven to romanticize the past retrospectively and remember its bright rather than its dark and gloomy side? Is this tendency a useful survival mechanism, enabling them to cope with difficult memories which otherwise might become intolerable?

TOPICS TO CONSIDER

1. The experience of war did not necessarily eradicate British **anti-Semitism**. In other portions of her recollections, Lazarus recounted how, when she and her mother went to the country as evacuees, their board and keep paid by the British government, host families would inspect their potential paying guests and reject those they did not want. Many country people "didn't like Jews because they were supposedly all the awful things that have ever been said about Jews." One woman "became hysterical" when she spotted a Star of David the mother had given her daughter "as a good luck charm to help keep me alive" and immediately expelled the young child and her mother from the house, "screaming that we had 'contaminated' everything we had touched—her dishes, her knives and forks—her very air!" Why, given the anti-Semitic and racist nature of Nazi ideology, did the British government make little if any effort to eradicate such popular attitudes?
2. Children generally have far less independence and freedom than adults, and—especially during wartime—often cannot really comprehend the reasons for the circumstances in which they find themselves. Does this lack of understanding, together with their powerlessness, make the experience of war particularly frightening to many children?

Further Information

Anderson, C. Leroy, Joanne R. Anderson, and Yunosuke Ohkura, eds. *No Longer Silent: World-Wide Memories of the Children of World War II: Autobiographic Essays.* Missoula, MT: Pictorial Histories, 1995.

Hylton, Stuart. *Their Darkest Hour: The Hidden History of the Home Front, 1939–1945.* Stroud, UK: Sutton, 2004.

Lewis, Peter. *A People's War.* London: Thames Methuen, 1986.

Longmate, Norman. *The G.I.'s: The Americans in Britain, 1942–1945.* New York: Scribner's, 1975.

Mackay, Robert. *The Test of War: Inside Britain 1939–45.* London: UCL Press, 1999.
Reynolds, David. *Rich Relations: The American Occupation of Britain, 1942–1945.* New York: Random House, 1995.
Werner, Emmy E. *Through the Eyes of Innocents: Children Witness World War II.* Boulder, CO: Westview Press, 2000.

Web Sites

BBC Primary History: World War 2. BBC Learning Web site. http://www.bbc.co.uk/schools/primaryhistory/world_war2/.
The "Blitz," September 7, 1940–1944. World War II Multimedia Database. http://www.worldwar2database.com/html/blitz.htm.
The Children's War: The Second World War Through the Eyes of the Children of Britain. Imperial War Museum London Web site. http://london.iwm.org.uk/upload/package/50/children/Exhibition/index.htm.
The Second World War 1939–1945. The National Archives Web site. http://www.nationalarchives.gov.uk/education/world-war-two.htm.

Films and Television

Dad's Army: The Complete Collection (1968–1977), starring Arthur Lowe, John Le Mesurier, Clive Dunn, John Laurie, and James Beck. BBC.
Dad's Army: The Movie (1971), starring Arthur Lowe, John Le Mesurier, Clive Dunn, John Laurie, and James Beck.
Fires Were Started (1943), directed by Humphrey Jennings. Starring George Gravett, Philip Dickson, and Fred Griffiths.
A Matter of Life and Death (1946), starring David Niven, Kim Hunter, Roger Livesey, and Raymond Massey.
Millions Like Us (1943), starring Eric Portman, Patricia Roc, Gordon Jackson, and Anne Crawford.

31. Women and Work: Oral History of Lola Weixel

INTRODUCTION

During World War II, the U.S. government actively encouraged American women to work, either at civilian jobs or in one of the auxiliary branches of the armed forces. At least temporarily, American women were employed in unprecedented numbers. One World War II iconic image was the poster of Rosie the Riveter, a woman worker in an aircraft plant often thought to epitomize American women's wartime contributions to the war effort. Among women who took a factory job was Lola Weixel, a young and highly politically conscious Jewish woman from New York.

KEEP IN MIND AS YOU READ

1. In the United States, a broad assumption existed that women's wartime employment was only a temporary emergency expedient, and that once the war ended, most women would gladly quit their jobs and resume life as homemakers.
2. From 1942 onward, the American government launched an aggressive publicity campaign to encourage women to take up jobs and free men to serve in the armed forces.
3. During the war, the number of American women working increased 60 percent, reaching 19 million in 1940, and the proportion of all American women employed rose from 28 to 37 percent. Of these, 72 percent of women joining the workforce during the war were married, with 60 percent aged 35 or above.

Oral History of Lola Weixel

I was a welder during World War II. I worked hard, was an anti-fascist—thought about that every day—and thought about my loved ones. I think that nobody can imagine the passion that we had, first as human beings, as anti-fascists, and, in my case, as a Jewish woman, to defeat fascism and save the world—save civilization from the plans of the Nazis that we all knew **Hitler** had outlined in his writings and in his ravings. . . . I wanted to become a welder because the boy across the street from my grandma's house was learning to be a welder, and he told me it was the most exciting thing on earth but that women couldn't do it. . . .

But aha! **Pearl Harbor** happened. Right away I got a letter, and there were lot of other women there overnight being trained. There were men in the program, too. We had a really good course. We had to take sheet-metal work before we could do welding; we had to learn to use tools. I was very bad. I was pretty dumb, but I was so determined, and they were so kind in that they didn't throw me out. They let me stay as long as it took, and it took me long compared to the other people, but then I got very good. We had two unusual teachers, and they were able to speak and tell me about what the heck I was doing there and what the function of welding was. I was never one who could learn something by imitating; I had to understand the process. Before I knew it, I was not only working as a welder, but I had a certificate that said I was a first-class welder. Lots of the women got that. We were very, very proud of it. It meant you were capable and could be trusted to work any kind of welding job. . . . Some people thought we were there to meet men. What men? We were there to get that "A" paper.

The women I worked with and the women I went to school with were largely, what we called at that time, working-class women. There's some talk saying that women came from every walk of life, and I suppose it's true, but women who chose to do hard, dirty work were working-class women whose fathers and brothers were often in the trades. They thought it was great. They knew about unions; they knew that they could make more money if they joined unions. Most of them were really down-to-earth, nice; I don't like to say ordinary or plain, but I mean that in the best sense of the words. Women who could be depended upon.

The first job I had as a welder was in a machine shop where they were making targets. We did the metal frames. They were round metal frames, and I understand that a colored sleeve would be put on it. They were towed up in the air on an airplane, and the men would do target practice on those. Now this was really very simple welding, and that made me a little unhappy because I felt that I could do more. I don't want to say that it was boring. It wasn't, because we had a lot of fun in the shop. We did a lot of singing, and the girls were swell. But I really wanted to do more skilled work.

There were some women who wanted to do what they called table work. They would sit, I guess these were some of the older women, and do small parts for the **glider**. The younger ones, and I was among them, wanted to do the climbing all over the glider, working in strange positions and doing more demanding work. That was fun. Now, the last job I had was very strange because they told us that we were making bomb cases. So I say we were making bomb cases. But I wouldn't swear to that. I don't know. They looked like metal coffins. . . .

Of the women I worked with, well, there were some more political than others, but they were all very much for the war and against Hitler. I must say that the feelings against the Japanese bordered on the racist. Everybody watched where the Red Army was every day on the maps. Everybody cared about that because they knew damn well we were giving our production, but they were giving their lives. We all knew it; everybody knew it. It hurts me today when I realize that there are so many young people growing up who don't even know that we were a partnership. . . .

My husband [away in the army] wrote to me at one time when I guess he was contemplating how we would get along after the war, because we were not rich people. We were not even comfortable people. We were very uncomfortable people as far as money was concerned. And he said: "You'll be a welder after the war. And you'll make a decent living and I'll do something and together we'll be okay. Don't worry." We did depend on it. So what

Pearl Harbor: U.S. naval base in Hawaii, where Japanese airplanes attacked the U.S. Pacific fleet on December 7, 1941, after which Japan, Germany, and Italy declared war on the United States

glider: engineless airplane, towed or winched up into the air

a shock to find out that it was not to be. I think that the question often is, Well, didn't you women expect to be thrown out after the war? Some women apparently, according to what they say, did. But people I worked with . . . thought we were learning a skill that would last us and be useful all our lives. We were very shocked and angry and hurt when we found that that was not true, that after the war they were finished with us, and we were gone—in spite of being a first-class welder and all that. It was not to be for the future.

I think the testimony of black women was especially touching, in that here they gained so much dignity and a feeling of self-worth from holding down these jobs in difficult situations. They were very good, very good. Black women wanted very much to excel because they had so much to gain. More than the rest of us, I would say. And to hear them say that they had to go back to cleaning somebody's house was really very, very maddening. You can imagine the frustration that went with that.

Source: Helene Keyssar and Vladimir Pozner, *Remembering War: A U.S.-Soviet Dialogue* (New York: Oxford University Press, 1990), 95–98. Used by permission.

AFTERMATH

Lola Weixel got married during the war. David, her husband, was serving in the armed forces. To her great regret, Weixel lost her job immediately the war ended. She became pregnant as soon as her husband returned. Later in life, she featured in the documentary *The Life and Times of Rosie the Riveter* (1983). Her family remained in New York and continued her tradition of progressive activism. Like Weixel, the majority of American female industrial workers lost their jobs when World War II ended. The assumption was that returning servicemen should automatically have priority for any available employment. By early 1947, approximately one million fewer American women held factory jobs than in 1945.

ASK YOURSELF

1. After training as a welder, Weixel believed that men greatly exaggerated the difficulty of their jobs, finding herself "that the skills were, so hard to learn, that, in fact, could be quickly learned." What tangible and intangible benefits did men gain by encouraging this kind of mystique?
2. After her marriage, Weixel decided to stick with her job rather than following her soldier husband from one military training camp to another. Later, she regretted that they had had so little time together, remembering "lots of letters and a lot of loneliness," but she still believed that her "own dignity depended on my carrying out of my responsibilities." Was she unusual in thinking her wartime job justified separation from her new husband?
3. Unlike men, women who worked still were expected to perform most domestic and household tasks. In another interview, Weixel remembered how she would "go home and cook and clean and do the laundry while my brother lay on the couch. We didn't question it much then. But I was angry about it for years." Why did masculine attitudes toward women who worked show so little change?
4. Weixel was a labor activist. She and fellow women workers set up a labor union in their workshop, whereupon the owner locked them out. When they joined the United Electrical Workers Union, they won an 80 percent pay rise. They also protested when black women were paid less than white women. Was Weixel fired

in 1945 because she was a woman, or because she was a highly effective trade unionist?

TOPICS TO CONSIDER

1. Although American women took up a wide variety of wartime jobs, they still faced massive and pervasive discrimination. Within the industrial labor force, in 1944 women held only 4.4 percent of positions as craftsmen, foremen, and skilled workers, up from 2.1 percent in 1940; they were often paid less for the same job, with wages only about 60 percent those of men, and rarely promoted. White-collar women workers also tended to be concentrated at the lower end of their professions. Why were women who were supposedly performing a patriotic duty routinely treated so unequally?
2. During and after World War II, in most countries a fundamental social assumption was that women should invariably and without question subordinate their own preferences and expectations to the broader dictates of a male-dominated state. What did these experiences contribute to the emergence of the women's movement in subsequent decades?

Further Information

Campbell, D'Ann. *Women at War with America: Private Lives in a Patriotic Era.* Cambridge, MA: Harvard University Press, 1984.

Colman, Penny. *Rosie the Riveter: Women Working on the Home Front in World War II.* New York: Crown Publishers, 1995.

Gluck, Sherna Berger. *Rosie the Riveter Revisited: Women, the War, and Social Change.* Boston: Twayne, 1987.

Hartmann, Susan M. *Home Front and Beyond: American Women in the 1940s.* Boston: Twayne, 1982.

Honey, Maureen. *Creating Rosie the Riveter: Class, Gender, and Propaganda during World War II.* Amherst: University of Massachusetts Press, 1984.

Honey, Maureen, ed. *Bitter Fruit: African American Women in World War II.* Columbia: University of Missouri Press, 1999.

Web Sites

American Women in World War II. History.com. http://www.history.com/topics/american-women-in-world-war-ii.

Partners in Winning the War: American Women in World War II. National Women's History Museum. http://www.nwhm.org/online-exhibits/partners/exhibitentrance.html.

Rosie Pictures: Select Images Relating to American Women Workers During World War II. The Library of Congress: Prints and Photographs Reading Room. http://www.loc.gov/rr/print/list/126_rosi.html.

Films and Television

The Life and Times of Rosie the Riveter (1980), directed by Connie Field. Clarity Films.
Rosie the Riveter (1944), starring Jane Frazee, Frank Albertson, and Barbara Jo Allen.
Swing Shift (1984), starring Goldie Hawn, Kurt Russell, and Christine Lahti.

32. Racial Conflicts in the U.S. Army: Recollections of Allen Thompson, 758th Tank Battalion

INTRODUCTION

Throughout World War II, racial conflicts bedeviled the U.S. Army. Especially in the south, racially motivated fights between black and white soldiers often disturbed the routine of military training camps. Allen Thompson of Cleveland, Ohio, from a part black, part Irish family, was studying history and political science at Wilberforce University when he was drafted in October 1941. It may well be significant that his grandfather had left the southern state of Mississippi to escape lynching after he had beaten up a white man who was cheating him. Thompson's all-black unit, the 758th Tank Battalion, proved assertive in insisting on training for combat service in tanks and resisting white troops' attempts to intimate them.

KEEP IN MIND AS YOU READ

1. When World War II began, African Americans throughout the United States faced pervasive discrimination, both formal and informal. In the southern states, Jim Crow laws forced blacks to use segregated public facilities, including schools, hospitals, transport, restaurants, sports grounds, cinemas, bathrooms, and hotels, that were separate from and almost invariably inferior to those provided for whites. Various legal and extralegal devices also made it extremely difficult for blacks to vote in elections.
2. Over one million African Americans served in the U.S. armed forces, 8 percent of total American military personnel. Many felt that they were fighting a double battle, not just against **fascism** abroad, but also against domestic racism and segregation.
3. The U.S. military was segregated. In 1940, the Marines and Air Corps would not accept African Americans, the navy would only take them as messmen, and the army segregated them rigidly, assigning black soldiers to separate combat and noncombat units. Black officers could not command white troops.
4. In the army, 78 percent of blacks but only 40 percent of whites were assigned to service units, where they often performed difficult and dangerous tasks, but lacked the acclaim and recognition of combat troops.

5. U.S. wartime rhetoric emphasized that the Allied powers were fighting for democracy, equality, and freedom, and condemned the racist ideology of the **Axis powers**, Germany, Japan, and Italy. Japanese propaganda sought to criticize Western colonialism and accused the Allies of fighting a "white man's war."

Recollections of Allen Thompson, 758th Tank Battalion

We were in tank training at **Fort Knox** when all of the sudden they told us they were going to put us into a **trucking company**. So we refused to eat. We did not go to the mess hall. We did it as a whole unit. There were a couple of lawyers in the group, and they got us organized. We just did not eat. And we said that we wanted to be trained as tankers and used as tankers, that was our demand. We did not want to be truck drivers or port battalion or loaders. We wanted to be tankers. Finally, they saw it our way. We even got black cooks because we complained that the white guys didn't know how to cook for us.

. . . .

When we got to **Camp Patrick Henry**, I saw it brewing. I could smell trouble, and I could see it too. When we went in for our indoctrination, the paratroopers on that base were antagonistic. They would gesture. They had shroud knives, the kind you use to cut your shroud when you drop in a parachute. They patted them, and they made gestures with those knives. We were told when we got there we could go anyplace on the post, because we are in the United States Army and all that. It was the post commander talking. "You are not confined to any area. You can go anywhere you want to." Well, that wasn't the case.

Some of our men had gone to the **PX** and were escorted out or run away from the area. The PX in our area was mixed, white and black soldiers. But the problem began because some white girls were overly friendly with the black soldiers, and the white paratroopers didn't like it. I was in the PX that night with a couple of sergeants, and I said, "Let's get out of here. I see some problems." So we got out.

The next night I was in charge of quarters, and oh, about fifty of those paratroopers came down the road in front of our **barracks**. They were making a lot of racket. I said, "What do you fellas want?"

"Well, your boys are trying to emulate paratroopers," they said. "They have their pants stuck down in their combat boots like us, and we feel that you all are trying to emulate paratroopers."

I said, "Well, these men are authorized for combat boots." And I told them to get back to their unit because they had no business over here. They left, but the next night about two hundred of them came back.

That night they said, "We're gonna kill some niggers tonight." Well, some shooting started. I don't know what side started it. But I do know that my company commander was supposed to have been knocked down, and the key to the **armory** was taken. And guns were taken out. And we had a small gunfight. It lasted about a hot minute. Because when the shots rang out and people fell, those guys cleared out in about two seconds. One of my men in the company got shot in the foot. One of theirs got killed. So they more or less quarantined the company, and there was a large investigation.

Fort Knox: U.S. Army base in southern state of Kentucky
trucking company: transport and delivery unit
Camp Patrick Henry: U.S. Army base in southern state of Virginia
PX: post exchange, store on army base for use of military personnel
barracks: accommodation for troops
armory: weapon storage facility

They took us in one by one and questioned us. They didn't have any evidence. None of the guns had fingerprints; nobody remembered nothing. But they busted the staff sergeant in my company, said that he had taken the key from the company commander. They couldn't figure out how my gun had been fired, and I said, "I don't know either."

We heard that paratrooper unit had jumped on every black unit that had come through. They found some excuse to jump on the black units, and they had never been stopped. One officer said, "Your outfit was the first to stop them." Yeah, my bunch of boys in the 758th Tank Battalion were crazy, I tell you. We had fellas from Chicago, New York, Detroit, Cleveland, Philadelphia, all, mostly, city boys, big city boys.

Source: Maggi M. Morehouse, *Fighting in the Jim Crow Army: Black Men and Women Remember World War II* (Lanham, MD: Rowman & Littlefield, 2000), 102, 106–108. Used by permission of Rowman & Littlefield.

AFTERMATH

During World War II, pressures for changes in military policy mounted. From April 1942 onward, the navy changed its policies, admitting blacks for general labor service and eventually integrating several ships, where African Americans served as radio and gunnery specialists. Twenty-two black combat units fought in Europe, the 758th Tank Battalion among them, and after the 1944–1945 Battle of the Bulge decimated various all-white infantry regiments, 2,500 African Americans were formed into platoons that joined white companies. In July 1941, the Air Corps also established a black training program at Tuskegee, Alabama, which eventually graduated 992 pilots, including those who made up the famous all-black 99th Fighter Squadron and 332d Fighter Group. In combat, African Americans generally performed at least as well as whites, receiving over 12,000 decorations and citations. In 1948 President **Harry S. Truman** desegregated the U.S. armed forces.

Though still doggedly opposed by many Americans, by the time the war ended civil rights and the struggle for black equality had become part of the national liberal agenda.

ASK YOURSELF

1. American military leaders were initially reluctant to send black troops overseas, fearing that if they encountered an egalitarian reception in other countries, especially the opportunity to date white women, this might prove unsettling to both black and white soldiers. They warned British and Australian officials not to allow African American military personnel to mix too freely with the local population. How did the British and Australians react to these suggestions?
2. Black servicemen who returned from fighting in World War II often became active in campaigns for voting rights and against segregation. In what ways did the experience of wartime service help to make them more assertive and self-confident in demanding these rights?
3. During World War II, membership in the National Association for the Advancement of Colored People (NAACP), the major American body representing African Americans, increased from 50,000 to 500,000, and a new organization, the interracial Congress of Racial Equality, also came into existence. Young African Americans in particular participated in boycotts and picketing against racist businesses, and many blacks were consciously committed to the

Double V for Victory campaign. In 1944 the Supreme Court declared all-white primaries, common in many southern states, unconstitutional, and the NAACP prepared to mount legal challenges to other segregationist practices. Had American political leaders anticipated these developments when the country entered World War II?

TOPICS TO CONSIDER

1. From World War II onward, the movement to win African Americans equal rights and end discrimination against them gained increasing momentum in the United States? Without the impact of the war, would the civil rights movement still have developed rapidly in the mid-20th century?
2. Did World War II prove an impetus for major social changes of any kind in other countries?
3. World War II helped to discredit colonial rule and accelerated the ending of Western imperialism in Asia and elsewhere. Did the same forces that weakened and undercut racism in the United States also threaten the continuation of Western colonialism? If so, how?

Further Information

Brandt, Nat. *Harlem at War: The Black Experience in World War II.* Syracuse, NY: Syracuse University Press, 1996.

Colley, David. *Blood for Dignity: The Story of the First Integrated Combat Unit in the U.S. Army.* New York: St. Martin's Press, 2003.

MacGregor, Morris J., Jr. *Integration of the Armed Forces, 1940–1965.* Washington, DC: Department of the Army, 1981.

McGuire, Philip. *Taps for a Jim Crow Army: Letters from Black Soldiers in World War II.* Santa Barbara, CA: ABC-Clio, 1983.

Morehouse, Maggi M. *Fighting in the Jim Crow Army: Black Men and Women Remember World War II.* Lanham, MD: Rowman & Littlefield, 2000.

Motley, Mary Pennick, ed. *The Invisible Soldier: The Experience of the Black Soldier, World War II.* Detroit: Wayne State University Press, 1975.

Wynn, Neil A. *The Afro-American and the Second World War.* Rev. ed. London: Holmes and Meier, 1993.

Web Sites

African Americans in the U.S. Army. Army.Mil: Features. http://www.army.mil/africanamericans/.

African American Odyssey. Library of Congress. http://memory.loc.gov/ammem/aaohtml/aohome.html.

Pictures of African Americans during World War II. U.S. National Archives. http://www.archives.gov/research/african-americans/ww2-pictures/.

Films and Television

Flying for Freedom: Untold Stories of the Tuskegee Airmen (2007). AMS Pictures.

Mutiny (1999), starring Michael Jai White, David Ramsey, and Duane Martin.

The Tuskegee Airmen: They Fought Two Wars (1995), starring Lawrence Fishburne, Alan Payne, and Malcolm-Jamal Warner.

Appendix 1: Biographical Sketches of Important Individuals Mentioned in the Text

Chamberlain, Neville (1869–1940): Conservative British politician, prime minister from 1937 to 1940. He became notorious for concluding the September 1938 Munich agreement with Adolf Hitler, under whose terms Germany annexed a large portion of Czechoslovakia's territory, the Sudetenland.

Churchill, Winston Leonard Spencer (1874–1965): Maverick British politician, the grandson of the Duke of Marlborough, son of Lord Randolph Churchill, a Conservative politician who served as chancellor of the exchequer in 1886, and his American wife Jennie Jerome. Winston, active in British politics from the early 1900s, switched parties twice, from the Conservatives to the Liberals in 1906, returning to the Conservative fold in the 1920s. Between 1906 and 1929 he served as home secretary, first lord of the admiralty, secretary of state for war, and chancellor of the exchequer. During the 1930s his strong support for British rearmament put him at odds with the Conservative administrations of Stanley Baldwin and Neville Chamberlain, who barred him from office. When World War II began, Churchill served briefly as first lord of the admiralty, becoming prime minister of a wartime coalition government in May 1940, and winning fame as a valiant and indomitable war leader who embodied Britain's fighting spirit. Voted out of office in July 1945, he returned as Conservative prime minister from 1951 to 1955.

De Gaulle, Charles (1890–1970): French general and statesman who broke with the French government in June 1940 over its surrender to Germany and went into exile, becoming the foremost leader of the Free French forces who decided to fight on against Germany. In 1958, he founded the Fifth French Republic, serving as its president from 1959 to 1969.

Eichmann, Adolf (1906–1962): Nazi official who took a leading role in drafting the "final solution" plan to exterminate all European Jews and in organizing the logistics of its implementation. After Germany's defeat in 1945, he fled to Argentina. Kidnapped by Israeli intelligence operatives in 1960, he stood trial in Jerusalem on charges of crimes against humanity and war crimes, and was convicted and executed in 1962.

Eisenhower, Dwight D. "Ike" (1890–1969): Five-star American general and supreme commander of Allied forces in Europe during World War II, responsible for planning and directing the invasions of North Africa in 1942 and France. After World War II, he served as chief of staff of the U.S. Army and the first supreme commander of North

Atlantic Treaty Organization (NATO) forces in Europe. From 1953 to 1961, he was the 34th president of the United States.

Goebbels, Josef (1897–1945): A fanatical Nazi and anti-Semite and early supporter of Adolf Hitler, Goebbels was German minister of propaganda from 1933 to 1945. He, his wife Magda, and six children remained with Hitler in the latter's Berlin bunker as the German capital fell to Russian troops, and after killing their children committed suicide themselves.

Goering, Hermann (1893–1946): Leading member of the Nazi Party, a former World War I fighter pilot, appointed head of the German Luftwaffe in 1935 and deputy Führer (German leader) in 1941. Tried for war crimes after Germany's defeat and sentenced to death, he committed suicide in his prison cell.

Hess, Rudolf (1894–1987): An early Nazi supporter and Adolf Hitler's deputy Führer, he fled to Britain in 1941 and spent the remainder of his life in various prisons.

Heydrich, Reinhard (1904–1942): Head of the *Reichssichterheitshauptamt* (RSHA), the major German security and police authority, appointed governor of German Czechoslovakia in September 1941, and assassinated by Czech resistance agents in June 1942.

Himmler, Heinrich (1900–1945): Leading Nazi Party official, as head of the German SS (*Schutzstaffeln* or Protection Police) and minister of the interior responsible for all Germany's internal and external security forces and for supervising all administrative matters, including concentration and extermination camps. Captured by Allied forces in May 1945, he committed suicide before he could stand trial for war crimes.

Hirohito, or the Shōwa Emperor (1901–1989): Emperor of Japan from 1926 until his death, Japan's head of state throughout World War II, who made the decision to surrender to the Allied powers in August 1945. The degree of his personal involvement in and support for Japanese military policies during the 1930s and 1940s remains controversial. Once the war ended, Allied occupation authorities retained the emperor as a useful political figurehead and symbol of stability and continuity, and therefore deliberately minimized his responsibility for earlier Japanese actions.

Hitler, Adolf (1889–1945): Austrian-born politician and World War I veteran who became head of the German Nazi (National Socialist German Workers) Party in 1921, and chancellor of Germany in 1933. As Führer (supreme leader) of Nazi Germany from 1933 to 1945, he installed a one-party dictatorship. Ultimate responsibility for all major German policies during this period rested on Hitler, who embarked on an accelerated German rearmament program during the 1930s and annexed Austria and Czechoslovakia in 1938 and 1939. Fanatically anti-Semitic, Hitler initially deprived German Jews of their rights as citizens, driving many to flee from Germany, and from 1940 onward implemented deportation and extermination policies designed to destroy all the remaining European Jews. After Germany invaded Poland in September 1939, fear of Hitler's continuing expansionist policies led Britain and France to declare war on Germany. Following rapid victories over Poland, Denmark, Norway, Belgium, the Netherlands, and France, all of which came under German occupation, in June 1941 Hitler declared war on Soviet Russia, embroiling his country in a lengthy, bloody, and ultimately disastrous conflict. Six months later, Germany also went to war with the United States, which spearheaded a second European front against German forces in July 1944. In spring 1945, Russian, American, and British forces converged on Germany. Facing defeat, on April 30, 1945, Hitler committed suicide in beleaguered Berlin.

Lindbergh, Charles Augustus (1902–1974): U.S. aviator who attained international celebrity status in 1927 when he became the first person to make a nonstop solo air flight across the Atlantic, from the United States to France. He then helped to pioneer the emerging U.S. aviation industry. After the kidnapping and murder of his eldest son in 1932, Lindbergh and his wife moved to Europe until 1939, when they returned to the United States. Before Pearl Harbor, Lindbergh, who believed that Great Britain and France were incapable of defeating Germany, became one of the most prominent opponents of U.S. intervention in World War II. Although nominally only a civilian consultant to the U.S. military, Lindbergh flew numerous combat missions in the Pacific theater of war. He later became an early supporter of the environmentalist movement.

MacArthur, Douglas (1880–1964): Leading U.S. general, commander of U.S. Armed Forces in the Far East, 1941–1942, who escaped to Australia after Japanese troops defeated American and Philippine forces and occupied the Philippine Islands. As supreme Allied commander of the Southwest Pacific Area, 1942–1945, directed an island-hopping campaign against Japan, retook the Philippines, and accepted Japan's official surrender on September 2, 1945. As supreme commander of the Allied Powers in Japan, from 1945 to 1950 MacArthur presided over major political, social, and economic reforms. From June 1950 to March 1951, he was commander in chief of United Nations forces in Korea.

Marshall, George Catlett (1880–1959): As chief of staff of the U.S. Army from 1939 to 1945 and chief military adviser to President Franklin D. Roosevelt, responsible for planning and directing overall U.S. military strategy in both Europe and Japan. Marshall subsequently became U.S. secretary of state from 1947 to 1949 and was secretary of defense from 1950 to 1951.

Mussolini, Benito (1883–1945): Italian politician, leader of the National Fascist Party, who became Italian prime minister in 1922. Known from 1925 as *Il Duce* (the leader), he made Italy into a one-party Fascist state and embarked on an aggressive nationalist program of expansion. In 1935 Italy invaded the North African state of Abyssinia. Mussolini aligned Italy with other fascist states, most notably Hitler's Germany, and in the 1936–1939 Spanish Civil War supported the ultimately victorious Nationalist military forces in their rebellion against the leftist government. After Hitler's successful conquest of most of Western Europe, in June 1940 Mussolini joined Germany in declaring war on Great Britain and France. In June 1941, Mussolini likewise supported the German invasion of the Soviet Union, sending Italian troops to fight on the Eastern front, and in December 1941 Italy joined Germany in declaring war on the United States. After Allied forces invaded Italy in July 1943, Mussolini's colleagues deposed him and placed him under arrest, negotiated an armistice with the Allies in September, and declared war on Germany in October 1943. Rescued from captivity in September 1943 by German paratroopers, Mussolini spent 18 months under German protection as a puppet ruler in north Italy. In late April 1945, Italian partisan fighters captured Mussolini and his mistress and summarily executed them.

Pu Yi Aisin Gioro (1906–1967): As a child he became the last emperor of China in 1908 and was deposed in 1912. When the Japanese took over Manchuria in 1932 and established the state of Manchukuo, they installed Pu Yi as a figurehead emperor, which he remained until 1945. Captured by Soviet forces in 1945, Pu Yi was repatriated to China after a Communist government took power there in 1949. After lengthy rehabilitation, he endorsed the Communist regime and spent the rest of his life in China.

Rommel, Erwin (1891–1944): Charismatic German field marshal who commanded German troops in Poland, France, and North Africa during World War II. Transferred to Normandy in late 1943 to prepare German forces to resist the anticipated Anglo-American second front invasion of France, while Soviet military units gradually advanced toward Germany, Rommel became increasingly disaffected from Hitler and by summer 1944 supported the Führer's overthrow. Implicated in an unsuccessful 1944 assassination plot against Hitler and seriously wounded soon after D-Day, in October 1944 Rommel was given the option of committing suicide, which he accepted.

Roosevelt, Franklin Delano (1882–1945): Democratic politician, from 1933 to 1945 32nd president of the United States. In the 1930s he implemented the New Deal, a major program of domestic social and economic reforms intended to combat the effects of the Great Depression. In international affairs, from the late 1930s onward he steered his country toward ever stronger opposition to the Axis powers, Germany, Italy, and Japan. In December 1941, all the three nations declared war on the United States. Under Roosevelt's leadership, the United States assertively headed the Allied coalition that won victory in both Europe and Asia in 1945.

Roosevelt, Theodore (1858–1919): Republican politician, 26th president of the United States from 1901 to 1909, a staunch believer that the United States should greatly expand its international role and become a leading great power.

Stalin, Josef Vissarionovich (1878–1953): Communist revolutionary who served as general secretary of the Soviet Communist Party from 1922 until his death in 1953, from the late 1920s unchallenged supreme ruler of the Soviet Union. Known for his ruthless elimination of political rivals and other opponents, both domestic and international, and his brutality in waging war.

Wilson, Woodrow (1856–1924): Democratic politician, from 1913 to 1921 28th president of the United States. As leader of his country during World War I, Wilson sought a declaration of war against Germany in April 1917 and enunciated a program of idealistic war aims that envisaged remaking the world's international system under American guidance along democratic, liberal capitalist, nonimperialist lines.

Yamamoto, Isoroku (1884–1943): Innovative Japanese Naval Marshal General, commander-in-chief of the Japanese Combined Fleet, who planned and supervised the December 1941 Pearl Harbor attack. He died in April 1943 when American fighters intercepted and shot down an airplane carrying him on an inspection tour of the South Pacific.

Appendix 2: Glossary of Terms Mentioned in the Text

Anti-Semitism: Hatred and prejudice against Jews.

Aryan: A term used by Nazi Germany to define racial purity. Aryans were supposedly blond, blue-eyed, fair-skinned, and physically fit.

Axis Powers: Germany, Italy, and Japan, the three major Fascist, totalitarian powers, linked from September 1940 in the Tripartite Pact, joined later by Hungary, Romania, and Bulgaria. During World War II, the Axis powers aligned themselves against the Allied powers, though not all nations in either camp were at war with all the others in the opposing group.

Blitz: Usually refers to the intensive German bombing of London, the British capital city, in 1940–1941.

Blitzkrieg, literally lightning war: the extremely swift mechanized campaigns in which German tanks, supported by heavy air power, swept across most of Western Europe in 1940.

D-Day: Opening day of the Anglo-American invasion of Western Europe, launched on June 6, 1944.

Destroyers-for-Bases Agreement (September 1940): An agreement whereby the United States gave beleaguered Britain 50 over-age destroyers, in exchange for naval base rights in Britain's Caribbean colonies.

Fascism: A rightwing authoritarian political movement, usually with strong ties to the military and to business interests.

Final Solution: Systematic German program to exterminate all European Jews, formally drafted at a January 1942 conference of top Nazi leaders in the Wannsee villa, Berlin.

Holocaust: German efforts to annihilate Europe's entire Jewish population, which resulted in an estimated 5,573,100 deaths between 1933 and 1945, the great majority in the period 1940–1945.

Lend-Lease program: U.S. military and economic aid program, established in the spring of 1941 by an Act of Congress, to provide assistance to any country whose defense was perceived as necessary to the security of the United States.

Luftwaffe: The German air force.

Manhattan Project: Massive U.S.-led international 1942–1946 scientific program to develop the world's first atomic weapons during World War II.

Munich Conference and Pact, September 1938: Meetings between German, Italian, French, and British leaders that resulted in an agreement to cede the Czech Sudetenland to Germany, in the hope of averting European war, praised by many at the time for maintaining peace. Within months Munich became a pejorative term, denoting the failure to withstand unacceptable demands by voracious dictators.

Nazi Party (NSDAP, or National Socialist German Workers Party): Extreme rightwing, anti-Semitic, and anti-Communist party founded by Adolf Hitler and other disaffected German veterans in 1919; from 1933 to 1945 the German ruling party.

Nazi-Soviet Non-Aggression Pact: Agreement between Nazi Germany and the Soviet Union, concluded in August 1939, whereby each agreed to remain neutral should the other go to war with other powers. Under a secret protocol, the two states agreed to divide Poland and Germany consented to Soviet annexation of the Baltic states, Latvia, Lithuania, and Estonia. The successful negotiation of this accord freed Germany to attack Poland, beginning World War II in Europe.

Pearl Harbor: The December 7, 1941 Japanese attack on the U.S. Pacific fleet, most of which was then anchored at the Pearl Harbor naval base in Oahu, Hawaii. After the raid, the three Axis powers, Japan, Germany, and Italy, declared war on the United States, making that country an outright belligerent at war against them.

Phony war: The period from September 1939 to April 1940 when, apart from the invasion and subjugation of Poland, no real hostilities occurred in Europe.

***Reich* (Empire)**: Hitler and the Nazis frequently used this word to describe not only Germany but the territories under German rule. Post-1933 Germany was, according to Hitler's calculations, the Third Reich, a terminology adopted to distinguished it from the First German Reich of the Emperor Charlemagne and the Second Reich headed by the Prussian monarchy from 1871 to 1918.

Selective Training and Service Act, September 1940: U.S. legislation that made all American men aged between 18 and 65 potentially liable to military conscription.

SA: *Sturm Abteilung* or Storm Section of the Nazi Party, a paramilitary unit that terrorized those the party considered to be political opponents or in some way undesirable.

SS: *Schutzstaffeln* or Protection Police. The much feared German security force, responsible for internal and subsequently external security.

Sudetenland: An area of the new state of Czechoslovakia, created in 1919, which had a substantial ethnic German population. In the late 1930s, Nazi Germany demanded that the Sudetenland be ceded to Germany. Under pressure from Britain and France, whose leaders still sought to avoid war with Germany, in September 1938 the Czechoslovak government eventually transferred this territory to Germany.

Versailles Peace Settlement (1919): The peace treaty between Germany and the Allied and Associated Powers that ended World War I. It stripped Germany of portions of German territory on both its western and eastern borders, as well as all Germany's former colonies, and imposed financial reparations upon Germany, which were intended to compensate nations attacked by Germany for the costs the war had imposed upon them.

Bibliography

Addison, Paul, and Angus Calder, eds. *Time to Kill: The Soldier's Experience of War in the West, 1939–1945.* London: Pimlico, 1997.

Addison, Paul, and Jeremy A. Crang, eds. *The Burning Blue: A New History of the Battle of Britain.* London: Pimlico, 2000.

Aldrich, Richard J. *Intelligence and the War against Japan: Britain, America and the Politics of Secret Service.* New York: Cambridge University Press, 2000.

Allen, Paul. *Katyń: The Untold Story of Stalin's Massacres.* London: Macmillan, 1991.

Alperovitz, Gar. *Atomic Diplomacy: Hiroshima and Potsdam—The Use of the Atomic Bomb and the American Confrontation with Soviet Power.* New York: Simon & Schuster, 1994.

Ambrose, Stephen E. *Band of Brothers: E Company, 506th Regiment, 101st Airborne, from Normandy to Hitler's Eagle's Nest.* New York: Simon & Schuster, 2001.

Ambrose, Stephen E. *Citizen Soldiers: The U.S. Army from the Normandy Beaches to the Bulge to the Surrender of Germany June 7, 1944 to May 7, 1945.* New York: Simon & Schuster, 1997.

Ambrose, Stephen E. *D-Day, June 6, 1944: The Climactic Battle of World War II.* New York: Simon & Schuster, 1994.

Asahina, Robert. *Just Americans: How Japanese Americans Won a War at Home and Abroad.* New York: Gotham Books, 2006.

Axelrod, Alan. *The Real History of World War II: A New Look at the Past.* New York: Sterling, 2008.

Bacque, James. *Crimes and Mercies: The Fate of German Civilians under Allied Occupation, 1944–1950.* Boston: Little, Brown, 1997.

Barrett, David, and Larry Shyu, eds. *Chinese Collaboration with Japan, 1932–1945: The Limits of Accommodation.* Stanford: Stanford University Press, 2002.

Bartov, Omer. *Hitler's Army: Soldiers, Nazis, and War in the Third Reich.* New York: Oxford University Press, 1991.

Bayly, Christopher, and Tim Harper. *Forgotten Armies: The Fall of British Asia, 1941–1945.* Cambridge, MA: Belknap Press, 2005.

Beevor, Antony. *D-Day: The Battle for Normandy.* New York: Penguin, 2010.

Beevor, Antony. *The Fall of Berlin 1945.* New York: Viking, 2002.

Beevor, Antony. *The Second World War.* Boston: Little, Brown, 2012.

Benz, Wolfgang. *A Concise History of the Third Reich.* Trans. Thomas Dunlap. Berkeley: University of California Press, 2006.

Berenbaum, Michael. *The World Must Know: The History of the Holocaust as Told in the United States Holocaust Memorial Museum.* Boston: Little, Brown, 1993.

Bergen, Doris L. *War and Genocide: A Concise History of the Holocaust.* Lanham, MD: Rowman and Littlefield, 2009.

Beschloss, Michael. *The Conquerors: Roosevelt, Truman and the Destruction of Hitler's Germany, 1941–1945.* New York: Simon & Schuster, 2002.

Bess, Michael. *Choices under Fire: Moral Dimensions of World War II.* New York: Alfred A. Knopf, 2006.

Bessel, Richard. *Fascist Italy and Nazi Germany: Comparisons and Contrasts.* New York: Cambridge University Press, 1996.

Bessel, Richard. *Germany 1945: From War to Peace.* New York: Harper, 2009.

Bessel, Richard. *Nazism and War.* New York: Modern Library, 2004.

Bessel, Richard, ed. *Life in the Third Reich.* 2nd ed. New York: Oxford University Press, 2001.

Biess, Frank, and Robert G. Moeller, eds. *Histories of the Aftermath: The Legacies of the Second World War in Europe.* New York: Berghahn Books, 2010.

Binney, Marcus. *The Women Who Lived for Danger: The Agents of the Special Operations Executive.* New York: William Morrow, 2003.

Bond, Brian. *War and Society in Europe 1870–1970.* New York: Palgrave Macmillan, 1984.

Bosworth, R.J.B. *Explaining Auschwitz and Hiroshima: History Writing and the Second World War.* New York: Routledge, 1993.

Bosworth, R.J.B. *Mussolini.* New ed. London: Bloomsbury Academic, 2010.

Bosworth, R.J.B. *Mussolini's Italy: Life Under the Fascist Dictatorship, 1915–1945.* New York: Penguin, 2006.

Breitman, Richard. *The Architect of Genocide: Himmler and the Final Solution.* New York: Alfred A. Knopf, 1991.

Breitman, Richard. *Official Secrets: What the Nazis Planned, What the British and Americans Knew.* New York: Hill and Wang, 1998.

Briggs, Asa. *Secret Days: Codebreaking in Bletchley Park.* Barnsley, South Yorkshire, UK: Pen and Sword Press, 2011.

Brody, J. Kenneth. *The Trial of Pierre Laval: Defining Treason, Collaboration and Patriotism in World War II France.* New Brunswick, NJ: Transaction Books, 2010.

Brokaw, Tom. *The Greatest Generation.* New York: Random House, 2004.

Brokaw, Tom. *The Greatest Generation Speaks: Letters and Reflections.* New York: Random House, 1999.

Browning, Christopher R. *Ordinary Men: Reserve Police Battalion 101 and the Final Solution in Poland.* New York: HarperCollins, 1992.

Bruscino, Thomas. *A Nation Forged in War: How World War II Taught Americans How to Get Along.* Nashville: University of Tennessee Press, 2010.

Buckley, John. *Air Power in the Age of Total War.* Bloomington: Indiana University Press, 1999.

Budiansky, Stephen. *Battle of Wits: The Complete Story of Codebreaking in World War II.* New York: Free Press, 2002.

Bullock, Alan. *Hitler and Stalin: Parallel Lives.* New York: Alfred A. Knopf, 1992.

Burleigh, Michael. *The Third Reich: A New History.* London: Macmillan, 2000.

Calder, Angus. *The People's War; Britain, 1939–45.* London: Jonathan Cape, 1986.

Calvocoressi, Peter. *Fall Out: World War II and the Shaping of Postwar Europe*. London: Longman, 1997.
Calvocoressi, Peter, Guy Wint, and John Pritchard. *Total War: The Causes and Courses of the Second World War*. 2nd rev. ed. New York: Pantheon, 1989.
Chang, Iris. *The Rape of Nanking: The Forgotten Holocaust of World War II*. New York: Basic Books, 1997.
Churchill, Randolph, and Martin Gilbert. *Winston S. Churchill: The Official Biography*. 8 vols. and 15 companion vols., with 8 additional companion vols. planned. Boston: Houghton Mifflin, 1961–1989, 1961–.
Churchill, Winston. *The Second World War*. 6 vols. London: Cassell, 1948–1953.
Cook, Haruko Taya, and Theodore F. Cook. *Japan at War: An Oral History*. New York: New Press, 1992.
Cotterell, Arthur. *Western Power in Asia: Its Slow Rise and Swift Fall, 1415–1999*. New York: Wiley, 2009.
Crane, Conrad C. *Bombs, Cities, and Civilians: American Airpower Strategy in World War II*. Lawrence: University Press of Kansas, 1993.
Davies, Norman. *No Simple Victory: World War II in Europe, 1939–1945*. New York: Viking, 2007.
Davies, Norman. *Rising '44: The Battle for Warsaw*. New York: Viking, 2004.
Davies, Peter. *Dangerous Liaisons: Collaboration and World War II*. New York: Longman, 2004.
Davies, Peter. *France and the Second World War: Resistance, Occupation, and Liberation*. New York: Routledge, 2000.
Daws, Gavan. *Prisoners of the Japanese: POWs of World War II in the Pacific*. New York: William Morrow, 1994.
Dower, John W. *Cultures of War: Pearl Harbor/Hiroshima/9–11/Iraq*. New York: Norton, 2010.
Dower, John W. *Embracing Defeat: Japan in the Wake of World War II*. New York: Norton, 1999.
Dower, John W. *War Without Mercy: Race & Power in the Pacific War*. New York: Pantheon Books, 1986.
Drea, Edward J. *Japan's Imperial Army: Its Rise and Fall, 1853–1945*. Lawrence: University Press of Kansas, 2009.
Ellis, John. *Brute Force: Allied Strategy and Tactics in the Second World War*. New York: Viking, 1990.
Ellis, John. *The Sharp End: The Fighting Man in WWII*. New York: Scribner's, 1980.
Erickson, John. *Stalin's War with Germany*. Vol. 1, *The Road to Stalingrad*; Vol. 2, *The Road to Berlin*. New Haven, CT: Yale University Press, 1983–1984, 2000.
Evans, David C., and Mark R. Peattie. *Kaigun: Strategy, Tactics, and Technology in the Imperial Japanese Navy, 1887–1941*. Annapolis, MD: Naval Institute Press, 1997.
Evans, Richard J. *The Coming of the Third Reich*. New York: Penguin, 2004.
Evans, Richard J. *Lying About Hitler: History, Holocaust, and the David Irving Trial*. New York: Basic Books, 2002.
Evans, Richard J. *The Third Reich in Power*. New York: Penguin, 2006.
Evans, Richard J. *The Third Reich at War: How the Nazis Led Germany from Conquest to Disaster*. New York: Penguin, 2009.
Favreau, Mark, ed. *A People's History of World War II: The World's Most Destructive Conflict, as Told by the People Who Lived Through It*. New York: Free Press, 2004.

Felton, Mark. *The Real Tenko: Extraordinary True Stories of Women Prisoners of the Japanese.* Barnsley, South Yorkshire, UK: Pen and Sword, 2011.

Fenby, Jonathan. *Alliance: The Inside Story of How Roosevelt, Churchill and Stalin Won One War and Began Another*. San Francisco: MacAdam/Cage, 2007.

Fenby, Jonathan. *The General: Charles de Gaulle and the France He Saved.* New York: Simon & Schuster, 2010.

Fenby, Jonathan. *Generalissimo: Chiang Kai-shek and the China He Lost.* Darby, PA: Diane Publishing, 2005.

Frank, Richard B. *Downfall: The End of the Japanese Imperial Empire.* New York: Random House, 1999.

Friedrich, Jörg. *The Fire: The Bombing of Germany, 1940–1945.* Trans. Allison Brown. New York: Columbia University Press, 2006.

Fritz, Stephen G. *Frontsoldaten: The German Soldier in World War II.* Lexington: University Press of Kentucky, 1995.

Fritz, Stephen G. *Ostkrieg: Hitler's War of Extermination in the East.* Lexington: University Press of Kentucky, 2011.

Fritzsche, Peter. *Life and Death in the Third Reich.* Cambridge, MA: Belknap Books, 2007.

Fujitani, T. *Race for Empire: Koreans as Japanese and Japanese as Americans during World War II.* Berkeley: University of California Press, 2011.

Fussell, Paul. *Wartime: Understanding and Behavior in the Second World War.* New York: Oxford University Press, 1989.

Gallicchio, Mark, ed. *The Unpredictability of the Past: Memories of the Asia-Pacific War in U.S./East Asian Relations.* Durham, NC: Duke University Press, 2005.

Gardiner, Juliet. *The Blitz: The British under Attack.* New York: Harper, 2010.

Gaskin, Margaret. *Blitz: The Story of December 29, 1940.* London: Faber and Faber, 2005.

Gerwarth, Robert. *Hitler's Hangman: The Life of Heydrich.* New Haven, CT: Yale University Press, 2011.

Gilbert, Martin. *The Day the War Ended, May 8, 1945: Victory in Europe.* London: HarperCollins, 1995.

Gilbert, Martin. *Final Journey: The Fate of the Jews in Nazi Europe.* Boston: Allen and Unwin, 1979.

Gilbert, Martin. *The Second World War: A Complete History.* Rev. ed. New York: Holt, 2004.

Glantz, David M. *The Battle for Leningrad, 1941–1944.* Lawrence: University Press of Kansas, 2002.

Glantz, David M. *Colossus Reborn: The Red Army at War, 1941–1943.* Lawrence: University Press of Kansas, 2005.

Glantz, David M. *Operation Barbarossa: Hitler's Invasion of Russia.* Stroud, UK: The History Press, 2011.

Glantz, David M. *Stumbling Colossus: The Red Army on the Eve of World War.* Lawrence: University Press of Kansas, 1998.

Glantz, David M., and Jonathan M. House. *When Titans Clashed: How the Red Army Stopped Hitler.* Lawrence: University Press of Kansas, 1995.

Goldhagen, Daniel Jonah. *Hitler's Willing Executioners: Ordinary Germans and the Holocaust.* New York: Alfred A. Knopf, 1996.

Goodwin, Doris Kearns. *No Ordinary Time: Franklin and Eleanor Roosevelt: The Home Front in World War II.* New York: Simon & Schuster, 1994.

Haffner, Sebastian. *The Meaning of Hitler.* Trans. Ewald Osers. New York: Macmillan, 1979.

Harries, Meirion, and Susie Harries. *Soldiers of the Sun: The Rise and Fall of the Imperial Japanese Army*. New York: Random House, 1992.
Harris, Carol. *Blitz Diary: Life Under Attack in World War II*. Stroud, UK: The History Press, 2011.
Harrison, Mark, ed. *The Economics of World War II: Six Great Powers in International Comparison*. Cambridge: Cambridge University Press, 1998.
Hastings, Max. *Armageddon: The Battle for Germany, 1944–1945*. New York: Alfred A. Knopf, 2004.
Hastings, Max. *Inferno: The World at War, 1939–1945*. New York: Alfred A. Knopf, 2011.
Hastings, Max. *Retribution: The Battle for Japan, 1944–45*. New York: Alfred A. Knopf, 2008.
Hastings, Max. *Winston's War: Churchill, 1940–1945*. New York: Alfred A. Knopf, 2010.
Heide, Robert and John Gilman. *Home Front America: Popular Culture of the World War II Era*. San Francisco: Chronicle Books, 1995.
Hersey, John R. *Hiroshima*. New York: Bantam Books, 1956.
Hersey, John R. *Men on Bataan*. New York: Alfred A. Knopf, 1942.
Hinsley, Francis Harry. *British Intelligence in the Second World War: Popular Edition*. London: Her Majesty's Stationery Office, 1993.
Hinsley, Francis Harry, et al. *British Intelligence in the Second World War: Its Influence on Strategy*. 4 vols. in 5 books. London: Her Majesty's Stationery Office, 1979–1988.
Hoenicke-Moore, Michaela. *Know Your Enemy: The American Debate on Nazism, 1933–1945*. New York: Cambridge University Press, 2009.
Honey, Maureen. *Bitter Fruit: African American Women in World War II*. Columbia: University of Missouri Press, 1999.
Ienaga, Saburo. *The Pacific War, 1931–1945*. New York: Pantheon, 2010.
Inada, Lawson Fusao, ed. *Only What We Could Carry: The Japanese American Internment Experience*. Berkeley, CA: Heyday Books, 2000.
Iriye, Akira. *The Origins of the Second World War in Asia*. New York: Longman, 1987.
Iriye, Akira. *Pearl Harbor and the Coming of the Pacific War: A Brief History with Documents and Essays*. Boston: St. Martin's Press, 1999.
Iriye, Akira. *Power and Culture: The Japanese-American War, 1941–1945*. Cambridge, MA: Harvard University Press, 1981.
Iriye, Akira, and Warren Cohen, eds. *American, Chinese, and Japanese Perspectives on Wartime Asia, 1931–1949*. Wilmington, DE: Scholarly Resources, 1990.
Jackson, Julian. *The Fall of France: The Nazi Invasion of 1940*. New York: Oxford University Press, 2003.
Jackson, Julian. *France: The Dark Years, 1940–1944*. New York: Oxford University Press, 2001.
Johnson, William Bruce. *The Pacific Campaign in World War II*. New York: Routledge, 2006.
Jones, R. V. *Wizard War: British Scientific Intelligence, 1939–1945*. New York: McCann, 1990.
Kaplan, Marion A. *Between Dignity and Despair: Jewish Life in Nazi Germany*. New York: Oxford University Press, 1999.
Keegan, John. *The Battle for History: Refighting World War II*. New York: Vintage Books, 1996.
Keegan, John. *The Second World War*. London: Hutchinson, 1989.
Kennedy, David M. *Freedom from Fear: The American People in Depression and War, 1929–1945*. New York: Oxford University Press, 2001.

Kennett, Lee B. *G.I.: The American Soldier in World War II.* New York: Scribner's, 1987.
Kennett, Lee B. *A History of Strategic Bombing.* New York: Scribner's, 1982.
Kerr, E. Bartlett. *Surrender and Survival: The Experience of American POWs in the Pacific, 1941–1945.* New York: William Morrow, 1985.
Kershaw, Ian. *The End: The Defiance and Destruction of Hitler's Germany, 1944–1945.* New York: Penguin, 2011.
Kershaw, Ian. *Hitler, 1889–1936: Hubris.* New York: W.W. Norton, 1999.
Kershaw, Ian. *Hitler, 1936–1945: Nemesis.* New York: W.W. Norton, 2000.
Judt, Tony. *Postwar: A History of Europe since 1945.* New York: Penguin, 2005.
Lanzman, Claude. *Shoah: An Oral History of the Holocaust.* New York: Pantheon, 1985.
Lary, Diana. *The Chinese People at War: Human Suffering and Social Transformation, 1937–1945.* Cambridge: Cambridge University Press, 2010.
Linderman, Gerald F. *The World Within War: America's Combat Experience in World War II.* Cambridge, MA: Harvard University Press, 1997.
Longerich, Peter. *Heinrich Himmler: A Life.* New York: Oxford University Press, 2012.
Longmate, Norman. *How We Lived Then: A History of Everyday Life During the Second World War.* New York: Random House, 2002.
MacDonogh, Giles. *After the Reich: The Brutal History of the Allied Occupation.* New York: Basic Books, 2007.
Manrich, Roger, and Heinrich Fraenkel. *Doctor Goebbels: His Life and Death.* New York: Skyhorse Publishing, 2010.
Martel, Gordon, ed. *"The Origins of the Second World War" Reconsidered: The A.J.P. Taylor Debate after Twenty-five Years.* Boston: Allen and Unwin, 2000.
Mawdsley, Evan. *December 1941: Twelve Days That Began a World War.* New Haven, CT: Yale University Press, 2011.
Mawdsley, Evan. *Thunder in the East: The Nazi-Soviet War 1941–1945.* New York: Bloomsbury, 2007.
Mawdsley, Evan. *World War II: A New History.* Cambridge: Cambridge University Press, 2009.
May, Ernest R. *Knowing One's Enemies: Intelligence Assessment before the Two World Wars.* Princeton, NJ: Princeton University Press, 1984.
May, Ernest R. *Strange Victory: Hitler's Conquest of France.* New York: Hill and Wang, 2000.
Mayer, Arno J. *Why Did the Heavens Not Darken? The "Final Solution" in History.* New York: Pantheon, 1988.
Mazower, Mark. *Dark Continent: Europe's Twentieth Century.* New York: Alfred A. Knopf, 1999.
Mazower, Mark. *Hitler's Empire: How the Nazis Ruled Europe.* New York: Penguin, 2008.
McIntosh, Elizabeth P. *Sisterhood of Spies: Women of the OSS.* Annapolis, MD: Naval Institute Press, 1998.
Mercatante, Steven D. *Why Germany Nearly Won: A New History of the Second World War in Europe.* New York: Praeger, 2012.
Miller, Christine A. *British Literature of the Blitz: Fighting the People's War.* New York: Palgrave Macmillan, 2009.
Moeller, Robert G. *War Stories: The Search for a Usable Past in the Federal Republic of Germany.* Berkeley: University of California Press, 1999.
Moore, Brenda L. *Serving Our Country: Japanese American Women in the Military during World War II.* New Brunswick, NJ: Rutgers University Press, 2003.

Motley, Mary P., ed. *The Invisible Soldiers: The Experience of the Black Soldier, World War II.* Detroit, MI: Wayne State University Press, 1975.
Murray, Williamson, and Allan R. Millett. *A War to be Won: Fighting the Second World War.* Cambridge, MA: Harvard University Press, 2001.
Myers, Ramon H., and Mark R. Peattie, eds. *The Japanese Colonial Empire, 1895–1945.* Princeton: Princeton University Press, 1984.
Nicholas, Lynn H. *Cruel World: The Children of Europe in the Nazi Web.* New York: Alfred A. Knopf, 2005.
O'Neill, William L. *A Democracy at War: America's Fight at Home and Abroad in World War II.* New York: Free Press, 1993.
Overy, Richard. *The Dictators: Hitler's Germany, Stalin's Russia.* New York: Norton, 2005.
Overy, Richard. *Interrogations: The Nazi Elite in Allied Hands, 1945.* New York: Penguin, 2002.
Overy, Richard. *1939: Countdown to War.* New York: Viking, 2010.
Overy, Richard. *The Origins of the Second World War.* 3rd ed. New York: Longman, 2008.
Overy, Richard. *Russia's War: A History of the Soviet War Effort: 1941–1945.* New York: Penguin, 1998.
Overy, Richard. *Why the Allies Won.* New York: Norton, 1997.
Peattie, Mark R. *Sunburst: The Rise of Japanese Naval Air Power, 1909–1941.* Annapolis, MD: Naval Institute Press, 2002.
Perret, Geoffrey. *There's a War to Be Won: The United States Army in World War II.* New York: Random House, 1991.
Perret, Geoffrey. *Winged Victory: The Army Air Forces in World War II.* New York: Random House, 1993.
Ponting, Clive. *Armageddon: The Second World War.* New York: Random House, 1995.
Ponting, Clive. *1940: Myth and Reality.* London: Hamilton, 1990.
Prange, Gordon W., with Donald M. Goldstein and Katherine V. Dillon. *At Dawn We Slept: The Untold Story of Pearl Harbor.* New York: McGraw Hill, 1981.
Prange, Gordon W., with Donald M. Goldstein and Katherine V. Dillon. *December 7, 1941: The Day the Japanese Attacked Pearl Harbor.* New York: Random House, 1991.
Rankin, Nicholas. *Churchill's Wizards: The British Genius for Deception 1914–1945.* New York: Faber and Faber, 2008.
Rees, Laurence. *Horror in the East: Japan and the Atrocities of World War II.* New York: Da Capo Press, 2002.
Rees, Laurence. *World War Two: Behind Closed Doors—Stalin, the Nazis and the West.* London: BBC Books, 2009.
Reid, Anna. *Leningrad: The Epic Siege of World War II.* New York: Walker and Company, 2011.
Reuth, Ralph Georg. *Goebbels.* Trans. Krishna Winston. New York: Harcourt, 1993.
Reynolds, David. *One World Divisible: A Global History since 1945.* New York: Norton, 2000.
Reynolds, David. *Rich Relations: The American Occupation of Britain 1941–1945.* New York: Random House, 1995.
Rhodes, Richard. *The Making of the Atomic Bomb.* New York: Simon & Schuster, 1986.
Roberts, Andrew. *Masters and Commanders: How Four Titans Won the War in the West.* New York: Harper, 2009.
Roberts, Andrew. *The Storm of War: A New History of the Second World War.* New York: Harper, 2011.

Roeder, George H., Jr. *The Censored War: American Visual Experience During World War II.* New Haven, CT: Yale University Press, 1993.

Roehrs, Mark D., and William A. Renzi. *World War II in the Pacific.* Armonk, NY: M. E. Sharpe, 2004.

Roseman, Mark. *The Wannsee Conference and the Final Solution.* New York: Penguin, 2002.

Rosenfeld, Gavriel D. *The World Hitler Never Made: Alternate History and the Memory of Nazism.* New York: Cambridge University Press, 2005.

Ryan, Cornelius. *The Last Battle.* New York: Simon & Schuster, 1966.

Ryan, Cornelius. *The Longest Day.* New York: Simon & Schuster, 1959.

Salisbury, Harrison E. *The 900 Days: The Siege of Leningrad.* New York: Harper & Row, 1986.

Samuel, Wolfgang W. E. *The War of Our Childhood: Memories of World War II.* Oxford: University of Mississippi Press, 2002.

Sarantakes, Nicholas Evan. *Allies Against the Rising Sun: The United States, the British Nations, and the Defeat of Imperial Japan.* Lawrence: University Press of Kansas, 2009.

Schaffer, Ronald. *Wings of Judgment: American Bombing in World War II.* New York: Oxford University Press, 1985.

Shepherd, Ben, and Juliet Pattinson, eds. *War in a Twilight World: Partisan and Anti-partisan Warfare in Eastern Europe, 1939–45.* New York: Palgrave Macmillan, 2010.

Shermer, Michael, and Alex Grobman. *Denying History: Who Says the Holocaust Never Happened and Why Do They Say It?* Revised and updated ed. Berkeley: University of California Press, 2000.

Sherry, Michael S. *The Rise of American Air Power: The Creation of Armageddon.* New Haven, CT: Yale University Press, 1988.

Sherwin, Martin J. *A World Destroyed: Hiroshima and Its Legacies.* 3rd ed. Stanford: Stanford University Press, 2000.

Shirer, William L. *The Rise and Fall of the Third Reich: A History of Nazi Germany.* New York: Simon & Schuster, 1960.

Shirley, Craig. *December 1941: 31 Days That Changed America and Saved the World.* New York: Thomas Nelson, 2011.

Snow, Edgar. *Red Star over China.* New York: Random House, 1978.

Snow, Philip. *The Fall of Hong Kong: Britain, China, and the Japanese Occupation.* New Haven, CT: Yale University Press, 2003.

Snyder, Timothy. *Bloodlands: Europe Between Hitler and Stalin.* New York: Basic Books, 2010.

Spector, Ronald H. *Eagle Against the Sun: The American War with Japan.* New York: Free Press, 1985.

Spector, Ronald H. *In the Ruins of Empire: The Japanese Surrender and the Battle for Postwar Asia.* New York: Random House, 2007.

Stafford, David. *Endgame, 1945: The Missing Final Chapter of World War II.* Boston: Little, Brown, 2007.

Stahel, David. *Operation Barbarossa and Germany's Defeat in the East.* New York: Cambridge University Press, 2009.

Stargardt, Nicholas. *Witnesses of War: Children's Lives under the Nazis.* New York: Vintage, 2007.

Steinberg, David Joel. *Philippine Collaboration in World War II.* Ann Arbor: University of Michigan Press, 1967.

Steiner, Zara. *The Triumph of the Dark: European International History 1933–1939.* Oxford: Oxford University Press, 2011.
Takaki, Ronald. *Double Victory: A Multicultural History of America in World War II.* Darby, PA: Diane Publishers, 2000.
Takaki, Ronald. *Hiroshima: Why America Dropped the Atomic Bomb.* Boston: Little Brown, 1995.
Tanaki, Yuki. *Hidden Horrors: Japanese War Crimes in World War II.* Boulder, CO: Westview Press, 1996.
Tarling, Nicholas. *A Sudden Rampage: The Japanese Occupation of Southeast Asia, 1941–1945.* Honolulu: University of Hawaii Press, 2001.
Taylor, A.J.P. *The Origins of the Second World War.* London: Hamish Hamilton, 1962.
Taylor, Frederick. *Dresden: Tuesday, February 13, 1945.* New York: Harper, 2004.
Terkel, Studs. *"The Good War": An Oral History of World War Two.* New York: Pantheon Books, 1984.
Terraine, John. *Business in Great Waters: The U-Boat War, 1916–1945.* New York: G. P. Putnam, 1989.
Thacker, Toby. *Joseph Goebbels: Life and Death.* New York: Palgrave Macmillan, 2009.
Thompson, Robert S. *Empires on the Pacific: World War II and the Struggle for the Mastery of Asia.* New York: Basic Books, 2001.
Thorne, Christopher. *Allies of a Kind: The United States, Britain, and the War against Japan, 1941–1945.* New York: Oxford University Press, 1978.
Thorne, Christopher. *The Issue of War: States, Societies, and the Coming of the Far Eastern Conflict of 1941–1945.* New York: Oxford University Press, 1985.
Tillman, Barrett. *Whirlwind: The Air War against Japan, 1942–1945.* New York: Simon & Schuster, 2010.
Toland, John. *The Rising Sun: The Decline and Fall of the Japanese Empire, 1936–1945.* New York: Random House, 1970.
Tomasevich, Jozo. *War and Revolution in Yugoslavia, 1941–1945: Occupation and Collaboration.* Stanford, CA: Stanford University Press, 2002.
Tooze, Adam. *The Wages of Destruction: The Making and Breaking of the Nazi Economy.* New York: Viking, 2007.
Trevor-Roper, Hugh. *The Last Days of Hitler.* London: Macmillan, 1947.
Tuttle, William M. *"Daddy's Gone to War": The Second World War in the Lives of America's Children.* New York: Oxford University Press, 1993.
Uchida, Jun. *Brokers of Empire: Japanese Settler Colonialism in Korea, 1876–1945.* Cambridge, MA: Harvard University Press, 2011.
Vinen, Richard. *The Unfree French: Life under the Occupation.* New Haven, CT: Yale University Press, 2006.
Walker, J. Samuel. *Prompt and Utter Destruction: Truman and the Use of Atomic Bombs Against Japan.* Chapel Hill: University of North Carolina Press, 1997.
Waller, Maureen. *London 1945: Life in the Debris of War.* New York: St. Martin's Press, 2005.
Watt, Donald Cameron. *How War Came: The Immediate Origins of the Second World War 1938–1939.* New York: Pantheon Books, 1989.
Weatherford, Doris. *American Women and World War II.* Secaucus, NJ: Castle Books, 2009.
Weinberg, Gerhard. *The Foreign Policy of Hitler's Germany: Starting World War II, 1937–1939.* Chicago: Chicago University Press, 1980.
Weinberg, Gerhard. *Germany, Hitler, and World War II: Essays in Modern German and World History.* Cambridge: Cambridge University Press, 1995.

Weinberg, Gerhard. *A World at Arms: A Global History of World War II.* 2nd ed. Cambridge: Cambridge University Press, 2005.

Weintraub, Stanley. *The Last Great Victory: The End of World War II, July/August 1945.* New York: Penguin, 1995.

Weintraub, Stanley. *Pearl Harbor Christmas: A World at War, December 1941.* New York: Da Capo Press, 2011.

Werner, Emmy E. *Through the Eyes of Innocents: Children Witness World War II.* New York: Basic Books, 1999.

Westad, Odd Arne. *Cold War and Revolution: Soviet-American Rivalry and the Origins of the Chinese Civil War, 1944–1946.* New York: Columbia University Press, 1993.

Wing, Sandra Koa, ed. *Our Longest Days: A People's History of the Second World War.* London: Profile Books, 2009.

Wynn, Neil A. *The African American Experience during World War II.* Lanham, MD: Rowman and Littlefield, 2010.

Yellin, Emily. *Our Mothers' War: American Women at Home and at the Front during World War II.* New York: Free Press, 2004.

Young, Louise. *Japan's Total Empire: Manchuria and the Culture of Wartime Imperialism.* Berkeley: University of California Press, 1998.

Yu Maochun. *OSS in China: Prelude to the Cold War.* New Haven, CT: Yale University Press, 1997.

Zahra, Tara. *The Lost Children: Reconstructing Europe's Families after World War II.* Cambridge, MA: Harvard University Press, 2011.

Ziegler, Philip. *London at War 1939–1945.* New York: Alfred A. Knopf, 1995.

Web Sites

BBC: World Wars in-depth. http://www.bbc.co.uk/history/worldwars/.

The National World War II Museum. http://www.nationalww2museum.org/.

The Second World War 1939–1945. The British National Archives Web site. http://www.nationalarchives.gov.uk/education/world-war-two.htm.

United States Holocaust Memorial Museum. http://www.ushmm.org/museum/.

World War II. EyeWitness to History.com. http://www.eyewitnesstohistory.com/w2frm.htm.

WorldWar-2.Net. http://www.worldwar-2.net/.

World War II Gallery. National Museum of the US Air Force. http://www.nationalmuseum.af.mil/exhibits/airpower/index.asp.

World War II Multimedia Database. http://www.worldwar2database.com.

Films and Television

BBC History of World War II (2009). BBC Warner.

Japan's War in Colour (2005). Rhino Theatrical.

Russia's War: Blood Upon the Snow (1997). PBS.

The World at War (1974). BBC.

World War II: Behind Closed Doors (2009). BBC Warner.

WWII in HD (2010). A & E Home Video.

Index

About the Editor

PRISCILLA ROBERTS read history as an undergraduate at King's College, Cambridge, where she also earned her PhD. Dr. Roberts then spent four years in the United States on a variety of fellowships, including one year at Princeton University on a Rotary graduate studentship and a year as a Visiting Research Fellow at the Smithsonian Institution, Washington, DC. She then moved to the University of Hong Kong, where she is now an associate professor of history. She is also honorary director of the University of Hong Kong's Centre of American Studies. She spent the year 2003 at George Washington University as a Fulbright Scholar and has received numerous other academic awards for research in the United States, Great Britain, and Australia. She specializes in 20th-century diplomatic and international history.